# Organisation and Everyday Life with Dyslexia and other SpLDs

*Organisation and Everyday Life with Dyslexia and other SpLDs* is about the wide range of impacts that dyslexia/ SpLD have in everyday life. All dyslexic/ SpLD people live with the possibility that their mind will function in a dyslexic/ SpLD way at any moment, regardless of strategies that they have acquired or developed. Even people with many strategies can suddenly find themselves struggling with their dyslexia/ SpLD again.

This book is addressed to dyslexic/ SpLD readers. Organisation is promoted as a tool to minimise the effects of dyslexia/ SpLD. The book covers:
- situations that might disrupt organisation
- a systematic approach to organisation
- everyday life, study peripherals and employment.

It has many life stories to help readers recognise the impacts of their own dyslexia/ SpLD.

Dyslexic/ SpLDs have the potential to offer skills and alternative approaches to tasks. Often, the solutions that they devise for themselves are very useful to the non-dyslexic/ SpLD people around them, which can enhance their self-confidence.

> When organisation suits the individual with SpLD
> innate intelligence and potential can be realised.

'This was an engaging read. I found the real-life examples in support of the observations and solutions particularly interesting as they bought the wider theory to life. This book offers numerous highly practical life strategies for dyslexics, but I also think that it has a broader application as many of the challenges described will be familiar to readers whether they perceive themselves to be dyslexic or not. Overall, I went away very impressed by the attention to detail, accessible style and reassuring tone.'
**– Dr James Fowler, Essex Business School, University of Essex, UK**

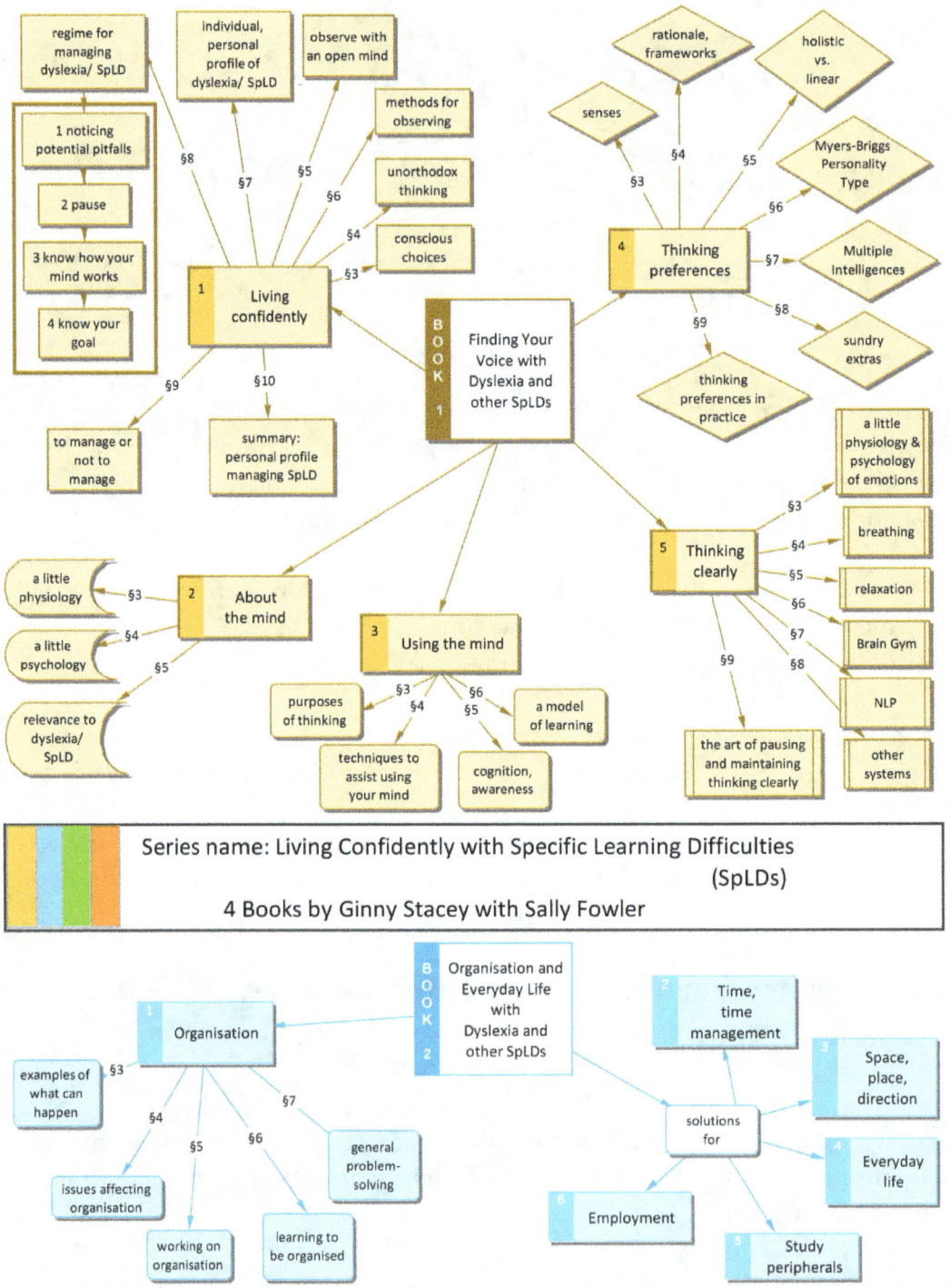

Different, larger maps of each book: Book 1: p 23; Book 2: p 25
Contents p xv    Where to start p viii

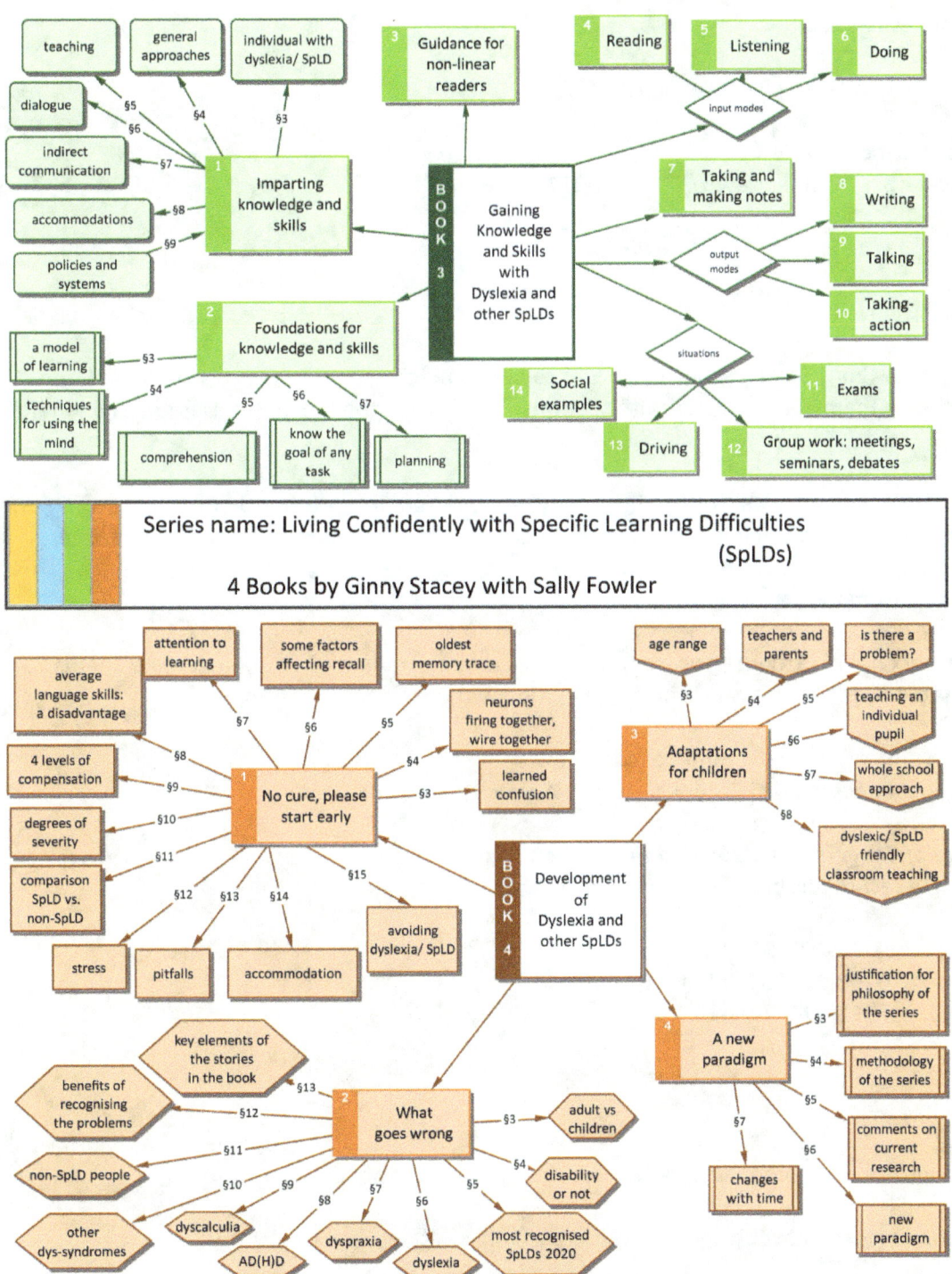

Different, larger maps of each book: Book 3: p 27; Book 4: p 29
Contents p xv    Where to start p viii

First published 2020
by Routledge
2 Park Square, Milton Park, Abingdon, Oxon OX14 4RN

and by Routledge
52 Vanderbilt Avenue, New York, NY 10017

*Routledge is an imprint of the Taylor & Francis Group, an informa business*

© 2020 Ginny Stacey

The right of Ginny Stacey and Sally Fowler to be identified as authors of this work has been asserted by them in accordance with sections 77 and 78 of the Copyright, Designs and Patents Act 1988.

All rights reserved. No part of this book may be reprinted or reproduced or utilised in any form or by any electronic, mechanical, or other means, now known or hereafter invented, including photocopying and recording, or in any information storage or retrieval system, without permission in writing from the publishers.

*Trademark notice*: Product or corporate names may be trademarks or registered trademarks, and are used only for identification and explanation without intent to infringe.

*British Library Cataloguing-in-Publication Data*
A catalogue record for this book is available from the British Library

*Library of Congress Cataloging-in-Publication Data*
A catalog record has been requested for this book

ISBN: 978-1-138-20240-5 (hbk)
ISBN: 978-1-138-20241-2 (pbk)
ISBN: 978-1-315-47397-0 (ebk)

Typeset in Calibri
by Ginny Stacey

This book has been prepared from camera-ready copy provided by the author.

Visit the companion website www.routledge.com/cw/stacey

# Organisation and Everyday Life with Dyslexia and other SpLDs

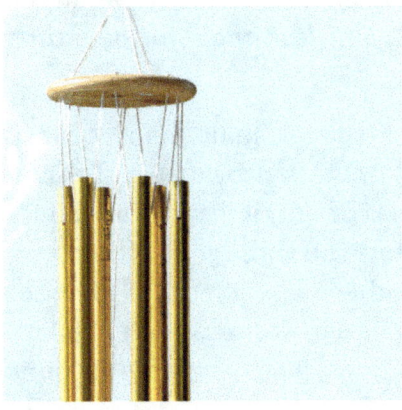

Wind chime music represents life flowing well
when organisation suits the individual concerned.

Ginny Stacey
with Sally Fowler

LONDON AND NEW YORK

'In this outstanding and unique new book, Ginny Stacey and Sally Fowler provide a wealth of tips and techniques, acquired over many years of living with dyslexia and working with people who have it, that can help dyslexics function more efficiently in their daily lives. Written by dyslexics for dyslexics, the book is organised and presented in a way that cleverly considers the different ways dyslexics process and assimilate information, acknowledging that there is not a "one-fits-all" approach to dealing with dyslexia. Central to their approach to coping with dyslexia is the notion of "metacognition", of reflecting on your own style of thinking to understand how dyslexia uniquely affects you, and what coping strategies and techniques work for you. Accordingly, by the time you have finished the book, you will not only have become more organised, productive and content with living with dyslexia; you will also be an expert on your unique style of thinking. Whether you are a student or a professional, I cannot recommend this book enough.'
– *James Tierney, LLB, BCL, LPC, Solicitor and a former student of Stacey*

'This book is packed with colour, shapes, mind maps, boxes and different "routes" through the material. Like everything in it, these provide excellent approaches for **everyone** whether individuals with an SpLD or not. It is possible to pick and choose what works for any one person, and key concepts run throughout the material strengthening the supportive approach. Similarly, these ingredients in the book are hugely helpful: lots of real examples, tips, models, resources and stories, as well as lots of headings, questions, alternatives, key concepts, solutions, insights, benefits, options and further references. A real gem, full of strategies.'
– *Sally Daunt, SpLD Tutor, Liverpool Institute of Performing Arts, UK*

**Ginny Stacey** did not realise she was dyslexic until her mid-20s. The challenge of learning to play classical guitar helped her to understand how her dyslexic mind works. Committed to helping other dyslexics achieve their potential, she developed a range of highly effective techniques for supporting dyslexic students in studying all subjects and coping with life in general. The techniques are widely used in universities and colleges. She has become a nationally-recognised expert in the field.

**Sally Fowler** stepped into the dyslexic world in her late 40s. It was a revelation to see the impacts of her dyslexia clearly. She became an approved teacher for the British Dyslexia Association with an M.A. in special education. She taught dyslexics, both children in schools and students at university. In Oxford, she met Ginny Stacey: the collaboration of two dyslexic minds has brought a wealth of experience to the *Living Confidently with Specific Learning Difficulties* series.

## **Dedication**

Dear fellow dyslexics,

The laughter we've shared tells me I'm on the right lines with my understanding of dyslexia. So do:
- the tears some of you have shed as you tell me your story and you know I hear
- the courage you've shown as you reveal your vulnerable side
- the joy you've known as you find ways to take charge of your dyslexia and run with it, not against it.

I hope this book will help many others to find their way through the trials and tribulations of dyslexia/ SpLD so that they can come out the other side to enjoy some of the good parts of being dyslexic/ SpLD.

SpLD = Specific Learning Difficulty
- dyslexia
- dyspraxia
- AD(H)D
- dyscalculia

see Ⓖ p 280 for descriptions

# Where to start:

- **Linear readers, who like to read straight through:**

In USEFUL PREFACE:

➤ Read THIS BOOK: ORGANISATION AND EVERYDAY LIFE WITH DYSLEXIA AND OTHER SpLDs.

➤ THE SERIES LIVING CONFIDENTLY WITH SPECIFIC LEARNING DIFFICULTIES (SpLDs), unless you have read another book of this series.

➤ Read sections marked with this book's icon.

Then read from Chapter 1.

- **Non-linear readers, who prefer to move around a book:**

A) Read the boxes in the USEFUL PREFACE
B) Choose one of these 5 suggestions:

1. Read the coloured boxes throughout the book and see what takes your interest.
2. Use the INDEX to find topics that interest you.
3. Use DIPPING-IN TO TRY OUT IDEAS, §1, in each chapter to find the most important topics.
4. Randomly move through the book to find what takes your interest.
5. Use the EXERCISE: INITIAL PURPOSE FOR READING to create your own list of what you want to read first.

THIS BOOK: ORGANISATION AND EVERYDAY LIFE WITH DYSLEXIA AND OTHER SpLDs: p 18

THE SERIES: LIVING CONFIDENTLY WITH SPECIFIC LEARNING DIFFICULTIES (SpLDs): p 21

USEFUL PREFACE: p 0

EXERCISE: INITIAL PURPOSE FOR READING: p 14

**Tip: Reading Styles**

It is useful to think about how you read.
See DIFFERENT WAYS TO READ: p 9

§ = subsection     Ⓖ = GLOSSARY     = Companion website
www.routledge.com/cw/stacey

>  **Tip:** This is a book to dip into.  Solid reading is not necessary.

## About the coloured boxes

### Meaning of Box Colours

There are coloured boxes throughout the book:

  orange for stories      orange for insights

    green for exercises      light blue for examples

 purple for tips     dark blue for text and diagrams

### Contents of boxes:

    story: a narrative
    insight: story with added information; or an important point
    tip: contains a suggestion to help you make progress
    example: usually more general than a story; sometimes directly expanding
            on some part of the preceding text
    exercise: instructions to try out some idea(s)

### Flow of boxes

The boxes are part of the text.  They are often split across pages.

---

### Tip:  Finding Information

The *INDEX* is organised alphabetically, with some particularly useful groups of entries listed at the beginning.

The Glossary ⓖ has all the acronyms and symbols, as well as explanations of words and phrases.  Page numbers are given for the relevant sections.

## Summary of the chapters

### Chapter 1 Organisation

The chapter has examples to show how organisation is often a problem for dyslexic/ SpLD people. There is a general model for developing organisation, with detailed steps for using it and a check-list. The model is applied to general problem solving. It is noted that a problem you are facing may be caused by something else, so the model is also adapted for finding the root cause of the problem you are trying to deal with.

### Chapter 2 Time and Time Management

The chapter discusses the problems with time and time management that are often encountered by dyslexic/ SpLD people. The sources can be a lack of time sense or that time words go wrong. There are suggestions for finding the solutions that suit you, including letting go of time.

### Chapter 3 Space, Place and Direction

Space, place and direction also cause problems for dyslexic/ SpLD people, and specifically for dyspraxic people. Again, the source can be a lack of the right senses or that words go wrong. There are suggestions for finding your solutions.

### Chapter 4 Everyday Life

Dyslexia/ SpLD affects everyday life, though this is not always recognised. The chapter looks at many different aspects of everyday life and what you can do to minimise the effects of your dyslexia/ SpLD.

### Chapter 5 Study Peripherals

You have to deal with many different systems in order to study. This chapter looks at these peripheral systems and what you can do to organise the details so that you have more time and energy for the study itself. It discusses choices made on a course. There are two worked examples in the chapter, NAVIGATING THE COURSE STRUCTURE and EXAM PROVISIONS. Both are annotated so that they can be applied to other situations.

### Chapter 6 Employment

Employment builds on everyday life and study. The chapter applies the work of the rest of the book to issues that can occur in employment. The importance of making the right choices is highlighted. NAVIGATING EMPLOYMENT STRUCTURES shows you how to make changes to the worked example NAVIGATING THE COURSE STRUCTURE so that it applies to employment. It is especially recognised that getting on with other people is very important during employment. Ways in which misunderstandings can occur are discussed with ideas of how to resolve them.

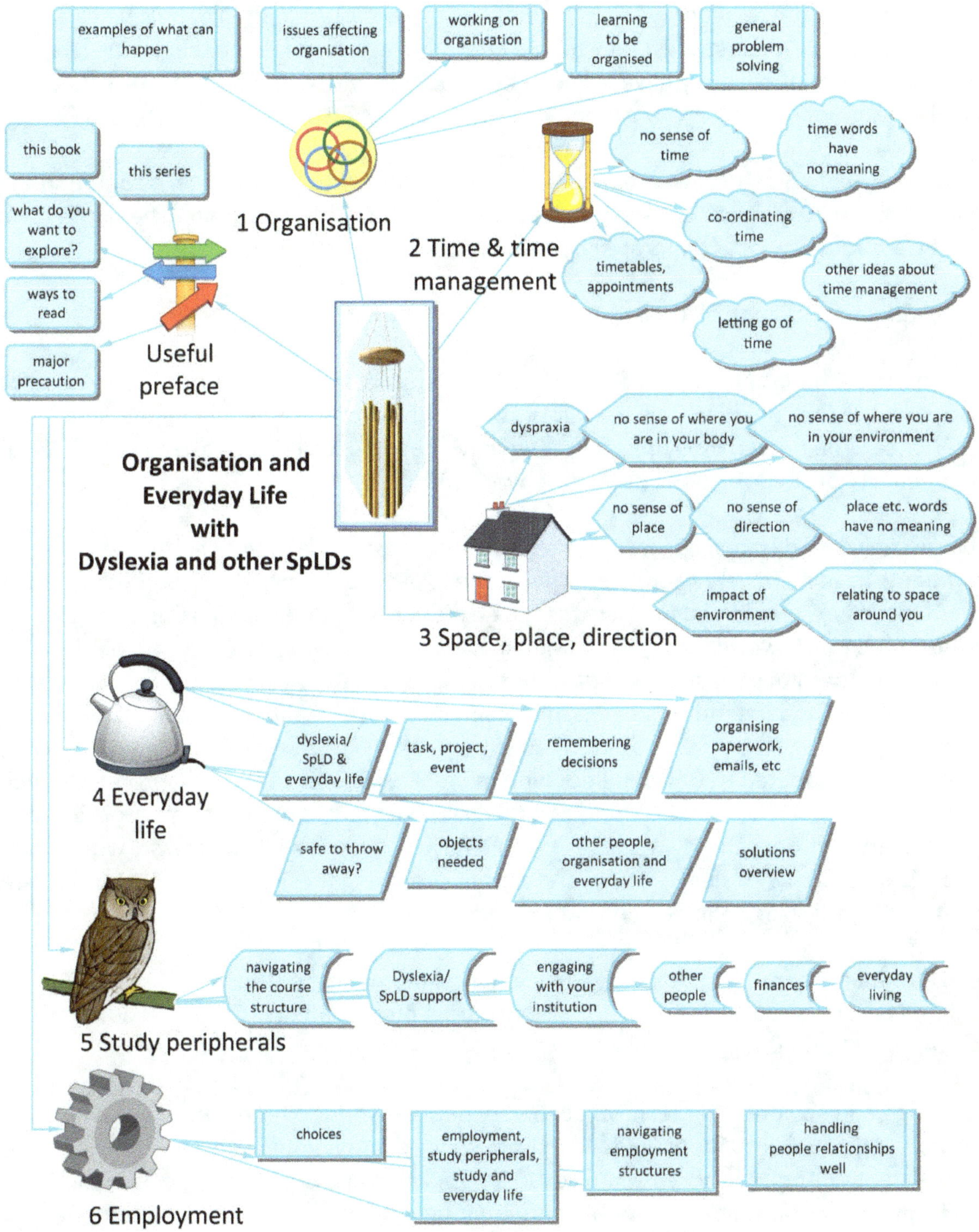

# Organisation and Everyday Life with Dyslexia and other SpLDs

## 1 Organisation
- examples of what can happen
- issues affecting organisation
- working on organisation
- learning to be organised
- general problem solving

## Useful preface
- this book
- this series
- what do you want to explore?
- ways to read
- major precaution

## 2 Time & time management
- no sense of time
- time words have no meaning
- co-ordinating time
- timetables, appointments
- other ideas about time management
- letting go of time

## 3 Space, place, direction
- dyspraxia
- no sense of where you are in your body
- no sense of where you are in your environment
- no sense of place
- no sense of direction
- place etc. words have no meaning
- impact of environment
- relating to space around you

## 4 Everyday life
- dyslexia/SpLD & everyday life
- task, project, event
- remembering decisions
- organising paperwork, emails, etc
- safe to throw away?
- objects needed
- other people, organisation and everyday life
- solutions overview

## 5 Study peripherals
- navigating the course structure
- Dyslexia/SpLD support
- engaging with your institution
- other people
- finances
- everyday living

## 6 Employment
- choices
- employment, study peripherals, study and everyday life
- navigating employment structures
- handling people relationships well

xi

## Acknowledgements

These books are the result of working with many, many dyslexia/ SpLD people since 1991. They have told me their stories; they have explored new ways of doing things; they have passed on the solutions they have found. I have worked with a few people with other disabilities or none. It has been a great adventure learning from them all.

I've also had conversations with many other people, sometimes deliberately, sometimes by chance – like a 20 minute conversation with a fellow passenger on a train. The books have benefitted from the ideas generated by the conversations.

My grateful thanks go to all these people.

I'd also like to thank colleagues in The Oxford SpLD Tutor Group, those at The University of Oxford and Oxford Brookes University for formal and informal exchange of ideas and experience. The network of support that we have between colleagues allows us to provide a high quality of support to the people we work with.

Several friends and colleagues have proof-read chapters for me in the final stages. Their comments have been very useful in clarifying the expression of my ideas. Sometimes their comments have re-enforced my view that the experience of dyslexia/ SpLD is foreign to the non-dyslexic/ SpLD world. If my expression occasionally seems strange to you, please wonder whether I'm saying something about dyslexia/ SpLD that is hard for a non-dyslexic/ SpLD person to understand since their minds simply don't give them the same experience.

I'm especially indebted to David Bullock who made 3 structures to lift my laptop, extended monitor, mouse and keyboard so that I worked standing and kept my brain's arousal system alert. Without these structures I would have struggled against the way words and my dyslexia send me to sleep. The final stages of preparing these books would have been months of awful struggle instead of the excitement I experienced.

I'd like to thank my family for their patience during the writing of these books. My husband deserves special mention for his encouragement, patience and his shed, which was my writing shed for many years.

Routledge and Taylor & Francis have been very patient with the time taken to convert the original single book into four stand-alone books. My commissioning editor, Lucy Kennedy, the assistant editors, Molly Selby and Lottie Mapp, and the production team leaders, Siân Cahill and Alison Macfarlane, have all done their best to understand and accommodate the unorthodox needs of dyslexic/ SpLD readers and my needs as a dyslexic author. My thanks to everyone who has been involved with this project.

I'd like to thank Carl Wenczek, of Born Digital Ltd., for tuition and much advice on dealing with my illustrations. I couldn't have managed all the visual components and figures without his guidance.

I have been extremely fortunate to benefit from Mike Standing's experience as a retired production manager of a printing company. He came and guided me through many details of the printing process as I undertook author typesetting of these books. Without his input, the typesetting process would have been a horrible struggle.

And finally, my thanks go to Sally Fowler who has accompanied me throughout the writing of the series. When I've been daunted or hit a blank patch, Sally's encouragement and enthusiasm have carried me through. Without Sally's belief in this work, the project would not have been finished.

## Illustrations – with page numbers

### Illustration acknowledgements and key to symbols

- ❖ Complete figures created using Inspiration® 9, a product of Inspiration Software®, Inc.
- ✍ Photos or drawings created by Ginny Stacey.
- ○ Material by Routledge/ Taylor and Francis.
- ⚑ Other figures whose sources are acknowledged in the text.

### Throughout the book

- ❖ Mind maps for USEFUL PREFACE and all the chapters
- ○ The icons for the series, books and chapters were created by Routledge/ Taylor & Francis and inserted into the mind maps or other diagrams as appropriate

### Front Matter

- ❖ The series mind map inside the cover    p ii, iii
- ❖ The book mind map    p xi

### Useful Preface    p 0

- ❖ 1    Mind map of book 1    p 23
- ❖ 2    Mind map of book 2    p 25
- ❖ 3    Mind map of book 3    p 27
- ❖ 4    Mind map of book 4    p 29
- ❖ 5    Living Confidently with Specific Learning Difficulties (SpLDs)    p 31

## Chapter 1  Organisation   p 36

- ❖ 1    Dipping-in   p 41
- ✍ 2    Feeling confident   p 45
- ❖ 3    Arrow position   p 46
- ❖ 4    Materials and methods   p 56
- ❖ 5    Model for developing organisation   p 58
- ❖ 6    Pile of stuff   p 63
- ✍ 7    Proof of the pudding   p 72

## Chapter 2  Time and Time Management   p 84

- ⚑ 1    Dates pulled down   p 91
- ❖ 2    Various solutions   p 94

## Chapter 3  Space, Place and Direction   p 104

- ❖ 1    Drawing while looking in a mirror   p 113
- ❖ 2    No short cut   p 116
- ❖ 3    Two different interpretations   p 117

## Chapter 4  Everyday Life   p 122

- ❖ 1    Steps in organising paperwork   p 145
- ❖ 2    Card marking a place   p 155
- ✍ 3    Post-it flag on important page   p 164

## Chapter 5  Study Peripherals   p 168

- ❖ 1    Navigating the course structure   p 176

## Chapter 6  Employment   p 206

- ❖ 1    Model for developing organisation applied to employment   p 219
- ❖ 2    Conflict resolution   p 228

## Appendix 2  Individual, Personal Profile of Dyslexia/ SpLD and Regime for Managing Dyslexia/ SpLD

- ❖ 1    Mental energy to monitor   p 249

# Contents

| | |
|---|---|
| Mind maps of the series ............ ii | Summary of the chapters ............ x |
| Where to start ............ viii | Map of this book ............ xi |
| Information and tip boxes ............ ix | Acknowledgements and illustrations ............ xii |

 **Useful Preface   This is worth reading**
📕 Marks sections where some or all of the text is specific to this book.

Mind map and Contents ............ 0
📕 What to expect from this book ............ 1
USEFUL PREFACE summary ............ 2
Templates on the website ............ 2
Appendix 1 ............ 2
1   Dipping-in to try out ideas ............ 2
2   Context, including PHILOSOPHY OF THIS SERIES ............ 3
3   Major precaution ............ 7
4   Different ways to read ............ 9
   4.1   Exercise: reading style   11
   4.2   Something goes wrong with reading   11
5   📕 What do you want to explore? ............ 12
   5.1   Initial purpose for reading   14
   5.2   Reader groups   15
   5.3   Reading to find out about a theme   17
6   📕 This book: *Organisation and Everyday Life with Dyslexia and other SpLDs* ............ 18
   6.1   Aims, outcomes and benefits   20
7   The series: *Living Confidently with Specific Learning Difficulties (SpLDs)* ............ 21
   7.1   Readership/ audience   21
   7.2   Summary of the series   21
   7.3   Aims and outcomes   31
   7.4   📕 Distinguishing between the different SpLDs   32
   7.5   The way forward   33
References and website information ............ 34

# Chapter 1  Organisation

| | |
|---|---|
| Mind map and contents | 36 |
| Vital for dyslexic/ SpLDs, good practice for all | 38 |
| Working with the chapter | 38 |
| Templates on the website | 39 |
| Appendix 1, 2 and 3 | 40 |

1 Dipping-in to try out ideas ..... 41
2 Context ..... 42
3 Examples of what can happen ..... 45
   3.1 Missing appointments ..... 46
   3.2 Not knowing what to take ..... 46
   3.3 Wrong preparation looks like being disorganised ..... 47
   3.4 Finding what you want ..... 47
   3.5 Out of sight is out of mind ..... 48
   3.6 Precisely wrong time or place ..... 48
   3.7 Ultra organised ..... 49
4 Issues affecting organisation ..... 50
   4.1 Other people choose to use the systems that are essential to dyslexic/ SpLDs ..... 51
   4.2 'New' can be problematic ..... 52
   4.3 Agreed checking of details ..... 52
   4.4 People who love being un-organised ..... 53
   4.5 Recognising the source of 'no organisation' ..... 53
   4.6 Benefit from what goes wrong ..... 54
5 Working on organisation ..... 55
   5.1 Materials and methods ..... 56
   5.2 Model for developing organisation ..... 57
      5.2.1 Initial Step 5 ..... 59
      5.2.2 Step 1: gather strengths ..... 60
      5.2.3 Step 2: assess hazards ..... 60
      5.2.4 Step 3: describe what needs organising ..... 61
      5.2.5 Useful questions ..... 61
      5.2.6 Step 4: recognise insuperable obstacles ..... 64
      5.2.7 Step 5: develop constructive ways forward ..... 65
      5.2.8 Recording your system of organisation ..... 65
   5.3 Hazards and obstacles ..... 66
      5.3.1 Pitfalls ..... 67
      5.3.2 Accommodation ..... 69
   5.4 To do lists, diaries and reminders ..... 69
   5.5 Check-list for using the MODEL FOR DEVELOPING ORGANISATION ..... 70
   5.6 Satisfaction: 'The proof of the pudding is in the eating' ..... 72
6 Learning to be organised ..... 73
   6.1 Dyslexia ..... 74
   6.2 Dyspraxia ..... 75
   6.3 AD(H)D ..... 77
   6.4 Dyscalculia and maths difficulties ..... 77
   6.5 Non-dyslexic/ SpLD ..... 79
7 General problem-solving ..... 79
   7.1 Working on a general problem ..... 80
   7.2 Finding the root cause of a problem ..... 82
References and website information ..... 83

## Chapter 2   Time and Time Management

| | |
|---|---|
| Mind map and contents ... 84 | 3  No sense of time ... 88 |
| Vital for dyslexic/ SpLDs, good practice for all ... 85 | 4  Time words have no meaning ... 91 |
| Working with the chapter ... 85 | 5  Co-ordinating time ... 92 |
| Templates on the website ... 86 | 6  Timetables and appointments ... 94 |
| Appendix 1, 2 and 3 ... 86 | 7  Other ideas about time management ... 98 |
| 1  Dipping-in to try out ideas ... 87 | 8  Let go of time ... 100 |
| 2  Context ... 87 | References and website information ... 103 |

## Chapter 3   Space, Place and Direction

| | |
|---|---|
| Mind map and contents ... 104 | 4  No sense of where you are in your environment ... 113 |
| Vital for dyslexic/ SpLDs, good practice for all ... 105 | 5  No sense of place ... 114 |
| Working with the chapter ... 106 | 6  No sense of direction ... 115 |
| Templates on the website ... 106 | 7  Words for space, place and direction have no reliable meaning ... 117 |
| Appendix 1, 2 and 3 ... 106 | 8  The impact of the environment ... 118 |
| 1  Dipping-in to try out ideas ... 107 | 9  Relating to the space around you ... 119 |
| 2  Context ... 108 | References and website information ... 120 |
|    2.1  Dyspraxia ... 110 | |
| 3  No sense of where you are in your body ... 111 | |

## Chapter 4   Everyday Life

| | |
|---|---|
| Mind map and contents ... 122 | 1  Dipping-in to try out ideas ... 126 |
| Vital for dyslexic/ SpLDs, good practice for all ... 123 | 2  Context ... 126 |
| Working with the chapter ... 124 | 3  Dyslexia/ SpLD and everyday life ... 127 |
| Templates on the website ... 124 |    3.1  Maintaining confidence ... 129 |
| Appendix 1, 2 and 3 ... 124 | 4  Solutions overview with examples ... 130 |
| | 5  Task, project, event ... 132 |

xvii

## Chapter 4   Everyday Life *continued*

6   Other people, organisation and everyday life  133
7   Objects needed for an event, task or general living  136
8   Remembering decisions  140
9   Organising paperwork, emails, etc.  144
   9.1   The flow of paperwork  146
   9.2   Gathering strengths to deal with paperwork, etc.  148
   9.3   Assessing hazards and insuperable obstacles in paperwork, etc.  149
   9.4   People you correspond with  150
   9.5   Describe the paperwork, etc., to be organised  150
   9.6   Attractive, constructive organisation of paperwork, etc.  151
   9.7   Filing  152
   9.8   Responding to the paperwork  156
10   When is it safe to throw something away?  159
   10.1   Objects  160
   10.2   Paperwork  161
   10.3   Computers, emails, and electronic devices – deleting  165
References and website information  167

## Chapter 5   Study Peripherals

Mind map and contents  168
Vital for dyslexic/ SpLDs, good practice for all  169
Working with the chapter  170
Templates on the website  170
Appendix 1, 2 and 3  170
1   Dipping-in to try out ideas  171
2   Context  172
3   Navigating the course structure (worked example)  175
   3.1   Preparation  176
      3.1.1   Step 1: gather strengths  176
      3.1.2   Step 2: assess hazards  177
      3.1.3   Step 3: describe what needs organising  180
      3.1.4   Step 4: recognise insuperable obstacles  181
      3.1.5   Step 5: develop constructive ways forward  181
   3.2   Course materials  181
   3.3   Meeting tutors  183
   3.4   Coursework  184
   3.5   Group work  185
   3.6   Your materials  186
   3.7   Timetable and study time  187
   3.8   Meeting deadlines  188
4   Dyslexia/ SpLD support  189
   4.1   IT: assistive technology  190
   4.2   Specialist 1:1 support  191
   4.3   Exam provisions (worked example)  194
5   Engaging with your institution's regulations, culture and departments  199
6   Other people  204
7   Finances  204
8   Everyday living  205
References and website information  205

## Chapter 6  Employment

| | |
|---|---|
| Mind map and contents ... 206 | 4  Employment, study, study peripherals and everyday life ... 215 |
| Vital for dyslexic/ SpLDs, good practice for all ... 207 | 4.1  Possible problematic issues in employment ... 217 |
| Working with the chapter ... 208 | 4.2  Learning new systems ... 218 |
| Templates on the website ... 208 | 4.3  Support at work ... 218 |
| Appendix 1, 2 and 3 ... 208 | 5  Navigating employment structures ... 219 |
| 1  Dipping-in to try out ideas ... 210 | 6  Handling people relationships well ... 223 |
| 2  Context ... 210 | 6.1  Culture at work ... 224 |
| 3  Choices ... 210 | 6.2  Dyslexic/ SpLD differences at work ... 226 |
| 3.1  To declare your dyslexia/ SpLD or not ... 212 | 6.3  Resolving interpersonal issues ... 228 |
| 3.2  Choices in employment ... 213 | 6.4  Dyslexic/ SpLD impossibilities ... 230 |
| 3.3  Keeping good records of your ideas ... 214 | References and website information ... 230 |
| 3.4  Choosing to change jobs ... 214 | |

## Appendix 1 Resources

| | |
|---|---|
| Contents ... 232 | 4  Generating useful questions ... 238 |
| Templates on the website ... 232 | 5  Surveying ... 241 |
| 1  General resources ... 233 | 6  Recording as you scan ... 242 |
| 2  Collecting information together ... 234 | 7  Monitoring progress ... 243 |
| 3  Prioritising ... 236 | References and website information ... 244 |

## Appendix 2  Individual, Personal Profile of Dyslexia/ SpLD and Regime for Managing Dyslexia/ SpLD

| | |
|---|---|
| Contents ... 246 | 1.4  Mental energy to manage dyslexia/ SpLD ... 249 |
| Templates on the website ... 247 | 2  Building up insights ... 250 |
| 1  Living confidently ... 248 | 3  The tool box for living confidently ... 253 |
| 1.1  Individual, personal profile of dyslexia/ SpLD ... 248 | 4  Updating the tool box ... 256 |
| 1.2  Regime for managing dyslexia/ SpLD ... 248 | 5  Negotiating accommodation ... 258 |
| 1.3  Testing and developing your profile and regime ... 249 | References and website information ... 261 |

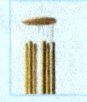

# Appendix 3 Key Concepts

Contents ............................................. 262
Templates on the website ............. 264
Context ............................................. 264
1  Thinking clearly (pausing) ......... 264
   1.1  Breathing                     265
   1.2  Relaxation                    266
2  Using the mind well ................... 267
   2.1  Mind set                      267
   2.2  Chunking                      267
   2.3  Recall and check              268
   2.4  Memory consolidation          268
   2.5  Concentration                 268
   2.6  Metacognition                 268
   2.7  Objective observation         268
   2.8  Reflection                    269
   2.9  Prioritising                  269
   2.10 A model of learning           269
3  Thinking preferences ................. 270
   3.1  The senses: visual, verbal and kinaesthetic  270
   3.2  Rationale or framework        271
   3.3  Holistic vs. linear           271
   3.4  Motivation                    271
         3.4.1  Myers-Briggs Personality Type  272
         3.4.2  Multiple Intelligences 272
   3.5  'Other'                       273

4  Useful approaches ..................... 273
   4.1  Materials and methods         273
   4.2  Model for developing organisation  274
   4.3  Comprehension                 274
   4.4  Key words                     274
   4.5  Know your goal                275
   4.6  Planning                      275
5  Aspects of dyslexia/ SpLD ......... 276
   5.1  Learned confusion             276
   5.2  Oldest memory trace           276
   5.3  Attention to learning         276
   5.4  Average level of language skills a disadvantage  276
   5.5  4 levels of compensation      276
   5.6  Pitfalls                      277
   5.7  Accommodation                 277
   5.8  Degrees of severity           278
   5.9  Stress                        278
   5.10 Benefits of recognising the problems  278
References and website information ......... 278

# Glossary

Contents ............................................. 280
1   Table: Symbols ............................... 280
2   Table: Specific Learning Difficulties
    (SpLDs) descriptions ..................... 280
3   Table: Acronyms ............................. 282
4   Table: Words and phrases, alphabetical
    list ............................................... 283
References and website information ..... 288

# List of Templates on the Website

List of templates ................................... 290

# Index

Useful groups of entries ................. 294     Alphabetic entries ............................. 295

# Useful Preface
## This is worth reading

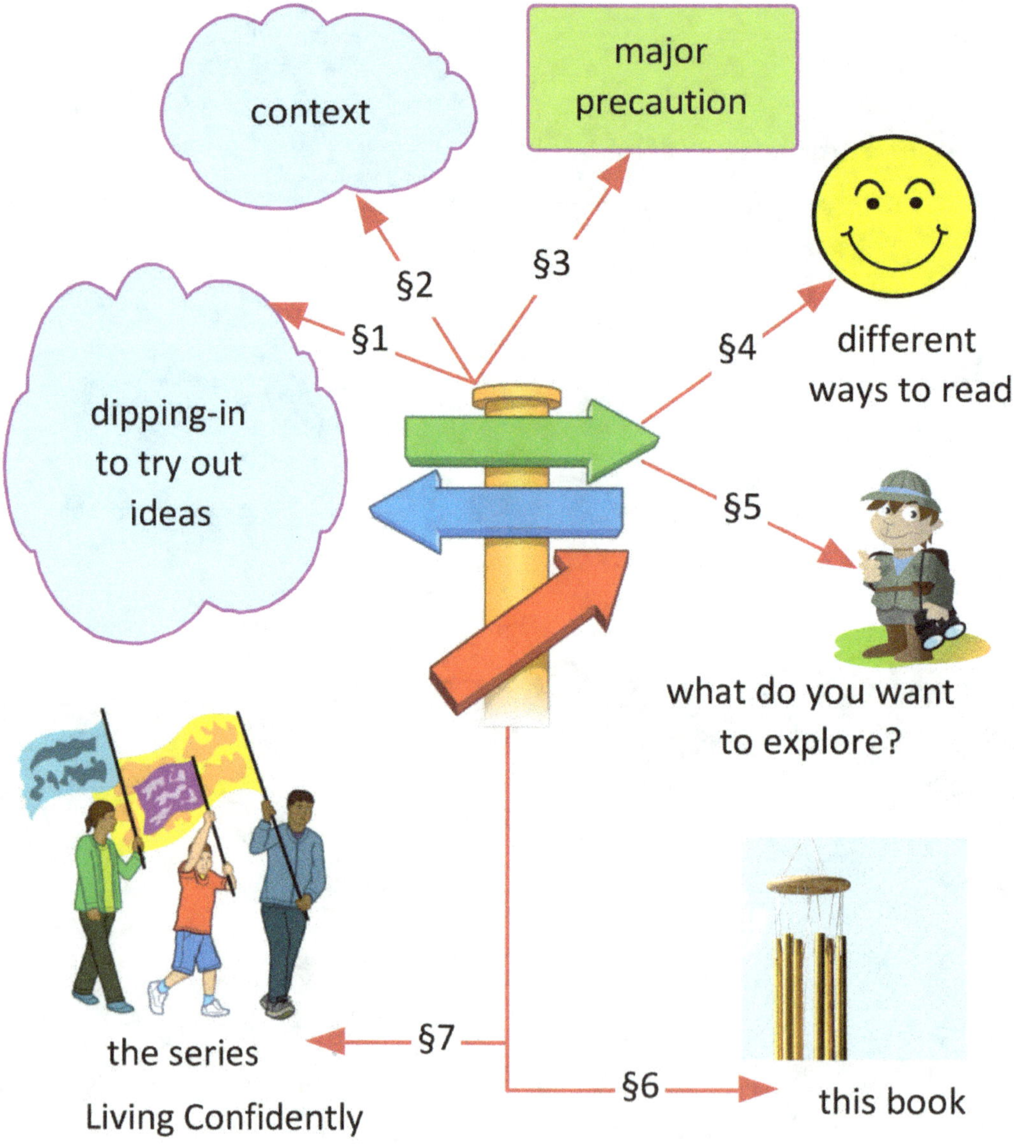

- §1 → dipping-in to try out ideas
- §2 → context
- §3 → major precaution
- §4 → different ways to read
- §5 → what do you want to explore?
- §6 → this book
- §7 → the series Living Confidently

# Contents

    What to expect from this book ........... 1
USEFUL PREFACE summary ............ 2
Templates on the website ............ 2
Appendix 1 ............ 2
1    Dipping-in to try out ideas ............ 2
2    Context, including PHILOSOPHY OF THIS SERIES ............ 3
3    Major precaution ............ 7
4    Different ways to read ............ 9
    4.1  Exercise: reading style    11
    4.2  Something goes wrong with reading    11
5    What do you want to explore? ............ 12
    5.1  Initial purpose for reading    14
    5.2  Reader groups    15
    5.3  Reading to find out about a theme    17

6    This book: *Organisation and Everyday Life with Dyslexia and other SpLDs* ............ 18
    6.1  Aims, outcomes and benefits    20
7    The series: *Living Confidently with Specific Learning Difficulties (SpLDs)* .... 21
    7.1  Readership/ audience    21
    7.2  Summary of the series    21
    7.3  Aims and outcomes    31
    7.4  Distinguishing between the different SpLDs    32
    7.5  The way forward    33
References and website information ............ 34

ⓖ p 282: SpLD: specific learning difficulty of which dyslexia is the best known and most widely researched

---

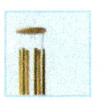 

### Insight:  What to expect from this book

Stories, insights and descriptions of everyday life that prompt you to recognise the ways your dyslexia/ SpLD has an impact on your own life.

We all have different experiences, so your precise situation may not be included; but how to explore what happens for you is at the heart of the book.

Taking charge of your dyslexia/ SpLD is a challenge you can accept, with the aim of minimising any disruptive effects and accentuating all the positive contributions you can make to anything you engage in.

# Useful Preface

## Useful Preface Summary

This preface is similar in the four books.

The book icon shows the sections that are particular to this book. The left margin blue line shows the length of these sections.

§1, DIPPING-IN TO TRY OUT IDEAS, suggests a quick way through.
§2, CONTEXT, shows my positive approach to dyslexia/ SpLD.
§3, MAJOR PRECAUTION, is about avoiding an increase in the effects of your dyslexia/ SpLD.
§4, DIFFERENT WAYS TO READ, is a first look at some of the issues with reading and will help you to read in different ways.
§5, WHAT DO YOU WANT TO EXPLORE, will help you decide how you want the book to help you.
§6, THIS BOOK: ORGANISATION AND EVERYDAY LIFE WITH DYSLEXIA AND OTHER SpLDS, sets the scene for this book.
§7, THE SERIES: LIVING CONFIDENTLY WITH SPECIFIC LEARNING DIFFICULTIES, gives a broad brush synopsis of the four books with details of the aims, outcomes and benefits.

§1: p 2
§2: p 3
§3: p 7

§4: p 9

§5: p 12

§6: p 18

§7: p 21

## Templates on the website

A1   JOTTING DOWN AS YOU SCAN
A2   BOOKMARK – PURPOSE
A4   JOTTING DOWN AS YOU READ
A5   COLLECTING IDEAS THAT INTEREST YOU

TEMPLATES

## Appendix 1  Resources

COLLECTING INFORMATION TOGETHER has ideas to help you be systematic about the way you gather information together.

COLLECTING INFORMATION TOGETHER: p 234

## 1   Dipping-in to try out ideas

Read INSIGHT BOX: WHAT TO EXPECT FROM THIS BOOK, above.
Read §3, MAJOR PRECAUTION.
Do the EXERCISE: AVOID MORE PROBLEMS WHEN LEARNING NEW SKILLS.
Read the 3 boxes in §2, CONTEXT.
Scan §4, DIFFERENT WAYS TO READ, then do the EXERCISE: READING STYLES, §4.1.

§3: p 7
EXERCISE: AVOID MORE PROBLEMS ... p 8

§2: p 3

§4: p 9
§4.1: p 11

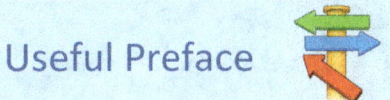

# Useful Preface

Read *§4.2, Something Goes Wrong with Reading.*

Read *Tip: Know Your Reason for Reading, §5.*

Do the *Exercise: Initial Purpose for Reading* in *§5.1.*

§4.2: p 11

§5: p 12
§5.1: p 14

## 2  Context

### Story: Two dyslexic sailors

*Scene*: sailing on a yacht belonging to John.  I had to learn the sequence for turning on the engine safely.

"I just can't do it that way!  I know how my mind works.  I've been teaching in the field for ages.  You've got to listen to me!  Let me ask my questions.  Let me understand.  Then I will be able to do it."

The frustration of being faced with another dyslexic person who WILL NOT LISTEN!

Both of us are fairly stubborn because we've individually worked out what we need to do to succeed and we're both teachers in different fields.  We just don't happen to have the same thinking preferences.

In this situation, I'm slightly at a disadvantage because I'm the novice in John's field and there's no way either of us want me to go into my professional role to analyse his strategies.

We simply both want me to learn to switch the engine on.

If I hadn't found my voice, there was no way I could find my way through my friend's view of how to learn (but see *Margin Note*).

*Margin Note*: I appreciated John's approach when he used it to help me up and down a 604m climb beside a Norwegian fjord.

As we learn we change the workings of our minds.  There are changes at the neuron level of the brain.  Efficient learning results in good neural networks.

Ⓖ  p 283:
 neural networks

# Useful Preface

The following analogy helps you to think about neural networks.

**Insight: Park paths and pruning neurons**

If a park has no fences round it, people will walk across in many different directions.

If a park has 2 gates on opposite sides of the park, people will walk across in a straight line between the gates. A definite path will show where the grass is worn away.

If the park has several gates either side, there will be a series of paths linking the various gates.

When a baby is born, the brain is like the unfenced park: few routes have been established through the brain to respond to the world around.

As a result of good learning, definite neuronal networks become established with use; this is the result of neuronal pruning. The single path is the analogy for non-dyslexia/ SpLD.

The park with several gates either side and many paths linking them is the analogy for dyslexia/ SpLD.

ⓖ p 283: pruning, neuron

Neuronal pruning: Kolb (1995)

**The philosophy of this series**

The philosophy of this series of books is that we, dyslexic/ SpLD people, can work out how our minds work, we can direct our thinking so that it is as effective as possible and we can enjoy contributing to the situations that we find ourselves in (see MARGIN NOTE).

We then have ownership of our thinking and actions. We can achieve to the level of our individual potential. We can confidently take our place alongside everyone else in the situations in which we find ourselves. We know how to MANAGE

MARGIN NOTE: As so often, this is good practice for everyone, but VITAL for dyslexic/ SpLDs.

# Useful Preface

OUR DYSLEXIA/ SpLD. We can co-operate with others to minimise the effects of our dyslexia/ SpLD on our own lives and on the lives of those who live, work or engage in action with us.

Dyslexia/ SpLD is not seen as a static phenomenon, like short-sightedness that only slowly changes with time. Dyslexia/ SpLD is seen as a collection of chaotic[1] neural networks that can exist alongside more useful networks.

Once the chaotic neural networks have established, dyslexia/ SpLD has developed. The chaotic neural networks are not destroyed when the more useful networks are established; they can lie dormant for a significant amount of time; they can be triggered into use in different ways. However well you manage it, you are always at risk of being as thoroughly dyslexic/ SpLD as ever.

The collection of chaotic neural networks will vary from person to person, even with the same dyslexia/ SpLD label.

Underlying the networks is a constitutional level of difference, which, when ignored, leads to the establishment of the chaotic neural networks. The constitutional level of difference is the permanent part of dyslexia/ SpLD. The chaotic neural networks are the source of the observed, problematic behaviours.

A child born with the differences at the constitutional level is 'at risk' of dyslexia/ SpLD. When recognised early in the development of learned networks, the constitutional differences do not have to lead to chaotic neural networks, though it may be impossible to prevent all of them. The unorthodox thinking processes that many successful dyslexic/ SpLDs enjoy will still develop, since they

*REGIME FOR MANAGING DYSLEXIA/ SpLD:* p 248

Ⓖ p 283: neural networks

---

[1]Chaos theory: when asked to spell a word, many dyslexic people have a collection of possibilities, for example sense, sens, cens, sns, scens. Each of these possibilities is the product of neural networks that connect the prompt to spell the word to the action of spelling it. By practice of the 'correct spelling' these alternative spellings are expected to be reduced (pruned) to only one, resulting in a stable neural network to achieve the correct spelling. That dyslexics continue throughout life with the variable spelling, shows this pruning isn't working for them and the implied collection of neural networks behind the variations is what I mean by 'chaotic neural networks'. The idea comes from my understanding of chaos theory (Gleick, 1997).

Ⓖ p 303: chaos theory

# Useful Preface

> are needed very early in learning to prevent establishment of the chaotic neural networks.

John is typical of many successful dyslexic/ SpLDs who have got through life without any special attention. They may have used:

- hard work
- sheer determination (John: bloody-mindedness)
- winging it
- the gift of the gab
- secretaries, parents, spouse or partner, children, friends
- one or two teachers with just the right approach
- pot luck
- apprenticeships, or other routes to the top from the shop floor, etc.
- 'other' (always a necessary option).

Whatever the route, they succeeded and they don't see what all the fuss is about now. They are the lucky ones; they made it to success. Many of their contemporaries didn't achieve very much; they can be dissatisfied with life and what they contribute.

*John is in TWO DYSLEXIC SAILORS: p 3*

**Dyslexia/ SpLD, education and beyond**

The educational system used to have elements that suited dyslexic/ SpLDs better than current systems do, and it was possible to get promotion without having to produce certificates that showed what qualifications you had.
There are changes afoot, but not ones that look likely to take us back to a regime that will suit most dyslexic/ SpLDs.

Society, workplace practices and education may change to be more sympathetic to dyslexic/ SpLD people (and to those with other disabilities); assistive technology allows access to modern communication systems; but without finding your own voice you aren't fully the person you could be; in using that voice to communicate with others you need listeners who can hear what you are saying: these last two objectives are the main aims of this series.

*Proverb: 'Give a man a fish and you feed him for a day; teach a man to fish and you feed him for a lifetime.'*

Useful Preface

### 3   Major precaution

**Protection from further dyslexic/ SpLD problems is an important aspect of managing dyslexia/ SpLD.**

**Insight:  Anything 'new' needs care**

You need to be very careful in the initial stages of a subject, or situation, even before you start to make sense of it.  You can too easily create an unhelpful memory that interrupts your thinking for a very long time.

**Example: A problem created at an initial stage**

After some 20 years of playing the guitar, my sight reading is still impaired by an early mistake.

One note (B on the treble clef) is an open string for a beginner, i.e. no left hand finger is needed to play it.  In musical notation, this note is a blob with a line through it (it is the middle line of the treble clef).

'Blob on a line' equated to 'finger on a string' when I first met it, and it still does.  I still have to work really hard to remember the note is an open string; I have to work hard to stop myself putting a finger on a string.

I didn't know then how to manage my dyslexia.  Now I know that I have to be careful, particularly at the beginning of something new.

# Useful Preface

### Exercise: Avoid more problems when learning new skills[2]

- What were the skills you learnt most recently?
- How did you learn them?
- What task was involved?
- How important are the skills to you?
- What made them easy to learn?
- What was hard about learning them?
- How easily have you been able to adapt the skills to other uses?

Reflection question: Is it a good idea to try out something new on tasks that are really important to you?

- It is OK if you can easily make changes to the way you do something later.

- It is not OK if you find the first way you tackle something leaves a strong impression.

- If this is your experience, try out new systems or skills on tasks that you don't mind about too much but that you are quite interested in.

- It is not OK if you are likely to think: "Can I trust this new approach? Will it muck up this task or topic?" Doubt like this will not allow you to explore the new approach freely.

- If in any doubt, use a task or topic that doesn't matter too much first; struggling with dyslexic/ SpLD tangles is such a pain, it's worth avoiding new problems.

- You won't give a new skill or system a fair trial, if you are worried about it or the task.

This green colour is recommended for colour blind people on the website of Okabe and Ito (Accessed 29 Jan 2017)

---

[2] The way many dyslexic/ SpLD people have to pay attention to learning may mean first learning makes more of an impression than it does for other learners.

# Useful Preface

## 4  Different ways to read

You may not like reading.  Many dyslexic/ SpLD people don't.
Do take notice of the message in SOMETHING GOES WRONG WITH READING: the author's style can cause problems.

SOMETHING GOES WRONG WITH READING: p 11

>
>
> **Tip:  Margin**
>
> You can use the right-hand margin to jot down your ideas as you scan or read the book.
>
> I have used it for cross-referencing and for references to help you find these when you want them.

The books in this series are written with several different styles of reading in mind.

You need to decide what your style of reading should be; do EXERCISE: READING STYLE.  You may find a new style that suits you.  Different styles might suit you at different times or for different purposes.

MARGIN NOTE: the different ways of reading relate to THINKING PREFERENCES: p 270 and in INDEX

EXERCISE: READING STYLE: p 11

The reading style is in green;
the writing styles in this book are in blue.

| | |
|---|---|
| Linear readers | People who read easily, starting at the beginning of a book. |
| | The books are written with a flow of information that can be read from beginning to end. |
| Spatial readers | People who would read best by moving about a book, finding the most relevant parts first. |
| | Each chapter starts with a DIPPING-IN section that helps the reader choose the best way to dip-in. |
| Framework readers | People who need an overview to be able to understand.  Some people's brains don't retain information unless they have thought about the framework, or schema, that holds it all together. |

Ⓖ p 283: framework schema

# Useful Preface

| | | |
|---|---|---|
| **Framework readers continued** | The P*HILOSOPHY OF THIS* S*ERIES* is one framework of the series. | P*HILOSOPHY OF THIS* S*ERIES*: p 4 |
| | Each chapter has a contents list and a mind map at the beginning to help people understand the author's overview. | |
| | R*ATIONALE, OR* F*RAMEWORK* outlines the importance of establishing a schema. | R*ATIONALE OR* F*RAMEWORK*: p 271 |
| **Sense-oriented readers** | Some people's understanding is dependent on the sense(s) they use. They may not use the senses equally. Vision, sound and the kinaesthetic sense are the most commonly used ones in education. People vary: of these three senses, sometimes one or another is very much more used, or one may be decidedly less used than the other two. Smell and taste are also senses and may need to be considered. | Senses: visual, verbal (oral/aural) kinaesthetic |
| | | Ⓖ p 283: kinaesthetic M*ARGIN* N*OTE*: The kinaesthetic sense uses body perception and physical movement to good effect |
| | 1) Visually: different layouts are used to indicate different types of information. For example: exercises for the reader are in green boxes. Cartoons and figures are used. | visual p 270 and in I*NDEX* |
| | 2) Orally/aurally: the language is direct, not complicated, but elegant (at least that is the intention). | verbal (oral/aural) p 270 and in I*NDEX* |
| | 3) Kinaesthetic: there are exercises for the reader which should engage the kinaesthetic sense; as should the anecdotes about the actions of others. | kinaesthetic: p p 270 and in I*NDEX* |
| **Interest-oriented readers** | Some people use their strongest interests in order to understand; they cannot retain information if these interests are not actively engaged. | |
| | 1) Some ideas about innate interests are listed in M*OTIVATION* in terms of Myers-Briggs Personality Type and Multiple Intelligences. Any reader for whom motivation is a key issue should use the ideas to work out what their particular motivation might be and deliberately use it while reading these books | M*OTIVATION*: p 271 |

# Useful Preface

| | |
|---|---|
| Interest-oriented readers *continued* | 2) Material can be written bearing in mind different motivations by presenting different perspectives. The suggested ROUTES on the WEBSITE for various reader groups are examples of catering for different perspectives. |
| Further comment | If two or more people are using the book together, the different styles of reading should be accommodated. |

ROUTES COMPANION WEBSITE

## 4.1 Exercise: reading style

**Exercise: Reading style**

Consider which styles of reading might suit you:
- Why might they suit you?
- Which have you tried already?
- Which work most of the time/ sometimes/ never?
- Which sound worth experimenting with?
- What do you know already about your way of reading?

See examples in *DIFFERENT WAYS TO READ*: p 9

## 4.2 Something goes wrong with reading

If you are struggling with reading, it is important to check whether there is anything that can be done about it.

For example, going to sleep over reading can indicate that the brain is taking in too much material that has not been understood properly.

There are many approaches to make reading effective that do not involve the mechanics of reading. The full discussion of reading is in *Gaining Knowledge and Skills with Dyslexia and other SpLDs* (Stacey, 2021). The discussion includes ways in which an author's style of writing is unhelpful to dyslexic/ SpLDs.

Stacey (2021)

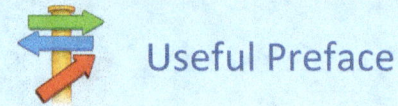 Useful Preface

**Insight: External factors hamper reading**

Reading difficulties can be made a lot worse by the way the text is written or presented. They aren't just from your dyslexia/ SpLD.

**Insight: Word changes cause doubt**

Some authors don't like to repeat the same word too many times, so they change the word even though the idea hasn't changed.

Do you ever find that you then start to doubt your reading ability? It's as if your mind is worrying because you may have missed some significant detail that the change of words indicates. Then gradually, your reading skill deserts you; you struggle; you end up sleeping over the text, even when you are very interested in it.

Sometimes in this series, I have deliberately not changed words, even though the repetition is rather tedious.

## 5   What do you want to explore?

One key tactic for making reading easier is to prime your mind, rather like warming up muscles. No serious sportsman would start their sport without warming up their muscles. The mind can be looked after in the same way.

# Useful Preface

> ➡️ **Tip: Know your reason for reading**
>
> When you identify your main purpose for reading anything, you give your mind some guidelines for understanding what you are reading.
>
> You then allow yourself to explore the text, looking to satisfy your purpose; reading is much easier.

 Dyslexia and the other specific learning difficulties (SpLDs) have wide-spread impact on our lives.

Ginny Stacey and Sally Fowler are both dyslexic, in different ways!

This book is worth reading because:
- it has many examples of the way organisation has an impact on the everyday life of dyslexic/ SpLD people
- it sets out a system for developing organisation
- it has a check-list for using the organisation
- it deals with problem solving
- it applies the ideas to organising:
    o time and time management
    o space, place and direction
    o everyday life
    o study peripherals
    o employment.

Any of these topics in the book could be part of your purpose for reading.

# Useful Preface

## 5.1  Initial purpose for reading

The following exercise is designed to help establish any reader's initial purpose: you are effectively creating your own dipping-in list.

### Exercise:  Initial purpose for reading

1  Use the TEMPLATE: A1 - JOTTING DOWN AS YOU SCAN to keep track of ideas.
   1.1  Remember you are scanning for this exercise, not reading. You are finding the sections most interesting to you now.

2  Scan the following places to find ideas that catch your interest:
   2.1  point 1.1 above, to remember to scan
   2.2  the orange insight boxes in this chapter
   2.3  the TABLE OF READER GROUPS, §5.2
   2.4  the themes in §5.3, READING TO FIND OUT ABOUT A THEME
   2.5  §6, THIS BOOK: ORGANISATION AND EVERYDAY LIFE WITH DYSLEXIA AND OTHER SPLDS
   2.6  §7, THE SERIES: LIVING CONFIDENTLY WITH SPECIFIC LEARNING DIFFICULTIES (SPLDS)
   2.7  the CONTENTS of the book
   2.8  the INDEX.

3  For each idea that catches your attention:
   3.1  note where in the book the idea is
   3.2  why the idea interests you
   3.3  how important the idea is to you immediately and in the longer-term.

4  Think about your life:
   4.1  What issues to do with dyslexia/ SpLD do you want to understand or solve?
   4.2  What situations in everyday life, employment or study are affected by your dyslexia/ SpLD, or might be affected?

5  Look at the list of ideas you have made.
   5.1  Are there any common threads that could be grouped together?  Use TEMPLATE: A5 - COLLECTING IDEAS THAT INTEREST YOU to gather the common threads.

---

TEMPLATES

§5.2: p 15
§5.3: p 17
§6: p 18
§7: p 21

CONTENTS: p xv
INDEX: p 295

NB: you are creating your personal dipping-in list.

TEMPLATES

# Useful Preface

> 5.2 Number the ideas in the order that you would like to explore them now.
>
> 5.3 Write the ideas on the *Template: A2 - Bookmark – Purpose* in the order that you want to explore them. The *Bookmark – Purpose* will remind you what you have decided to explore.
>
> 6 Start reading. Use *Template: A4 - Jotting Down as You Read*, or any other template, to capture insights as you read.

 ## 5.2 Reader groups

One way of giving your mind the guidelines that assist reading is to recognise why you want to acquire any new information.

I have thought about different reader groups with slightly different reasons for reading this book. These are shown in the *Box: Reader Groups*.

This section gives the profile of each group.

 The *website companion* has further reader groups for the whole series.

---

**Reader groups**

| | | |
|---|---|---|
| A | Dyslexic/ SpLD readers wanting: | |
| A1 | | to understand what happens to them |
| A2 | | to solve problems |
| A3 | | to apply how they think best. |
| B | Non-dyslexic/ SpLD people wanting: | |
| B1 | | to understand more about ways dyslexic/ SpLDs manage their lives |
| B2 | | to use the many ideas that are good practice for all while being VITAL for dyslexic/ SpLDs. |

---

Decide which reader group(s) you belong to.

Why do you choose the group(s)?

What information are you looking for? Use *Reading to Find Out about a Theme*, below, and *Aims, Outcomes and Benefits* to help you decide.

*Aims, Outcomes and Benefits:* p 20

# Useful Preface

**A1-A3: Dyslexic/ SpLD people**

These groups include those who have formal diagnostic assessments and those who suspect they belong to the dyslexic/ SpLD group. They need to know as much as possible about themselves in order to gain autonomy.

*autonomy: control over your life by self-determination: acting and thinking for yourself; independent; free; self-governing*

The groups are distinguished by three approaches:
- wanting to understand what happens
- wanting to solve problems
- wanting to apply how they think best.

As far as final outcomes are concerned, there is no difference between these three groups. The initial approach is likely to be quite different.

**The A3 group** – dyslexic/ SpLD people whose primary interest is finding out how they think – should start with the 1st book of the series, *Finding Your Voice with Dyslexia and other SpLD* (Stacey, 2019) and then apply their best thinking by using this book. It is important to acknowledge the different approach that suits people in group A3. If you belong to this group, you may find you have questions that need answering before you can make progress with this book and they are questions that this book is not intended to address.

*Stacey (2019)*

**B1:    Non-dyslexic/ SpLD people**

   wanting to understand more about ways dyslexic/ SpLDs manage their lives

The art of living with differences is fundamental to good relationships between people across the dyslexic/ SpLD and non-dyslexic/ SpLD divide.

*MARGIN NOTE FOR READER GROUPS A1-A3: the world around you needs to understand what is happening to you.*

Non-dyslexic/ SpLD people who live with dyslexic/ SpLDs often feel they don't understand how the dyslexic/ SpLDs function. There can be considerable tension when communication is not straightforward.

Those working with dyslexic/ SpLDs or engaging with them in other everyday activities (i.e. 'in action with') may need the same level of knowledge of dyslexia/ SpLD as those living with them. Reactions due to lack of clear communication could be easier to deal with when the people involved are not living in the same place.

# Useful Preface

Good signage and communication styles can make a significant improvement to the ease with which dyslexic/ SpLD people can gain information. Communicators should know the techniques, often simple, that improve the clarity of communication for dyslexic/ SpLD people.

These are all people whose communication and dealings with dyslexic/ SpLD people can have long-reaching affects on the lives of the dyslexic/ SpLD people. It is usually really important that any impact of the dyslexia/ SpLD is clearly and fairly dealt with. Misunderstandings and difficulties in communication may be obvious to both sides but they can also be hidden because neither group of people is paying any attention to different interpretations during the communication.

Dyslexia/ SpLDs are hidden: you cannot look at one of this group of people and say, "That person has dyslexia/ SpLD, I need to be aware of that." Much of the general approach to dyslexia/ SpLD is about courtesy between people; an increase in courtesy would be beneficial to society at large. Policy makers and politicians, especially, need to be well informed at a general level of interest because policies built on incomplete knowledge can be harmful and expensive.

**B2:    Non-dyslexic/ SpLD people**

    to use the many ideas that are good practice for all while being VITAL for dyslexic/ SpLDs

There are many ideas that apply to people in general. Non-dyslexic/ SpLD readers can find ideas to improve their approach to many tasks or situations.

## 5.3  Reading to find out about a theme

Dyslexia/ SpLD impacts on the whole of life. There may be a particular aspect of your life that you want to explore first. In thinking how a dyslexic/ SpLD person might approach the material, I put together several different themes. The themes relevant to this book are listed below. The full list of themes in the series is on the *Website*, with where to find the discussions.

THEMES

# Useful Preface

 The themes that are relevant to this book include:
Organisation
- Using your strengths
- Recognising hazards and obstacles

Creating satisfying systems for organising
- Time and time management
- Space, place and directions
- Everyday life
    - Tasks, projects, events
    - Objects
    - Remembering decisions
    - Paperwork, emails, etc.
    - Throwing away or deleting
- Study peripherals
    - Navigating course structures
- Employment
    - Navigating employment structures
- Making choices
- Relating to other people

The themes for the rest of the series come under the general headings of:

Living with confidence
- Individual, personal profile of dyslexia/ SpLD
- Regime for managing dyslexia/ SpLD

Thinking, knowledge and skills

Understanding and dialogue

## 6   This book: *Organisation and Everyday Life with Dyslexia and other SpLDs*

Organisation underpins so much of what we do and think, even when very young.  Child development is a subsection of Social Psychology with a large literature.  As babies explore their environment, they make schemas from the multitude of signals received by their senses.

ⓖ p 283:  schema

# Useful Preface

Learning involves organising thoughts. It continues throughout life; for example, when the local supermarket changes its shelving, you have to learn the new system. Organisation has a central position in managing dyslexia/ SpLD, especially as it is one of the manifest behavioural problems of dyslexia/ SpLD (Stacey, 2020b).

Dyslexia/ SpLD is noticed most often when you are expected to learn something. Teachers or parents have expectations that are not being met by your performance. The other groups of people who are concerned about performance are employers and managers at work. These are simply times when other people are paying particular attention. The person living with dyslexia/ SpLD knows it affects the whole of life.

This book describes many situations which are affected by the impact of organisation on the lives of dyslexic/ SpLD people. The hope is that you will recognise some as being very similar to your own experience. Those stories that are unfamiliar are an opportunity to observe what happens in your life and work out how your own dyslexia/ SpLD affects you.

Anything to do with time and place often causes difficulty in organisation for dyslexic/ SpLDs. The problems often relate to the way the senses of time and space, place and direction have developed in your brain.

This book uses a particular model for developing organisation and then applies it to:
- time and time management
- space, place and direction
- everyday life
- study peripherals
- employment

with the last two being recognised as special cases of everything else.

There are 2 annotated examples in the book. NAVIGATING THE COURSE STRUCTURE has been annotated to show how to adapt the processes to NAVIGATING EMPLOYMENT STRUCTURES. EXAM PROVISIONS has been annotated to adapt the processes to much more general situations.

Stacey (2020b)

NAVIGATING THE COURSE STRUCTURE: p 175
NAVIGATING EMPLOYMENT STRUCTURES: p 219

EXAM PROVISIONS: p 194

# Useful Preface

## 6.1 Aims, outcomes and benefits

The aim of this book is to give you much more control over the ways your dyslexia/ SpLD affects your life, any study you undertake and the way you conduct your work.

You should have a greater understanding of the breadth of the impact and some insights that allow you to take your dyslexia/ SpLD in your stride. If you work with the book, you can develop your own strategies so that you can readily use them. You should also have a clearer idea as to when and how you might struggle more than usual with dyslexia/ SpLD.

Many students have benefitted from this greater understanding and more proficient control. They have reached a stage of enjoying the positive sides of their potential and not minding about the dyslexia/ SpLD. It is my hope that you will also find such benefits.

### Insight: Freedom to be at your best

Dyslexia/ SpLD can hamper people in their everyday life, study or employment.

Recognising the effects and managing them is possible and rewarding.

To be organised is not promoted as a desirable end, rather organisation is seen as a tool to use to put your dyslexia/ SpLD in its place so that:

### You Are Free To Be At Your Best

# Useful Preface

## 7  The Series: *Living Confidently with Specific Learning Difficulties (SpLDs)*

### 7.1  Readership/ audience

*Living Confidently with Specific Learning Difficulties (SpLDs)* is a series of books that look at the whole of the experience of living with these specific learning difficulties.

| Descriptions in ⓖ p 280 of 4 SpLDs: dyslexia, dyspraxia, AD(H)D, dyscalculia |

The ideas described in this series draw on work over 25 years helping individuals to find out how their minds work and how to use them effectively in study or everyday life.

*Finding Your Voice with Dyslexia and other SpLDs* and *Organisation and Everyday Life with Dyslexia and other SpLDs* are both written addressing dyslexic/ SpLD people.

*Gaining Knowledge and Skills with Dyslexia and other SpLDs* and *Development of Dyslexia and other SpLDs* both address people in roles alongside a dyslexic/ SpLD person.

Each book can be used on its own, but there are some concepts that spread over the four. The KEY CONCEPTS are summarised in APPENDIX 3.

*APPENDIX 3:* p 262

### 7.2  Summary of the series

Life is a journey. We need to find our way through it.

We need our own voice to help us navigate.

*Living Confidently with Specific Learning Difficulties (SpLDs)* is about living life to the full and enjoying the journey, each person using her maximum potential and minimising the effects of her dyslexia/ SpLD.

# Useful Preface

Book 1: *Finding Your Voice with Dyslexia and other SpLDs* (Stacey, 2019)
The book is written for dyslexic/ SpLD people and contains:

- building a personal, individual profile
    - thinking preferences
    - pitfalls
    - ways to pause well
    - accommodations
- four steps for managing dyslexia/ SpLD
    - recognising your pitfalls
    - pausing
    - using your thinking preferences
    - knowing your goal
- ideas from physiology and psychology that
    - relate to dyslexia/ SpLD
    - help make sense of some effects of dyslexia/ SpLD
- techniques for using the mind well
    - mind set
    - chunking
    - recall
    - memory consolidation
    - concentration
    - metacognition
    - objective observation
    - reflection
    - making connections
    - prioritising
- thinking preferences
    - senses: visual, aural/oral (verbal), kinaesthetic
    - framework or rationale
    - holistic vs. linear thinking
    - Myers-Briggs Personality Type, especially motivation
    - Multiple Intelligences
- thinking clearly: techniques for using maximum mental capacity
    - emotional hi-jacking
    - emotional states of mind
    - confidence
    - self-esteem
    - breathing
    - relaxation
    - Brain Gym
    - Neuro-Linguistic Programming (NLP)
    - the art of pausing and maintaining clear thinking.

# Useful Preface

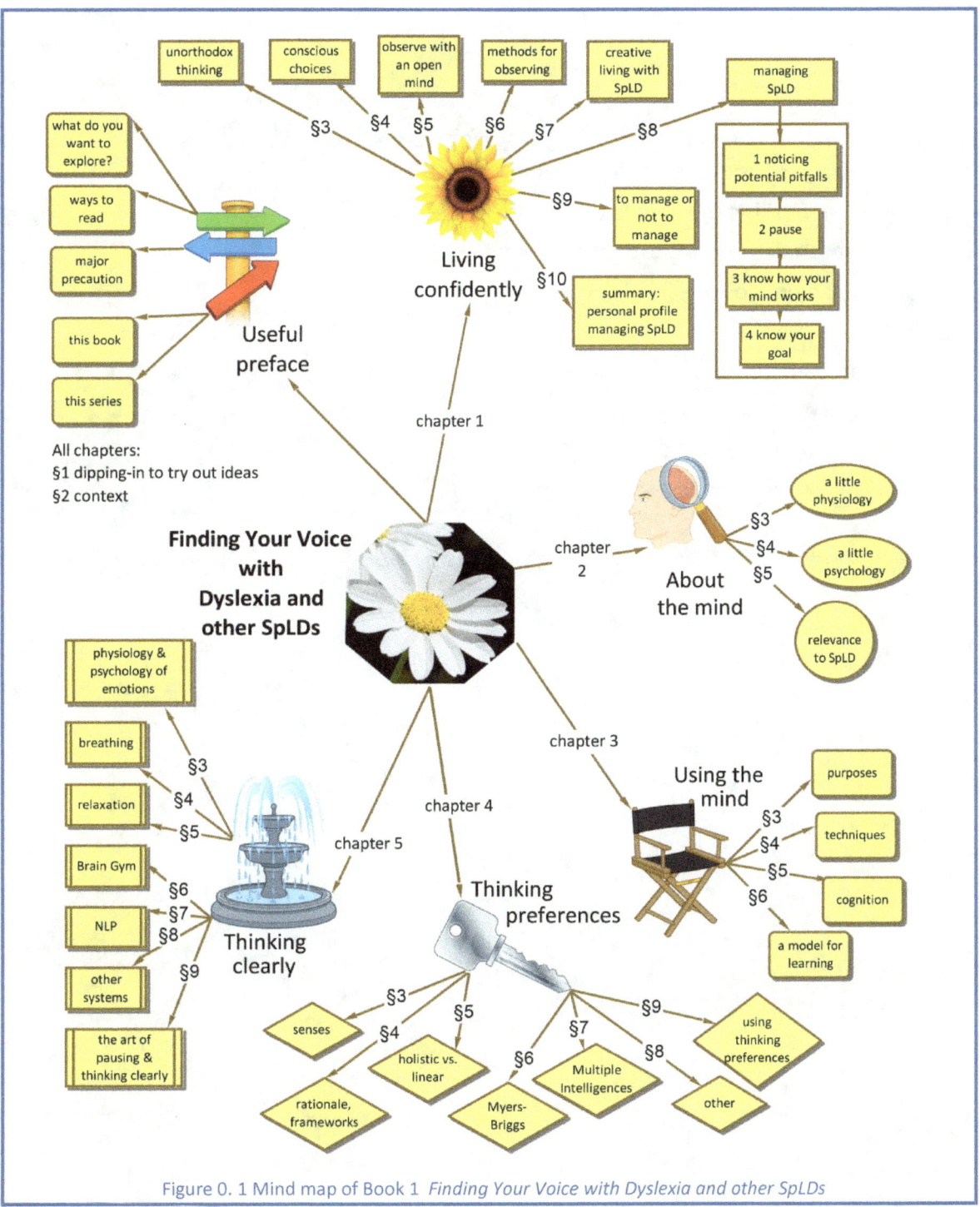

Figure 0. 1 Mind map of Book 1 *Finding Your Voice with Dyslexia and other SpLDs*

# Useful Preface

Book 2: *Organisation and Everyday Life with Dyslexia and other SpLDs* (Stacey, 2020a)
The book is written for dyslexic/ SpLD people and contains:
- a model for working out issues to do with organisation
    - materials and methods for working on any ideas
- general problem-solving
- solutions applied to
    - time and time management
    - space, place and direction
    - everyday life
    - study peripherals
    - employment.

# Useful Preface

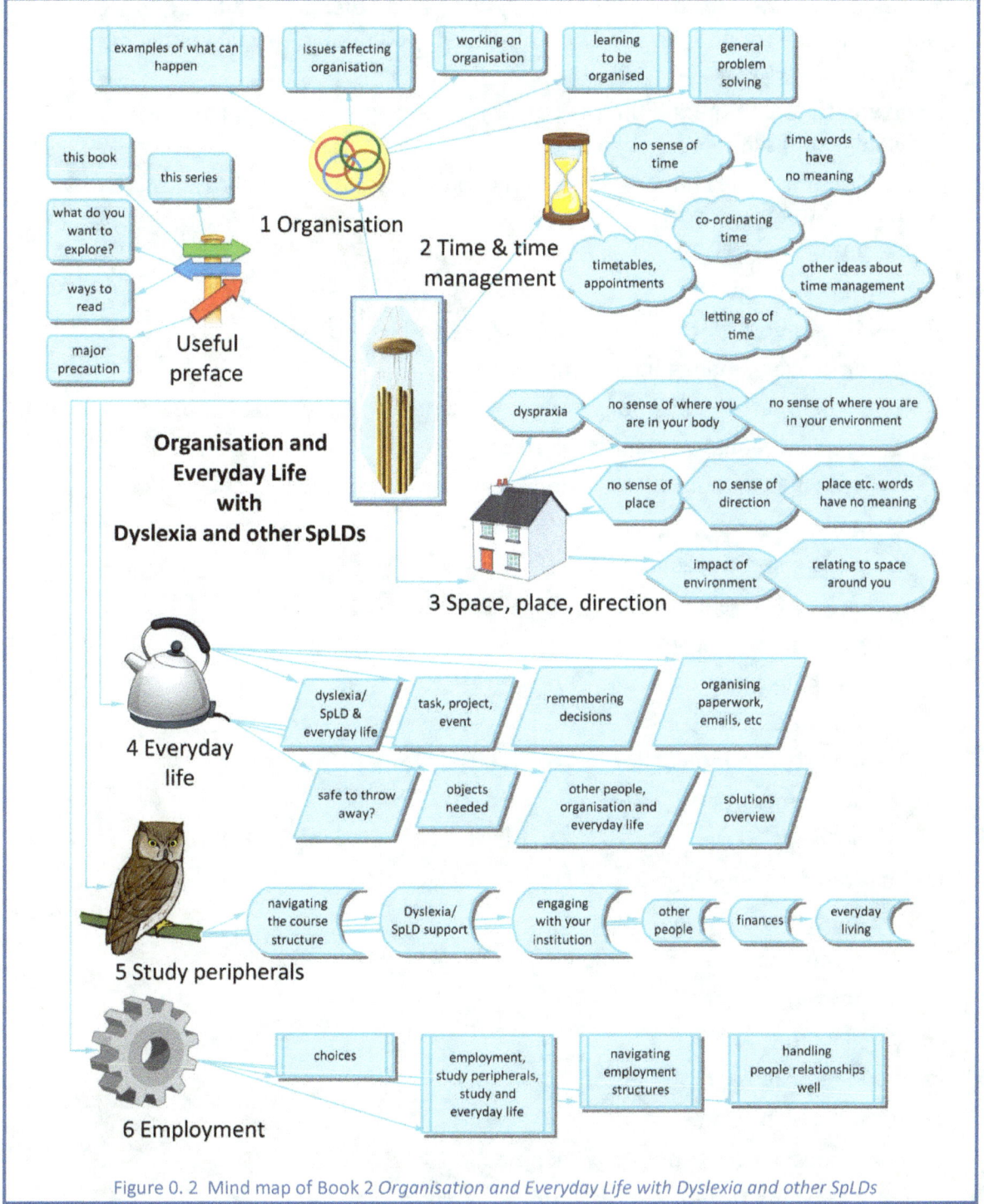

Figure 0.2 Mind map of Book 2 *Organisation and Everyday Life with Dyslexia and other SpLDs*

# Useful Preface

Book 3: *Gaining Knowledge and Skills with Dyslexia and other SpLDs* (Stacey, 2021)
The book is written for people who assist dyslexic/ SpLD people to gain knowledge and skills, which includes everyone:
- when you tell someone the time of day or how to cook an egg, you are passing on knowledge and skills
- you can't immediately tell whether the person you are talking to is dyslexic/ SpLD.

The book contains:
- different roles people have:
    - 1-1 support teachers, subject teachers and lecturers
    - employers, managers and supervisors
    - professionals in positions of influence and authority: healthcare, legal, financial
    - family, friends, acquaintances, work colleagues
    - designers and producers of indirect communications
    - policy makers
    - people in the media
- imparting knowledge and skills:
    - general approaches
    - teaching
    - dialogue
    - indirect communication
    - accommodation
    - policies and systems
- foundations for knowledge and skills:
    - model for learning
    - comprehension
    - knowing the goal
    - planning
- input modes: reading, listening, doing
- taking and making notes
- output modes: writing, speaking, taking-action
- situations: exams, group work (meetings, seminars, debates), driving
    - social examples: travel, job applications, eating out, finances.

# Useful Preface

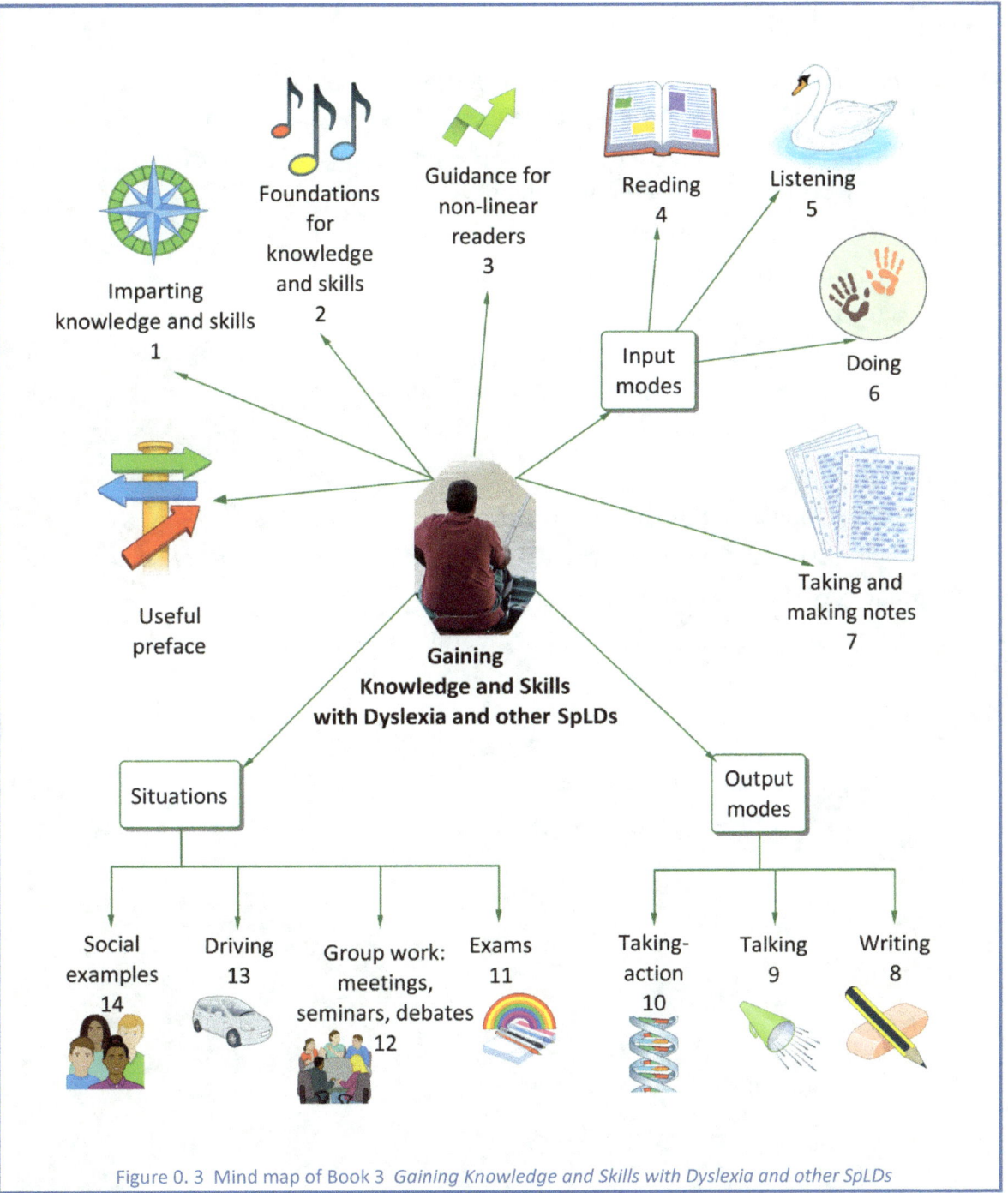

Figure 0.3 Mind map of Book 3 *Gaining Knowledge and Skills with Dyslexia and other SpLDs*

# Useful Preface

Book 4: *Development of Dyslexia and other SpLDs* (Stacey, 2020b)
The book is written for those alongside dyslexic/ SpLD people and contains:

- ideas about the persistence of dyslexia/ SpLD and reasons to take dyslexia/ SpLD into account earlier rather than later, including:
    - learned confusion
    - neurons firing together, wire together
    - the persistence of dyslexia/ SpLD
    - problems masked by average language skills
    - levels of compensation
    - degrees of severity
- what goes wrong
    - discussion about the different SpLDs
    - discussion about similar problems experienced by non-dyslexic/ SpLD people
- adaptations of the ideas for younger children
- how to approach matching an individual's learning to what they are good at.

# Useful Preface

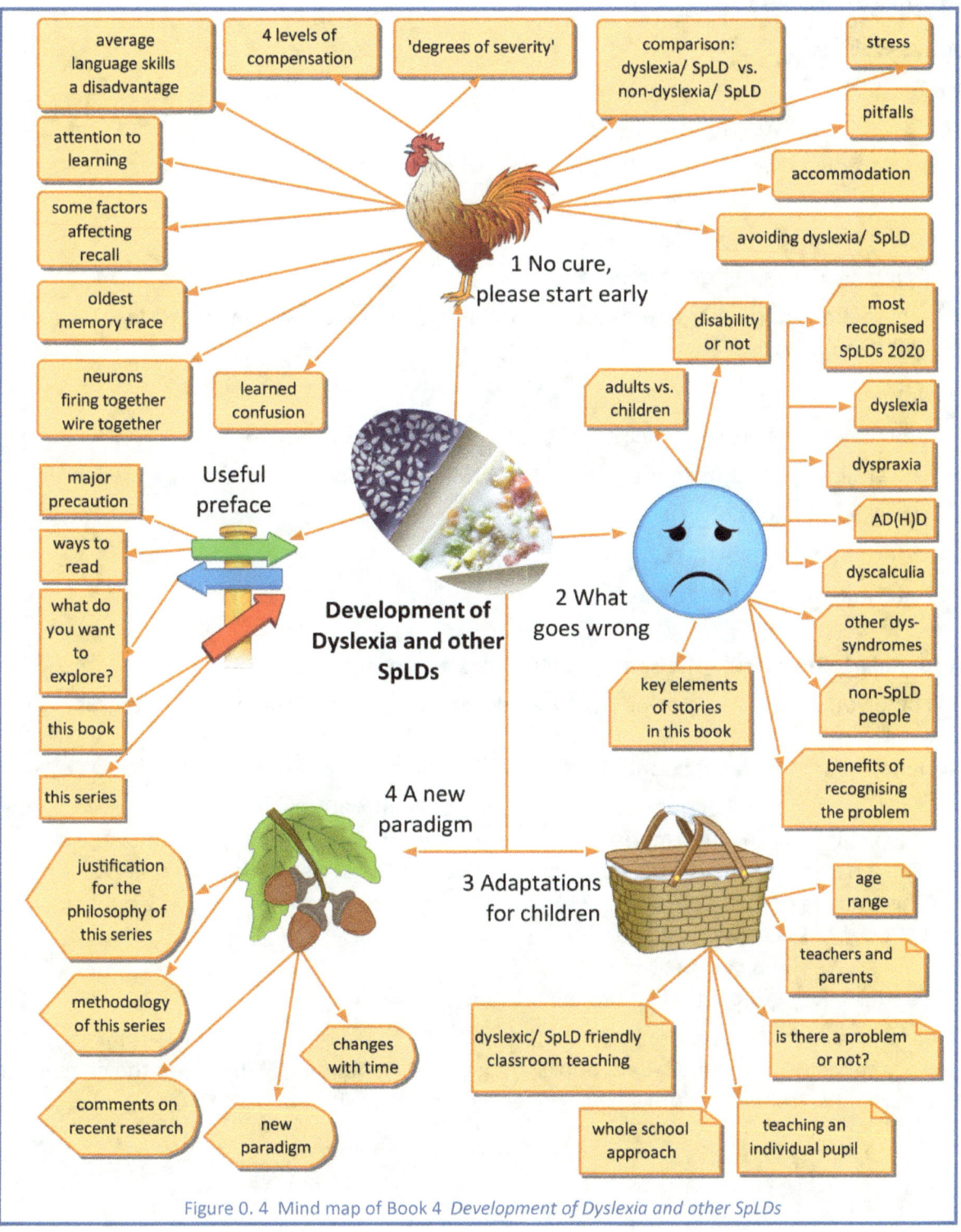

Figure 0. 4 Mind map of Book 4 *Development of Dyslexia and other SpLDs*

# Useful Preface

## Applicable to all books in the series

**Series website**
- has material to assist with using the books:
    - templates and check-lists
    - different ways to select the material most useful to you.

**Useful Preface**
- is mostly the same for each book
- the sections particular to each book are marked by the book icon and a blue line on the left hand margin.

It contains:
- the philosophy of the series
- a warning to avoid further dyslexic/ SpLD traits developing as new things are learnt
- some suggestions to make reading easier
- information about the book in question
- information about the series.

**Appendix 1  Resources** (The same in all 4 books except for referencing.)
will help you collect information together, decide on priorities and monitor progress.

**Appendix 2  Individual, Personal Profile and Regime for Managing Dyslexia/ SpLD**
(The same in all 4 books except for section 1 and referencing.)
will help you build the information about your dyslexia/ SpLD and how you manage it. Section 1, LIVING CONFIDENTLY, starts by stating the aim for dyslexic/ SpLD people to be as autonomous as possible.  In books 2 - 4, a summary of the material in book 1 is included so that these books can be used independently of each other.

**Appendix 3  Key Concepts** (The same in all 4 books except for referencing.)
In order to allow the separate books of the series to be used on their own, summaries of the key concepts of the individual books are given in Appendix 3.  These are the concepts I think are most important for living confidently with dyslexia/ SpLD.

# Useful Preface

Figure 0. 5  Living Confidently with Specific Learning Difficulties (SpLDs)

The book cover images:

The daisy represents growth.

Wind chime music represents life flowing well when organisation suits the individual concerned.

The fisherman recalls the saying: 'Give a man a fish, you feed him for a day; teach a man to fish, you feed him for a lifetime'.

The slices of cake represent changing 'That's the way the cookie crumbles' to 'It's a piece of cake'.

## 7.3  Aims and outcomes

The first group of aims of this series is that dyslexic/ SpLD people can:

- find out what their best ways of thinking are, how to use them and maintain their use
- understand how their specific learning difficulty affects them
- be able to pause when they recognise a pitfall has occurred
- know how to deal with the pitfall
    - by using best ways of thinking
    - knowing what needs to happen
- negotiate with those around them so that they are able to fulfil their potential in any situation and so that the dyslexic/ SpLD effects are minimised.

The general attitude at the end of the process is almost:

- OK, I'm dyslexic/ SpLD; I really enjoy the way I process information and the way I am
- everyone has some problems, mine just happen to have a label
- it's no big deal; I'll do well 'with a little help from my friends'.

In order to achieve this group of aims, a group of specialist support providers will need in-depth knowledge of dyslexia/ SpLD. Their knowledge and experience are usually a major contribution to the progress made by any dyslexic/ SpLD person.

31

# Useful Preface

The second group of aims is that:

- non-dyslexia/ SpLD people can understand better what the issues are for the people with dyslexia/ SpLD
- communication between the two groups can be improved to the benefit of all parties.

These two sets of aims produce different outcomes depending on whether you are dyslexic/ SpLD or alongside a dyslexic/ SpLD person. The WEBSITE has OUTCOMES for various reader groups more finely classified.

They have been divided into:

- the Skills and Knowledge
- the Benefits, including changes of behaviour
- and some thoughts about the Potential Possibilities.

There can be a lot of laughter and joyful living once good communication is established across the differences of dyslexia/ SpLD.

*OUTCOMES*

## 7.4   Distinguishing between the different SpLDs

Most of the series is not marked as more or less relevant to a particular SpLD. People are so varied even when their problems are given the same labels. The clearest separation I know is that organisation is the major problem for dyspraxic adults when it comes to thinking (the motor side of dyspraxia is not covered). But even in this group, I'm aware of one student with no dyslexic problems who needs to be aware of his thinking preferences in order to do justice to his knowledge.

Out of respect for the overlap of experiences (problems and solutions), most of this book makes no distinction between the different SpLDs, with exceptions in 2 places. In CHAPTER 1, ORGANISATION, some differences for the 4 different SpLDs are discussed in LEARNING TO BE ORGANISED. In CHAPTER 3, SPACE, PLACE AND DIRECTION, the special importance of the physical aspects of DYSPRAXIA is briefly discussed.

*LEARNING TO BE ORGANISED:* p 73

*DYSPRAXIA:* p 110

# Useful Preface

## 7.5 The way forward

The whole series is about the autonomy that allows dyslexic/ SpLD people to get out from under the difficulties. These difficulties have a label, may have various labels, but they aren't the only difficulties that people face. Negotiating accommodations should be done with understanding of the issues for all parties involved. The way forward could benefit many groups of people.

ⓖ p 283: autonomy

What I hope people will get from the series:

Dyslexic/ SpLD people:
> a systematic way of observing strengths and weaknesses and using the strengths to help you manage the problems you face because of your dyslexia/ SpLD; the confidence to contribute to work, life, in your study, in a way that fulfils your innate potential and which is not masked or hampered by your dyslexia/ SpLD.

Those in supporting roles, whether in a 1-1 relationship or in a more general type of relationship:
> resources to understand the impact of dyslexia/ SpLD on the whole lives of dyslexic/ SpLD people and ways of making necessary adjustments to facilitate better communication.

Those who have to think about public communication and use of public spaces:
> an understanding of the difficulties encountered by dyslexic/ SpLD people and a recognition that making communication and access easier for them will also help many other people.

Politicians, other policymakers and people in the media:
> an understanding that dealing with dyslexia/ SpLD effectively as early as possible is the right thing for society to do; that done well it has cost benefits in many different ways and is therefore worth carrying through properly; that mutual respect and consideration between all members and levels of society are enhanced through the best approaches to dyslexia/ SpLD.

# Useful Preface

What I hope will happen for dyslexic/ SpLD children:
> that adults will listen to them and observe them so that they can grow up with maximum autonomy and management of their dyslexia/ SpLD; that many of the recognised problems might not develop for them.

What I hope will happen in general education is that the new paradigm I have put forward (Stacey, 2020b) will be seen as teacher-friendly, effective, sensible, satisfying and cost saving.

Ⓖ p 283: paradigm (Stacey, 2020b)

The new paradigm is:
- that systems are developed, and used, to explore how individuals, children and adults, learn
- that learners have the opportunities to tailor their learning tasks so that they can achieve the knowledge and skills being taught
- that teaching programmes are flexible enough to accommodate all learner approaches.

**Final comment**

When people are confident of their skills and not afraid to own and manage their weaknesses, they have many of the tools necessary to face the various situations in their life, see the TOOL BOX FOR LIVING CONFIDENTLY.

TOOL BOX FOR LIVING CONFIDENTLY: p 253

The voice is found; the potential is unlocked; living with dyslexia/ SpLD is done with confidence.

## References

Gleick, James, 1997, *Chaos, The Amazing Science of the Unpredictable*, Minerva, London

Kolb, Bryan, 1995, *Brain Plasticity and Behaviour*, Lawrence Erlbaum Associates, Mahwah, NJ

Stacey, Ginny, 2019, *Finding Your Voice with Dyslexia and other SpLDs*, Routledge, London

Stacey, Ginny, 2020a, *Organisation and Everyday Life with Dyslexia and other SpLDs*, Routledge, London

Stacey, Ginny, 2020b, *Development of Dyslexia and other SpLDs*, Routledge, London

Stacey, Ginny, 2021, *Gaining Knowledge and Skills with Dyslexia and other SpLDs*, Routledge, London

## Website information

Okabe, Masataka, Ito, Kei, 2008, *Color Universal Design (CUD) - How To Make Figures and Presentations That Are Friendly to Colorblind People*,
http://jfly.iam.u-tokyo.ac.jp/color/ Accessed 29 January 2017
Series website: www.routledge.com/cw/stacey

# 1 Organisation

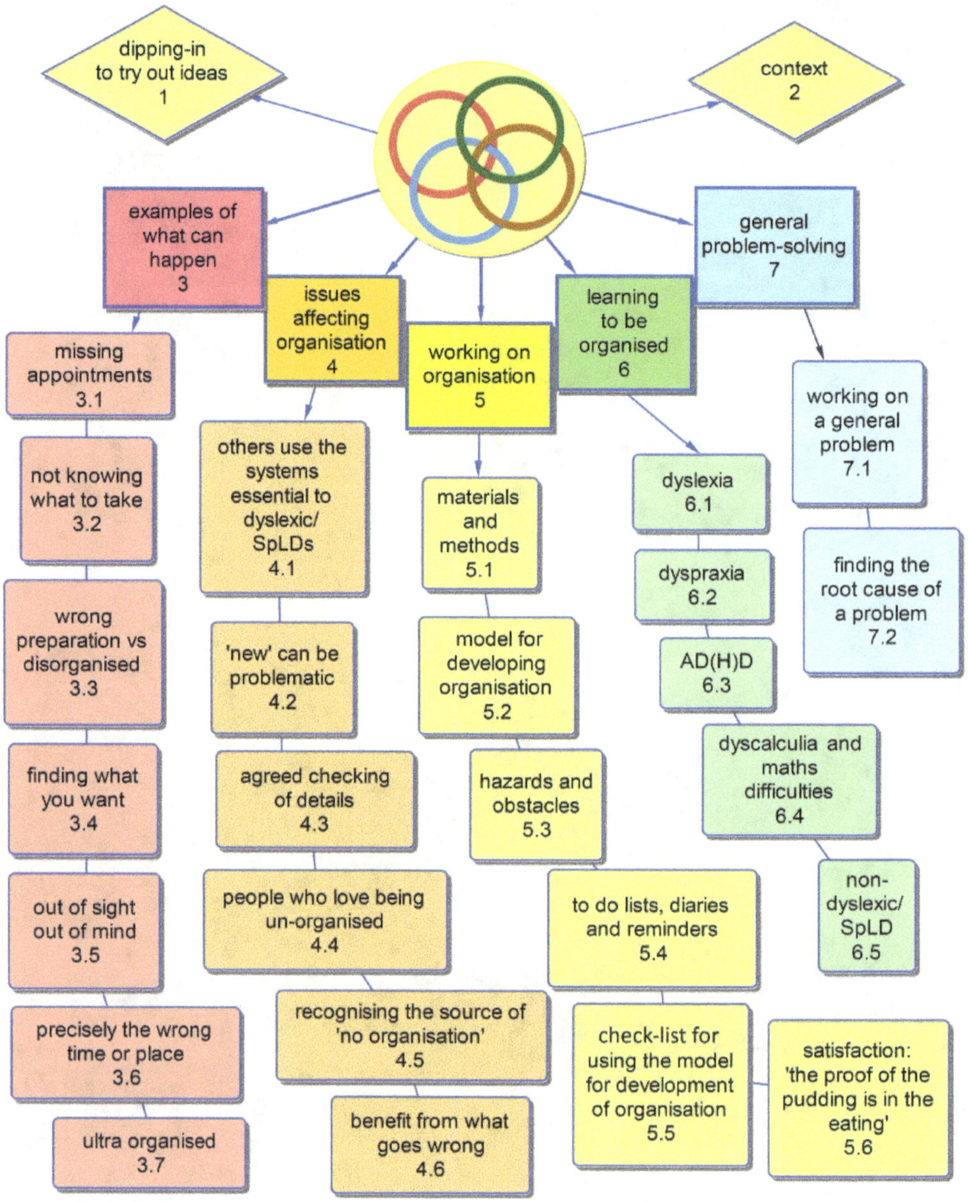

- dipping-in to try out ideas — 1
- context — 2
- examples of what can happen — 3
  - missing appointments — 3.1
  - not knowing what to take — 3.2
  - wrong preparation vs disorganised — 3.3
  - finding what you want — 3.4
  - out of sight out of mind — 3.5
  - precisely the wrong time or place — 3.6
  - ultra organised — 3.7
- issues affecting organisation — 4
  - others use the systems essential to dyslexic/SpLDs — 4.1
  - 'new' can be problematic — 4.2
  - agreed checking of details — 4.3
  - people who love being un-organised — 4.4
  - recognising the source of 'no organisation' — 4.5
  - benefit from what goes wrong — 4.6
- working on organisation — 5
  - materials and methods — 5.1
  - model for developing organisation — 5.2
  - hazards and obstacles — 5.3
  - to do lists, diaries and reminders — 5.4
  - check-list for using the model for development of organisation — 5.5
  - satisfaction: 'the proof of the pudding is in the eating' — 5.6
- learning to be organised — 6
  - dyslexia — 6.1
  - dyspraxia — 6.2
  - AD(H)D — 6.3
  - dyscalculia and maths difficulties — 6.4
  - non-dyslexic/SpLD — 6.5
- general problem-solving — 7
  - working on a general problem — 7.1
  - finding the root cause of a problem — 7.2

# Contents

Vital for dyslexic/ SpLDs, good practice for all .......... 38
Working with the chapter .......... 38
Templates on the website .......... 39
Appendix 1, 2 and 3 .......... 40
1 Dipping-in to try out ideas .......... 41
2 Context .......... 42
3 Examples of what can happen .......... 45
    3.1 Missing appointments 46
    3.2 Not knowing what to take 46
    3.3 Wrong preparation looks like being disorganised 47
    3.4 Finding what you want 47
    3.5 Out of sight is out of mind 48
    3.6 Precisely wrong time or place 48
    3.7 Ultra organised 49
4 Issues affecting organisation .......... 50
    4.1 Other people choose to use the systems that are essential to dyslexic/ SpLDs 51
    4.2 'New' can be problematic 52
    4.3 Agreed checking of details 52
    4.4 People who love being un-organised 53
    4.5 Recognising the source of 'no organisation' 53
    4.6 Benefit from what goes wrong 54
5 Working on organisation .......... 55
    5.1 Materials and methods 56
    5.2 Model for developing organisation 57
        5.2.1 Initial Step 5 59
        5.2.2 Step 1: gather strengths 60
        5.2.3 Step 2: assess hazards 60
        5.2.4 Step 3: describe what needs organising 61
        5.2.5 Useful questions 61
        5.2.6 Step 4: recognise insuperable obstacles 64
        5.2.7 Step 5: develop constructive ways forward 65
        5.2.8 Recording your system of organisation 65
    5.3 Hazards and obstacles 66
        5.3.1 Pitfalls 67
        5.3.2 Accommodation 69
    5.4 To do lists, diaries and reminders 69
    5.5 Check-list for using the MODEL FOR DEVELOPING ORGANISATION 70
    5.6 Satisfaction: 'The proof of the pudding is in the eating' 72
6 Learning to be organised .......... 73
    6.1 Dyslexia 74
    6.2 Dyspraxia 75
    6.3 AD(H)D 77
    6.4 Dyscalculia and maths difficulties 77
    6.5 Non-dyslexic/ SpLD 79
7 General problem-solving .......... 79
    7.1 Working on a general problem 80
    7.2 Finding the root cause of a problem 82
References and website information .......... 83

## 1 Organisation

**Vital for dyslexic/ SpLDs, good practice for all**

It is vital for you, as a dyslexic/SpLD person, to recognise the wider impact of dyslexia/ SpLD on your life, to organise yourself and so become autonomous. Then you can minimise the effects of your dyslexia/ SpLD while enhancing your strengths.

Learning to be organised is one of those skills that most dyslexic/ SpLD people must actively learn; it is one of the skills they are unlikely to learn subliminally while doing other work.

It is good practice for all to recognise what happens in their lives and to organise themselves to minimise problems and to enhance strengths. So the solutions presented in this chapter can be useful to many non-dyslexic/ SpLD people.

Ⓖ p 283: autonomous

Ⓖ p 283: subliminal

### Working with the chapter

**Key ideas**

- What are your own experiences?
- You are not alone.
- Your best materials and methods.
- Hazards and obstacles.
- 'New' can make dyslexia/ SpLD worse.
- System that suits you.
- Satisfaction.

It is not worth creating more problems in your organisation systems. Read MAJOR PRECAUTION. Do the EXERCISE: AVOID MORE PROBLEMS WHEN LEARNING NEW SKILLS. Learning to be organised is a new skill.

The 2 sections dealing with solutions are:
   WORKING ON ORGANISATION
   GENERAL PROBLEM-SOLVING.

MAJOR PRECAUTION: p 7

EXERCISE: AVOID MORE PROBLEMS WHEN LEARNING NEW SKILLS: p 8

WORKING ON ORGANISATION: p 55

GENERAL PROBLEM-SOLVING: p 79

# Organisation 1

If you only recognise dyslexia/ SpLD as the core difficulties[1], you will miss many of the situations when these syndromes have an important impact on your life. Much of this chapter is an opportunity for you to reflect on other people's experience and realise what happens in your life.

As you gather insights, record them and collect them together in such a way that you will be able to use them. Use the TEMPLATES and APPENDICES to help you.

It is equally important for others who live or work with dyslexic/ SpLD people to know the wider impact these syndromes can have.

## Templates on the website

In the initial stages of working with this chapter use:
A1      JOTTING DOWN AS YOU SCAN
A2      BOOKMARK – PURPOSE
A3      JOTTING DOWN AS YOU READ
B1      COLLECTING IDEAS THAT RELATE TO YOU

TEMPLATES

As you work with the MODEL FOR DEVELOPING ORGANISATION, use one of:
F1      DEVELOPING ORGANISATION - MIND MAP
F2      DEVELOPING ORGANISATION - SPATIAL
F3      DEVELOPING ORGANISATION - LINEAR

MODEL FOR DEVELOPING ORGANISATION: p 57

As you try out your organisation systems, record what happens and reflect on it to make improvements, using:
B3      COMPARE EXPECTATIONS AND REALITY
B4      ACTIONS, RESULTS, NEXT STEP
B8      RECORDING TEMPLATE - 4

To explore any difficulties and find the core problem(s), use one of:
F7      ROOT CAUSE OF A PROBLEM - MIND MAP
F8      ROOT CAUSE OF A PROBLEM - SPATIAL
F9      ROOT CAUSE OF A PROBLEM - LINEAR

Check your progress using:
B11     MONITORING PROGRESS

---

[1] Core difficulties:    dyslexia: words            dyspraxia: movement
                          dyscalculia: maths         AD(H)D: attention
Descriptions of these 4 specific learning difficulties are in the GLOSSARY, ⓖ p 280.

# 1 Organisation

### Appendix 1  Resources

This appendix will help you collect information and make progress as you learn to be organised.

APPENDIX 1: p 232

### Appendix 2  Individual, Personal Profile of Dyslexia/ SpLD and Regime for Managing Dyslexia/ SpLD

APPENDIX 2: p 246, including:
TOOL BOX,
PROFILE,
REGIME

**Tip:** ORGANISATION **and building your profile and regime**

As you work on organisation, you will learn more about the way dyslexia/ SpLD impacts on your life and about your best ways to deal with it. You can record the insights and build them into a TOOL BOX FOR LIVING CONFIDENTLY, which includes your own INDIVIDUAL, PERSONAL PROFILE OF DYSLEXIA/ SPLD and your REGIME FOR MANAGING DYSLEXIA/ SPLD.

### Appendix 3  Key Concepts

APPENDIX 3: p 262

I cover these key concepts when doing an audit of skills and knowledge with a dyslexic/ SpLD student. The appendix shows which of the 4 books in the series covers each idea in full.

**Tip: The skills and knowledge you can gain from this series**

APPENDIX 3: KEY CONCEPTS has a list of the main skills and knowledge that you can gain from this series of books. They fall into the categories of
  THINKING CLEARLY
  USING THE MIND WELL
  YOUR THINKING PREFERENCES
  ASPECTS OF DYSLEXIA/ SPLD

THINKING PREFERENCES are highlighted in orange in this chapter.

# Organisation 1

## 1 Dipping-in to try out ideas

Step 1:

- Read EXAMPLES OF WHAT CAN HAPPEN, §3, and ISSUES AFFECTING ORGANISATION, §4.

  §3: p 45
  §4: p 50

- Look at LEARNING TO BE ORGANISED, §6, for brief guidance relating to different SpLDs or none.

  §6: p 73

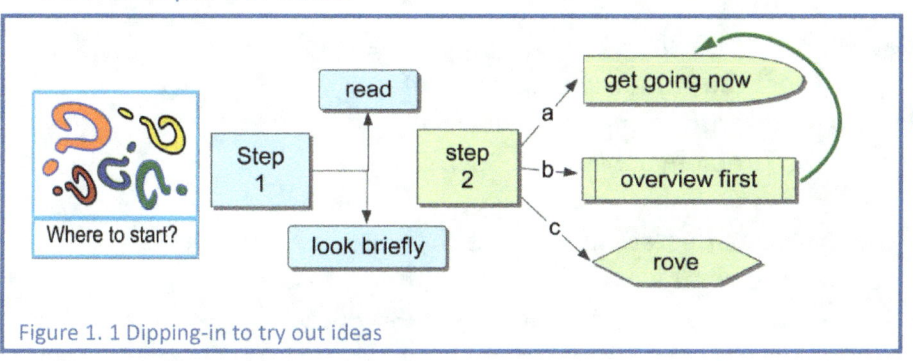

Figure 1.1 Dipping-in to try out ideas

Step 2a:   If you feel happier getting going immediately:

- decide on something (see MARGIN NOTE) to organise
    - if you aren't very good at organising, choose a task at level 2 on a scale of 1 - 5, where 1 is something that is easy to organise and 5 is something difficult to organise
- work on the organisation of your selected task using CHECK-LIST FOR USING THE MODEL FOR DEVELOPING ORGANISATION, §5.5.

MARGIN NOTE: 'something' could be anything such as objects, situations, tasks, ideas, people, planning

§5.5: p 70

Or step 2b:   If you like to have an overview of what you are doing:

- read WORKING ON ORGANISATION, §5
- then do step 2a.

§5: p 55

Or step 2c:   If you like to rove over text to see what it's about:

- look for experiences that match your own
- look at the STORY, INSIGHT and EXAMPLE BOXES in this chapter
- reflect how close they are to your experience, and how your experience is different
- read the sections that relate to your immediate needs and note the others for future work
- decide on something to organise now and try out what you have picked up.

# 1  Organisation

## 2  Context

Dyslexia/ SpLD are often first identified in an educational setting, or parents may be aware that a child is not learning in quite the expected way.  As a result, the dyslexic/ SpLD patterns of processing are primarily seen as being educational, and suitable teaching is expected to put any problems right.

However, anyone with dyslexia/ SpLD knows that it affects the whole of life.  Also, it doesn't just affect the standard categories of symptoms that can be associated with each specific learning difficulty.  Organisation is a very common problem across all 4 SpLDs.

I've known people whose dyslexia affected much more than spelling and reading.  They were unaware what was at the root of their problems; therefore, they were at the mercy of their dyslexia/ SpLD.

I've watched dyslexic adults not owning the effects of their dyslexia and creating a lot of extra hassle for themselves and others.

I've known students come to university quite unprepared to take care of themselves because one of their parents always did the organisation for them, including generally taking care of the effects of the dyslexia/ SpLD.

The following insight describes several ways in which organisation can be sabotaged.

**Insight: Child footballer assembling kit for a game**

If Mum's put everything away, she will have put clothes in drawers and the boots somewhere else in the house.  The boots could easily get left behind, as follows.

A check-list of all the necessary gear could be used by the footballer to put the gear into the sports bag; the items are checked off as they are retrieved from drawers.  Once everything is collected from the drawers, the job feels done.

Organisation 1

The possibilities for the boots to get left behind are:
1. The fact that the boots haven't been included among the rest of the kit gets overlooked because everything else is ticked off.
2. The footballer assumes he will remember the boots and takes no action to make sure he does remember.
3. He intends to go straight from getting gear out of the drawers to finding the boots and putting them in, but some other idea comes into his mind and in following it, the need to collect the boots gets erased[2].

The process of collecting the gear has to be designed to avoid all possible ways that the boots could be left behind.

Situations like this can occur during education, employment or in life in general, at any time.

**Insight: Taking everything, just in case**

Many dyslexic/ SpLD people end up taking everything because they cannot be sure what they will need for the day and they know that they will not be able to do tasks without the necessary equipment.

It is very important that you understand enough about your dyslexia/ SpLD to discuss the problems with any other people involved so that you can focus on the possible problems and resolve them by talking about them.

---

[2] My non-dyslexic/ SpLD proof-reader suggested replacing 'erased' by 'overlooked'. So I want to stress the experience of a thought being erased; it feels like the thought is no longer in your mind; it is not even there to be overlooked. Erasing doesn't happen all the time, but enough times to be worth highlighting.

# 1  Organisation

Being organised is about being as autonomous as you can be and using ways round problems whenever possible.  You can create systems so that you have a good level of stable organisation.

There will be some problems that have no solution for some people and there will be times when habitual good organisation disintegrates.

The effort involved in organisation ranges from substantial down to minimal.

⒢ p 283: autonomous

**Insight: Anything 'new' disturbs organisation**

Any new situation makes your organisation systems vulnerable.  'New' includes:
- starting a new subject
- new school
- new job
- living with a new person, even a baby
- having a new bank account
- moving between different office stations
- in fact anything for which you have to re-think your patterns of behaviour.

*'New' Can Be Problematic:* p 52

Education, at any level, is likely to increase the occurrence of difficulties because it is about learning new knowledge and new skills.  It also has far-reaching implications as academic achievement is part of the evidence presented for new jobs.  Therefore, appropriate support during education is very important.

Employment is increasingly being recognised as a situation that creates problems for dyslexic/ SpLD people.  There is a growing expectation that accommodations will be put in place that enable dyslexic/ SpLD people to fulfil their potential, in different working environments.

⒢ p 283: accommodation

Organisation 1

In any setting, support and accommodation should be appropriate.  It can be detrimental when helpers take over and do tasks for you; it is often better to wait until all possibilities have been exhausted and there is no other option.  There will come a time when the helper is not there to step in; you are then very vulnerable and may not know how to deal with the unfolding situation.  It is much better for you to be the organiser of what happens to you, as far as possible.

Providing you are aware of the wide-spread implications, you can be effective and you can negotiate accommodation when essential.  It is not a very good long-term solution to pretend, or forget, that your dyslexia/ SpLD has no impact on your life.

There is joy once dyslexia/ SpLD is managed well.  People go on to feel confident and to enjoy using their own way of doing things.  They often have a lot to offer the communities in which they work or live.

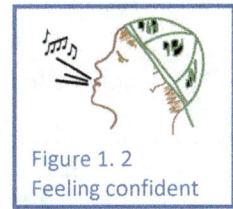
Figure 1. 2
Feeling confident

This chapter has:
> some examples of people's experiences
> discussion about
>> issues related to organisation
>> working on organisation
>> organisation and the 4 SpLDs or none
>> general problem-solving.

## 3   Examples of what can happen

The following are just a few of the ways dyslexic/ SpLD people experience organisation.  You may have similar or quite different stories.  Again, read the stories and notice which parts relate to you, and which parts don't and then reflect on why they don't.

Non-dyslexic/ SpLD people will have experiences that mirror those of the dyslexic/ SpLD group and it is sometimes difficult to pinpoint why there is any difference that needs to be taken into account.

As you begin to understand what happens for you and how you can best deal with it, it can become easier to deal with the responses of others.

TEMPLATES

Use *B1 - COLLECTING IDEAS THAT RELATE TO YOU*

**1 Organisation**

## 3.1 Missing appointments

>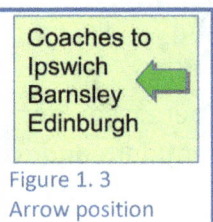
> 
> Figure 1.3
> Arrow position

> **e.g.**
> 
> **Example: Missing appointments**
> 
> People who turn up for appointments, meetings, one-off lectures, etc. one week too early or too late (or another time period: an hour, a day). A series of lectures at the same time is likely to be less of a problem after the first.
> 
> People who cannot stop themselves from setting out at the time they are supposed to arrive.
> 
> Not being able to read signs correctly, and taking the wrong route to an appointment:
> A34 instead of A43
> bus number 49 instead of 64
> seeing a left-hand arrow on the right side of a notice and going right, see FIGURE 1. 3.

## 3.2 Not knowing what to take

>
> 
> **Example: Not knowing what to take**
> 
> Never being able to get the sports kit right; or having extremely careful strategies to make sure it is complete.
> 
> Taking absolutely everything, just in case it's needed.

# Organisation 1

## 3.3 Wrong preparation looks like being disorganised

**Example: Wrong preparation looks like being disorganised**

An idea can be discussed at a formal meeting and seem to be adopted.

You then go away and prepare for the next meeting on the basis of the discussion, only to find out at the next meeting that the other people didn't understand it the same way as you did, and all your preparation has been a waste of time and effort.

## 3.4 Finding what you want

**Example: Finding what you want**

Even if you have been dealing with something in the last 5 minutes, or less, it can be very difficult to remember what you have done.

If you change where you keep anything, you may have difficulty finding it again. Time and again you will go to the old place and not find the object, and you won't remember where the new place is.

## 3.5 Out of sight is out of mind

You can only think about anything on the top; anything not on the top is simply ignored, even if it was on top just a moment ago.

**Story: Out of sight is out of mind**

One colleague could not put her books or papers away while she was writing her thesis, nor could she put them in piles. She had to have them all laid out and visible at the same time. If she didn't do that, she could not recall the information in them.

Filing systems are difficult to use. You daren't put something away, especially papers, because 'out of sight is out of mind': anything put away will not be attended to.

The opposite is also experienced: there are some who know very well where they have put things or papers even when they get buried.

It is very important not to clear up for dyslexic/ SpLD people in either group.

## 3.6 Precisely wrong time or place

Miles (1993) discussed confusion over left and right. He remarked that the errors are not random and 'inconsistency is easy to achieve; consistency in getting the wrong answer is not'. His case descriptions show the subjects of his research working to try to reach the right answers. Dyslexic/ SpLD people can devote considerable energy and attention to get somewhere at precisely the wrong time or place.

Miles (1993, p 90)

# Organisation 1

**Story: The effort to arrive at precisely the wrong time**

One student discovered that the more she tried the worse the problems became and the more people emphasised any complications the more difficulty she had.

On one occasion, a tutor stressed that he had to go to a meeting at 3pm, so he would have time to see her at 2pm. The stress on '3pm' eclipsed the session start at 2pm.

The student was very pleased with herself to arrive exactly at 3pm; she had taken a lot of trouble to get herself there on time, to no avail.

## 3.7 Ultra organised

**Insight: Ultra organised**

I have met many dyslexic/ SpLD students who have described their individual ways of being organised.

Some have a system that doesn't take too much effort; others have more complicated systems.

Almost all say that they cannot afford to let their organisation slip in any way and that, if they do, they very rapidly become completely disorganised. Being organised is the only way they can deal with life.

These students are among the most organised people; also see *'New' Can Be Problematic*.

*'New' Can Be Problematic:* p 52

# 1 Organisation

## 4 Issues affecting organisation

Being disorganised is not a result of being lazy nor of being indifferent to the consequences of the disorganisation. I have hardly ever come across a dyslexic/ SpLD person who has a middling level of organisation that simply happens without conscious effort.

Lazy or indifferent: see also INSIGHT: UNDERLYING DYSLEXIA/ SPLD ISSUES: p 226

### Insight: Varying levels of organisation

Some dyslexic/ SpLD people are ULTRA ORGANISED as in the INSIGHT BOX above.

There are others who are extremely organised at work and not at all at home.

Anything new is likely to undermine the organisation system for a while, for the very organised people.

There are some who never achieve a satisfactory method of creating a system for organisation, but they benefit when a system is developed with them.

There are some who are disorganised and life does not run smoothly for them. Even when someone else devises a system for them and with them, they are not able to gain anything from it.

There are some who are un-organised, see PEOPLE WHO LOVE BEING UN-ORGANISED.

The distinction between disorganised and un-organised is worth recognising; I've put the hyphen in 'un-organised' deliberately to call attention to the distinction.

PEOPLE WHO LOVE BEING UN-ORGANISED: p 53

Organisation 1

If you struggle with organisation, it is often some part of your dyslexia/ SpLD profile that is causing the problems. You have to find out exactly where the problem lies in order to find the solution. It could be reading notices that is causing problems; or misunderstanding the tone of voice, as above in STORY: THE EFFORT TO ARRIVE AT PRECISELY THE WRONG TIME. The solutions won't be robust unless any underlying problem has been sorted out in advance, see FINDING THE ROOT CAUSE OF A PROBLEM.

 p 283: profile

STORY: THE EFFORT TO ARRIVE AT PRECISELY THE WRONG TIME: p 49

FINDING THE ROOT CAUSE OF A PROBLEM: p 82

## 4.1 Other people choose to use the systems that are essential to dyslexic/ SpLDs

**Story: Others using a system essential to a dyslexic**

A dyslexic person had volunteered to operate the lights for an amateur production. He was asked to switch various lights on and off while the producer decided what he wanted. The dyslexic person couldn't remember which switch belonged to which light, even if he was operating the same couple of lights in fairly quick succession.

He numbered the switches and named the lights, related the switches to the lights and had a list alongside the row of switches, which was found by everyone else to be better than relying on memory. He also made charts of the lighting changes in the manuscript at the cues; again this was used by everyone operating the lights.

Others would have done a good enough job without these memory aids, but the whole lighting effects were much more precise because others were using the system the dyslexic person HAD TO use.

# 1 Organisation

## 4.2 'New' can be problematic

Anything you are encountering for the first time might be a potential hazard to your dyslexic/ SpLD organisation system: new job; new banking system; new interactive web site; new topic in a course; new school; new house; new car; new piece of music.

>
>
> **Tip: Pay attention to newness**
>
> This insight applies to any first time event that might be repeated several times.
>
> It is worth getting the way you deal with the situation right for you at the start of the event. It is often difficult or impossible to delete any errors from your memory by getting the processes right on the second run through. See the INDEX for other discussion about aspects of 'new'.

INDEX: p 294

If you can negotiate what you need to do while learning about the new system, it is possible to start in a way that steadily builds up what you need to know and the long-term dyslexic/ SpLD problems will be minimal. Often the difficulty is that you have got some way into working with the new material before you fully understand the impact of your dyslexia/ SpLD; by then your memories for the initial stage are confused and it is sometimes impossible to remove these initial-stage-memories and replace them with a more effective set of memories for the new system (Stacey, 2020).

Stacey (2020)

## 4.3 Agreed checking of details

Instructions can easily be misunderstood, whether they are spoken or written. Sometimes words are misread or misunderstood; sometimes people just have different, valid internal interpretations of the words. It is worth having an agreement with the person giving the instructions that you will put your understanding into your own words. It may take several situations to evolve before effective rapport is developed between the pair of you.

# Organisation 1

**Story: Monitoring individual understanding**

There was a series of emails between a meeting organiser and an attendee, trying to clarify what the attendee 1) had already done, 2) had to do before the meeting and 3) what she should bring to the meeting.

A brief 10 minute face-to-face discussion took place after the attendee had done her preparation; the attendee found she'd misinterpreted some of the emails and she had to work into the early hours to produce what was needed.

The attendee needed to know that the organiser accepted that she should summarise the whole situation after each detail was added so that the organiser could monitor that they both had the same ideas. The meeting organiser needed to recognise that he should keep reviewing the summary to check for alternative interpretations between the pair of them.

## 4.4  People who love being un-organised

There are some people who are not organised, dyslexic/ SpLD or non-dyslexic/ SpLD, and they love the way their life is. They can be a joy to be with. I hope they have the self-confidence to resist any pressure to become organised, providing they don't create burdens for other people or themselves.

## 4.5  Recognising the source of 'no organisation'

If you struggle with organisation as a result of dyslexia/ SpLD, there is a tendency to take responsibility, or take the blame, for anything that is amiss in terms of organisation. You need to recognise those times when you are not the source of the confusion, but someone else is. You may not be able to do anything about it, and it may be holding you up quite a bit.

The first thing to do is not feel guilty, which would only increase your difficulties.
The second is to make sure you are organising everything you can to make life work for you; see whether others are affected too and whether you can help each other.

 **1 Organisation**

The third suggestion comes from trying to stop situations sapping my energies: I try to find something I can learn or gain from the situation, often by looking at life from other perspectives. I sometimes gain insights into the difficulties non-dyslexic/ SpLD people have with the way I function and these insights can lead to more tolerance and co-operation.

The final suggestion, though not the least important, is to find someone who understands your difficulties and who can listen in such a way that you can cope with a situation you can't change.

## 4.6   Benefit from what goes wrong

You can benefit from the way things go wrong and the way you solve them. You can learn more about the ways in which it would be easier for you to do things.

**Insight: What goes wrong is useful**

Although I use visual thinking preferences very well on many occasions, I can't use Post-it reminders the same way that others can.

Many people put notices to themselves where they will see them at strategic moments: e.g. notes stuck on the door to see as they go out of the house.

I don't 'see' such notes; I have to put the notes where they will be in my way, so that they obstruct my physical movements; that way they work for me.

This pattern shows me that what I do (moving over the Post-its) is more powerful than what I see. I need to focus on using my kinaesthetic sense.

THE SENSES: VISUAL, VERBAL, KINAESTHETIC: p 270

# Organisation 1

## 5 Working on organisation

You need to be able to THINK CLEARLY in order to organise something. It can be very important to know your THINKING PREFERENCES.

The MATERIALS AND METHODS you use for working out your organisation may make a difference.

It is good to have some guiding principles that give you a consistent framework for developing a system, see MODEL FOR DEVELOPING ORGANISATION. You need to monitor its effectiveness, see SATISFACTION: 'THE PROOF OF THE PUDDING IS IN THE EATING'.

Be sure that you want to put in the effort to be organised. If you are not intrinsically motivated or if there are no incentives, you are unlikely to sustain the effort needed to be organised.

For some, the incentives come from the benefits in saved time and energy, and the reduction in frustration. When trying to become organised you need to give yourself long enough for these benefits to become established.

If you don't have enough motivation to become organised, you might as well stop before you start.

You need to find the level of disorganisation that you feel comfortable with.

You shouldn't rely on others to do the organisation for you. They can't be there with you all the time; you become vulnerable in their absence and your independence is reduced if people organise things for you.

However, there are some occasions when having others doing things for you, including organisation, is the only way forward, see the discussion of insuperable obstacles in STEP 4: RECOGNISE INSUPERABLE OBSTACLES.

---

THINK CLEARLY (PAUSING): p 264
THINKING PREFERENCES: p 270
MATERIALS AND METHODS: p 56

MODEL FOR DEVELOPING ORGANISATION: p 57

SATISFACTION: 'THE PROOF OF THE PUDDING IS IN THE EATING': p 72

STEP 4: RECOGNISE INSUPERABLE OBSTACLES: p 64

# 1 Organisation

## 5.1 Materials and methods

There are many tasks which are made easier by choosing the right materials and methods, not just organisation. It is convenient to include the discussion here and to focus on organisation.
You can experiment with the suggestions and find what suits you best. You may find that you use different materials and methods for different tasks.

>
>
> **Tip: Materials and methods**
>
> While working on anything, it is important to select the materials and method(s) that suit you best.

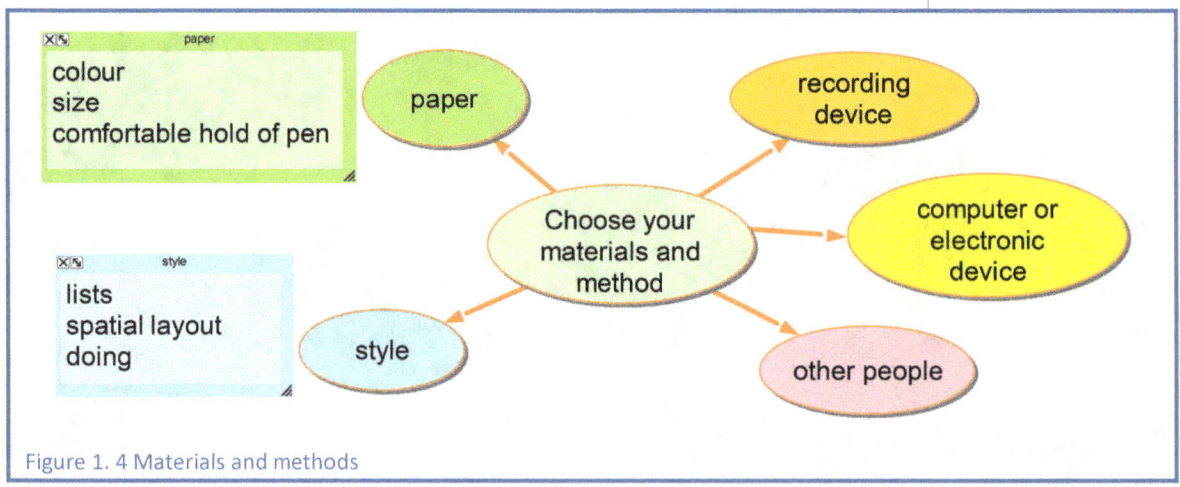

Figure 1. 4 Materials and methods

**Some ideas about materials:**

Paper: Choose the colour and size that suits you; choose the writing (or drawing, etc.) tool that suits you: think about colour of the ink, size of the line and comfort of holding the tool (<mark>visual</mark>, <mark>kinaesthetic</mark>). Give yourself space to spread out, which may help you deal with short-term memory problems, see STORY: OUT OF SIGHT IS OUT OF MIND.

Recording device (<mark>oral</mark>, <mark>aural</mark>): Use one which allows you to put tags or markers at significant places.

THE SENSES: VISUAL, VERBAL, KINAESTHETIC: p 270

STORY: OUT OF SIGHT IS OUT OF MIND: p 48

Computers or electronic devices: use any programmes or devices that you know help you to record what you are working on and how you are thinking about it.

**Some ideas about methods:**

**Linear** thinkers: You are most likely to work with lists.

**Holistic** thinkers: You are likely to use mind maps, flow diagrams or drawings.

**Kinaesthetic** people (those who learn by doing) need to do or to use 'doing memory': assemble objects or use materials to represent ideas; or use imagination to call to mind the task to be organised and the problems encountered, and then imagine the possible solutions. Use paper or a recording device to store the ideas and thinking for later access.

Other people: Bouncing ideas off others is necessary for some in order to know what they themselves are thinking (Myers-Briggs, **extrovert**, **feeling**). Talk through the task to be organised, the problems and the development of solutions with another person, preferably someone with understanding of the effects of your dyslexia/ SpLD. As you go, summarise points you have understood. The discussion can be captured for later access either on paper or a recording device.

*Holistic vs. Linear:* p 271

ⓖ p 283: mind map, doing

*Myers-Briggs Personality Type:* p 272

## 5.2 Model for developing organisation

The following model for organisation is a means of talking about different aspects. There may well be times when only part of it applies, or you may want to create your own methods for being organised.

The approach used in THE MODEL FOR DEVELOPING ORGANISATION has many other applications. WORKING ON A GENERAL PROBLEM shows how to use the approach in a more general way.

*Working on a General Problem:* p 80

TEMPLATES ON THE WEBSITE suggests those that will help you develop the methods for organising that suit you.

*Templates on the Website:* p 39

# 1 Organisation

The table gives the steps and where information may be found to help you use the model.

| | |
|---|---|
| **Steps for model for developing organisation:** | |
| 1   gather strengths | |
| 2   assess hazards | APPENDIX 2: p 246 |
| These 2 steps are mainly about how you manage your dyslexia/ SpLD (use APPENDIX 2). | LEARNING TO BE ORGANISED: p 73 |
| LEARNING TO BE ORGANISED has some comments dealing with different SpLDs or none. | |
| CHAPTERS 2 AND 3, TIME AND TIME MANAGEMENT, and SPACE, PLACE AND DIRECTION, include underlying hazards. | CHAPTER 2: p 84  CHAPTER 3: p 104 |
| 3   describe what needs organising | |
| What you need to organise and how you do it may involve ideas from other chapters in the book: | |
| CHAPTER 2 TIME AND TIME MANAGEMENT | |
| CHAPTER 3 SPACE, PLACE AND DIRECTION | |
| CHAPTER 4 EVERYDAY LIFE | CHAPTER 4: p 122 |
| CHAPTER 5 STUDY PERIPHERALS | CHAPTER 5: p 168 |
| CHAPTER 6 EMPLOYMENT. | CHAPTER 6: p 206 |
| 4   recognise insuperable obstacles | |
| Insuperable obstacles will probably emerge as the other steps are completed; they are likely to be very individual. | HAZARDS AND OBSTACLES: p 66 |
| 5   develop constructive ways forward | |
| Same chapters as for Step 3. | |

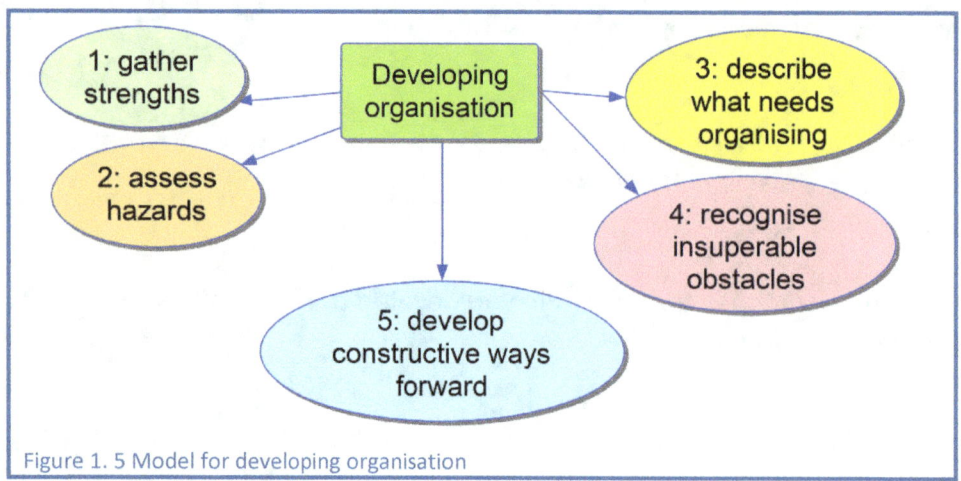

Figure 1. 5 Model for developing organisation

# Organisation 1

**The role of other people**

The model is written in terms of a single person, but it could be expanded to include others, or others may have an effect on the organisation that you, as a single individual, want to put in place.

Examples being:
1. others may have strengths they can contribute to a project
2. your organisation of a project may require someone to provide materials at a specific time and they don't manage to do so.

The second example is easier to adjust to with good organisation, than with none.

There are times when other people have to do some part of the organisation for you, see STORY: LEFT-HANDED ACCOMMODATION IN A COFFEE SHOP, STORY: DICTATING INSTRUCTIONS and DYSPRAXIA.

STORY: LEFT-HANDED ACCOMMODATION IN A COFFEE SHOP: p 213

STORY: DICTATING INSTRUCTIONS: p 230

DYSPRAXIA: p 75

## 5.2.1  Initial Step 5

Sometimes, you don't initially know the best way of organising, say, the paperwork for a new project.

If you have no system, everything gets into a muddle and it takes a long time to put straight once you decide how you'd like to do it.

It is sometimes better to have a simple initial system until you realise how it would best be done.

Again, individual experience matters: some have difficulty forgetting an initial system and it is better to accept the muddle until a good system is thought through and to take the extra time to resolve the muddle into a system.

# 1 Organisation

**Exercise: Realise your present organisational skills**

Think of something that you organise or plan reasonably well already (even if it is getting others to do it for you).

Relate the 5 steps of the model to the organisation:
- What strengths do you use?
- What are the difficulties from your dyslexia/ SpLD?
- What needs organising?
- What obstacles need avoiding?
- What organisation is in place already?

Adapt the results of this exercise to give you an initial way forward for a given task.

## 5.2.2 Step 1: gather strengths

Final solutions often depend on your innate strengths so they will be individual; what works for one person will not do for another.
- What are your THINKING PREFERENCES?
- How can you use any of them for a given organisational task?
- What MATERIALS AND METHODS do you prefer?

THINKING PREFERENCES: p 270

MATERIALS AND METHODS: p 56

## 5.2.3 Step 2: assess hazards

A hazard is a danger or a risk. In this context, it could be anything that puts your organisation at risk.

HAZARDS AND OBSTACLES: p 66

Acknowledging that you have a difficulty with organising can be essential to sorting out any solution. You need to find the answer to:
- What stops you from organising XXX? Where XXX means anything that needs organising, see STORY: INSUPERABLE OBSTACLE CHANGED TO HAZARD.

STORY: INSUPERABLE OBSTACLE CHANGED TO HAZARD: p 64

# Organisation 1

**Insight: Possible reasons for organisation not working well**

- For some, being organised is a delight and they can think up any number of ways of organising a subject or an area of their lives. The difficulty is that no particular way dominates their preferences and each day a different approach is used, resulting in confusion.

- Others seem to have no concept of organisation.

- Others simply spend a lot of time and effort on organisation, with variable results.

- There can be direct effects from your dyslexia/ SpLD that interfere with attempts to be organised; it is important to be aware of them; LEARNING TO BE ORGANISED discusses the importance of organisation to people with the different SpLDs. Dealing with TIME AND TIME MANAGEMENT and SPACE, PLACE AND DIRECTION can also interfere with organisation.

LEARNING TO BE ORGANISED: p 73

TIME AND TIME MANAGEMENT: p 84

SPACE, PLACE AND DIRECTION: p 104

Having unreasonable expectations of yourself can also create problems. Being content with the way you organise anything may make a considerable difference to your effectiveness.

## 5.2.4 Step 3: describe what needs organising

You need to be as clear as possible about what needs organising. The other chapters in this book each deal with different areas that may need deliberate organisation; use them in conjunction with the questions below.

## 5.2.5 Useful questions

It is useful to have some guiding questions, or expectations, that allow you to work out what needs organising, what's currently not working for you and what to develop to improve matters.

USEFUL QUESTIONS is an entry in the INDEX: p 295

# 1 Organisation

From the following list[3], choose the ones that you think apply to the task you want to organise:

- What needs to be organised?
    - Give specific details; use the other chapters in the book to help you identify details.
    - Group the details by looking for relationships between them (chunking).
    - Work with *Key Words* to distinguish main themes from details.
- What are you trying to achieve?
- What goes wrong with your present set up?
- Can you find everything you need without fruitless searching?
- Do you take everything you need, or only what you need, when you go out somewhere, or to another part of the house/ workplace/ other place?
- Do you achieve the task in hand so that you are satisfied and it doesn't take too much time?
- Are your expectations realistic? (See *Margin* for *Templates*.)
- Do you meet deadlines in a way that feels right for you?
- Do you use your resources of time and energy well?
- Do you remember what you:     decided to do
  
                                                agreed to do
  
                                                need to do?
- Do you feel the task in hand is progressing well?
  
  What are you trying to achieve? (For the second time, it may be clearer once you've thought for a while.)
- Do you think, "I can see what to do. Why am I not doing it?" See *Story: Insuperable Obstacle Changed to Hazard*.

---

Ⓖ p 267 chunking

*Key Words:* p 274

Templates

Use *B3 - Compare Expectations and Reality* and
*B4 - Action, Results, Next Step*

*Story: Insuperable Obstacle Changed to Hazard:* p 64

---

[3] Or design your own set of questions,
see the two *Exercises: To Practise Generating Useful Questions:* p 240.

## Organisation 1

 **Example: Brainstorming about a pile of stuff, a list version** FIGURE *1.6*

I have this pile of stuff that accumulates.
I'd be interested to look at it; some of it is hobby.
Some of it I need to scan for important, career implications.

I never give time to going through it – I just hope!
I hate the pile that looms at me: "You haven't read us!"

Set of useful questions, with answers:
Are my expectations realistic?   No.
What goes wrong with the present set up?   It depresses me.
What am I trying to achieve?   Not to miss anything.

Decision: Add a 'Reading Magazines' section to my monthly diary notes; list the magazines as they arrive and put them in the already existing WORK, HOBBY, GENERAL magazine racks.  Tick the magazines when read.  Once a month see if any work ones haven't been read and make time for them.  Abandon any that haven't been read and start enjoying the new arrivals.

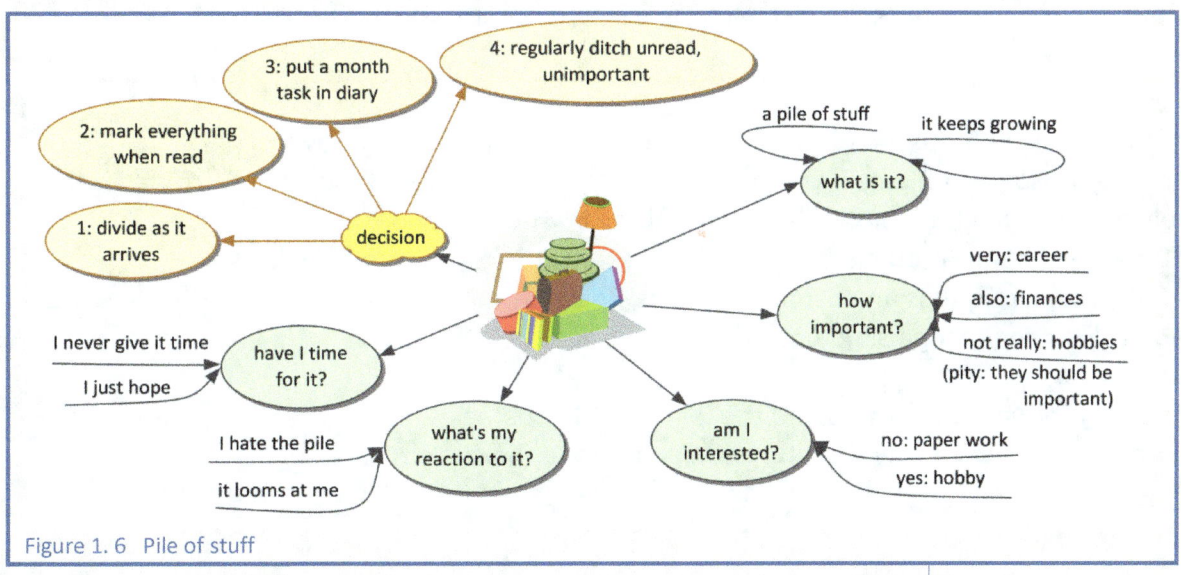

Figure 1.6  Pile of stuff

When you brainstorm about something, you often find that the obvious action to take emerges out of the brainstorming.

## 1 Organisation

### 5.2.6 Step 4: recognise insuperable obstacles

See also HAZARDS AND OBSTACLES.

By 'insuperable obstacle'[4] I mean something that blocks progress. Until you work on describing what needs organising, Step 3, and how to organise it, Step 5, it won't be clear what is going to be an insuperable obstacle for any given system. It may be that nothing is insuperable.

Insuperable obstacles may arise from your dyslexia/ SpLD or from something that cannot be arranged. It is possible that the dyslexia/ SpLD contribution is from something you normally have ways of avoiding, but the added constraints of the situation make your usual strategy ineffective.

HAZARDS AND OBSTACLES: p 66

**Story: 'Insuperable obstacle' changed to 'hazard'**

The boiler wasn't working. The house owner worked out what needed doing and organising. A week later, the boiler still wasn't working and nothing had been done. Reflecting on the situation, he said: "I know exactly what to do. I just don't like phoning. Ah! So that's why the boiler is still off." While unrecognised, the phoning phobia is an 'insuperable obstacle'; recognised, its status can be altered to 'hazard'.

As you work on Steps 3 and 5, recognise anything that will be almost impossible to rely on, e.g. if you have NO SENSE OF PLACE, it is not worth relying on yourself to know where something is. There may be obstacles that are nothing to do with dyslexia/ SpLD; for example, lack of physical strength is an obstacle to lifting heavy furniture. These obstacles need recognising too.

NO SENSE OF PLACE: p 114

The way forward needs to avoid the insuperable obstacles, or deal with them in such a way that they don't sabotage the system.

---

[4] The phrase 'insuperable obstacle' is repeated too much for good literary taste, but in this section it represents a particular idea and, for clarity, I have not changed the wording.

### 5.2.7 Step 5: develop constructive ways forward

The ways forward will depend on what is to be organised. Key elements have been divided among the remaining chapters of this book:

>TIME AND TIME MANAGEMENT, CHAPTER 2
>SPACE, PLACE & DIRECTION, CHAPTER 3
>EVERYDAY LIFE, CHAPTER 4
>STUDY PERIPHERALS, CHAPTER 5
>EMPLOYMENT, CHAPTER 6.

CHAPTER 2: p 84
CHAPTER 3: p 104
CHAPTER 4: p 122
CHAPTER 5: p 168
CHAPTER 6: p 206

The comments here are general ones.

---

**Tip: Attractive organisation**

The ways forward have to be such that the person using them will want to use them. They may need to be attractive to the person or satisfying, or have some other particular quality.

---

**Simple or complex**

Think about the level of complexity that's needed or will be helpful.

- Sometimes it is essential to think of quite minor details because if they are ignored nothing is going to work.
- Sometimes different people will need different levels of detail in order to follow the organisation of a situation/ task.
- Sometimes only a broad outline of the organisation system is needed because too much detail complicates the situation unnecessarily.

### 5.2.8 Recording your system of organisation

---

**Insight: You forget your wonderful system**

Many dyslexic/ SpLD people are quite good at working out a system, but forget what it was, and so invent another the next day.
The result can be chaos.

 **1 Organisation**

It's useful to record the system in a way that you will understand in several days' time. Keep your notes in a useful place, e.g. in the front of the ring binder containing the organised paperwork, see also REMEMBERING DECISIONS.

REMEMBERING DECISIONS: p 140

Record how well the system works and modify it when necessary.

## 5.3 Hazards and obstacles

A hazard is a danger or a risk whereas an obstacle is something that blocks one's way or prevents progress. A hazard you have to take steps to deal with, an obstacle you have to go round, or avoid. Both of them could be caused by yourself, others or the situations you find yourself in. You need to be as objective as possible about hazards and obstacles, without being unkind to yourself or others.

**Insight: Contrast between insuperable obstacle and hazard**

I have a very good system of using my diary for notes, but out of sight is out of mind (an insuperable obstacle)
→ leave the diary open on my desk; simply don't close it even overnight.

I can misread (hazard), especially when I try to read too quickly
→ allocate a time in my diary for noting what is coming up. The time needs to be when I can expect to be calm and not under pressure.

'Misreading' is only a hazard, since it doesn't always happen; whereas 'out of sight, out of mind' happens in a pretty reliable way!

I can't completely eradicate the impact of these two effects of my dyslexia. I have to let people know and discuss with them how we minimise the effects.

Organisation 1

>
> 
> **Tip: To find out what is being problematic**
> 
> 1  You can create a mind map about what you are trying to achieve and search for the hazards and obstacles; you can question why they cause problems; don't just stop with the obvious ideas, keep probing; see FINDING THE ROOT CAUSE OF A PROBLEM.
> 
> 2  You can keep a notebook in which you collect information over time in order to do the same probing work.
> 
> 3  You can explain to a suitable person; talking things through with others often allows ideas to surface that you miss on your own.

FINDING THE ROOT CAUSE OF A PROBLEM: p 82

In 1) you are thinking about what you know on your own

2) you are collecting information over time

3) you are working with another person.

Any way that suits you of doing these processes should help you to identify either a hazard or an obstacle.

Once you have discovered the hazard or obstacle, you can use any of the methods in this chapter or book to work out how best to deal with it. You may have to negotiate with others to find the best way forward. Or you may have to seek help from a completely different source.

## 5.3.1  Pitfalls

Hazards and obstacles that arise out of your dyslexia/ SpLD are the pitfalls element of your INDIVIDUAL, PERSONAL PROFILE OF DYSLEXIA/ SPLD and your REGIME FOR MANAGING DYSLEXIA/ SPLD. As you engage with becoming autonomous and you observe what happens to you, you will gain a clearer understanding of your pitfalls. On the surface, they will often have a lot in common with the problems encountered by non-dyslexic/ SpLD people. Stress in dialogue with others can be eased when you know how your experience of dyslexia/ SpLD underpins the way any problem affects you.

The PROFILE and REGIME are both in APPENDIX 2: p 246

ⓖ p 283: autonomous

 **1 Organisation**

Many of the stories, insights and examples in this book are about a hazard or an obstacle, including:

| | | |
|---|---|---|
| hazard: | STORY: OTHERS USING A SYSTEM ESSENTIAL TO A DYSLEXIC | STORY: p 51 |
| | EXAMPLE: PROBLEMS IN EVERYDAY LIFE | EXAMPLE: p 127 |
| obstacle: | STORY: SYSTEM DISRUPTED | STORY: p 139 |
| | STORY: AN INCONSISTENT MEMORY FOR SPACE AND DIRECTION | STORY: p 109 |
| both: | INSIGHT: CHILD FOOTBALLER ASSEMBLING KIT FOR A GAME | INSIGHT: p 42 |
| | EXAMPLE: MISSING APPOINTMENTS | EXAMPLE: p 46 |

One person's pitfall may be no problem at all to another person with the same dyslexic/ SpLD label. Whether a pitfall is a hazard or an obstacle depends on the circumstances.

Thus, there are considerable variations in the pitfalls listed in people's *INDIVIDUAL, PERSONAL PROFILES OF DYSLEXIA/ SPLD*.

These variations contribute to the difficulties in getting non-dyslexic/ SpLD people to recognise the full impact of these syndromes.

### Exercise: To be clear about a pitfall

- Use a mind map or *B8 - RECORDING TEMPLATE 4*.
  - Headings for the *TEMPLATE*, or arms of the mind map:
    A = date; B = event; C = what was happening;
    D = problem; E = impact from your dyslexia/ SpLD.
  - Use key words or brief sentences, if you can; or highlight the main points.
- C: What was happening: give an overview of the event.
- D: Problem: describe how you experienced the problem you encountered.
- E: Impact from your dyslexia/ SpLD: set out how you think your dyslexia/ SpLD contributed to the problem.
- Keep your records.
- Gradually build a picture of your main pitfalls.

TEMPLATES

# Organisation 1

- For each entry:
  - What is it?
  - When is it problematic?
  - How is your dyslexia/ SpLD at the root of it?
  - How do you manage it when it is a hazard?
  - What turns it from a hazard to an obstacle?
  - What accommodation do you need when it is an obstacle?
- Add your insights to your PROFILE and REGIME.
- Work with the insights to manage your dyslexia/ SpLD and to negotiate any necessary accommodations.

The PROFILE and REGIME are both in APPENDIX 2: p 246

## 5.3.2 Accommodation

There are certain situations when you know you are unlikely to be able to deal with a pitfall. In such cases you need accommodations, or provisions, to enable you to avoid the pitfall while being able to do the rest of the task in hand. Provisions for exams are widely recognised as accommodations that 'level the playing field', i.e. they enable all students equal opportunity to demonstrate knowledge and skill. The EXAM PROVISIONS section has been written as a WORKED EXAMPLE, with guidelines in the margin so that the example can be adapted to other situations. NEGOTIATING ACCOMMODATION has suggestions about making the case for accommodations to the people who will need to agree to them.

(G) p 283: accommodation

EXAM PROVISIONS: p 194
INSIGHT: WORKED EXAMPLE: p 174
NEGOTIATING ACCOMMODATION: p 258

## 5.4 To do lists, diaries and reminders

Organisation includes putting the system(s) into action.

- Some people are able to remember what needs doing; they won't be reading this section but it is important for others to realise they just have minds that work that way.
- Others have to-do lists or to-do maps in some shape or form.
- Others use their diary.
- Others use electronic devices: computers, mobiles, recorders.

You also have to make sure that everything gets into the to-do list, diary or electronic device.

# 1 Organisation

> **e.g.**
>
> **Example: Making sure nothing gets missed**
>
> Everything that comes in and that needs organising is put in an in-pile.
>
> - The pile is checked every couple of days and entries made in the diary for processing; once entered, papers and objects can be put away.
> - It's important not to allow the in-pile to mount too high.

With electronic devices, you need to work out the best system for you, so that you are not over-loaded by endless distracting signals.

## 5.5 Check-list for using the MODEL FOR DEVELOPING ORGANISATION

This is a check-list for working on organisation.

| | | |
|---|---|---|
| 1 | Identify what you need to organise.  Choose some KEY WORDS, or a phrase, that act as a brief, specific title, examples being:<br>　　remembering people's birthdays<br>　　help with essay-writing.<br>Use these words to replace the words in green in the rest of this check-list. | KEY WORDS: p 274 |
| 2 | Start by selecting your best MATERIALS AND METHODS;<br>then understand the Steps of the MODEL FOR DEVELOPING ORGANISATION, especially the USEFUL QUESTIONS in Step 3; adapt them as necessary to fit what you need to organise. | MATERIALS AND METHODS: p 56<br><br>MODEL FOR DEVELOPING ORGANISATION: p 57<br>USEFUL QUESTIONS: p 61 |
| 3 | Steps 1 & 2 of the model:<br>Brainstorm what you already know about your THINKING PREFERENCES and the PITFALLS of your dyslexia/ SpLD; don't at this point get distracted into exploring these aspects of your thinking or dyslexia/ SpLD. | ⓖ p 283: brainstorm<br><br>THINKING PREFERENCES: p 270<br>PITFALLS: p 69 |

# Organisation 1

| | | |
|---|---|---|
| 4 | Step 3 of the model:<br>Brainstorm what you need to organise.<br>    If STUDY PERIPHERALS or EMPLOYMENT are part of what you need to organise, scan the relevant chapters for extra ideas. | STUDY PERIPHERALS: p 168<br>EMPLOYMENT: p 206 |
| 5 | If what you need to organise includes finding information or sifting through information to find whether any of it is relevant or important or urgent:<br>    you need to create some keywords or research/ guiding questions or internet search phrases that will help you process the information effectively. It helps to KNOW YOUR GOAL and to capture it in KEY WORDS. | KNOW YOUR GOAL: p 275<br><br>KEY WORDS: p 274 |
| 6 | Steps 4 & 5 of the model:<br>Decide which sections are relevant to what you need to organise from<br>    TIME AND TIME MANAGEMENT, CHAPTER 2<br>    SPACE, PLACE AND DIRECTION, CHAPTER 3<br>    EVERYDAY LIFE, CHAPTER 4 sections:<br>        §5    TASK, PROJECT, EVENT<br>        §6    OTHER PEOPLE, ORGANISATION AND EVERYDAY LIFE<br>        §7    OBJECTS NEEDED FOR AN EVENT, TASK OR GENERAL LIVING<br>        §8    REMEMBERING DECISIONS<br>        §9    ORGANISING PAPERWORK, EMAILS, ETC.<br>        §10   WHEN IS IT SAFE TO THROW SOMETHING AWAY?<br>    STUDY PERIPHERALS, CHAPTER 5<br>    EMPLOYMENT, CHAPTER 6 | CHAPTER 2: p 84<br>CHAPTER 3: p 104<br><br>CHAPTER 4:<br>§5: p 132<br>§6: p 133<br>§7: p 136<br><br>§8: p 140<br>§9: p 144<br>§10: p 159<br><br>CHAPTER 5: p 168<br>CHAPTER 6: p 206 |
| 7 | Step 4: Do you recognise any insuperable obstacles? | |
| 8 | Step 5: Describe your plan for organisation and keep it where you will use it. | |
| 9 | Keep applying the MODEL FOR DEVELOPING ORGANISATION. You may want to work with the Steps out of order, for instance you may find you need to change your research questions for Step 3 once you have started working on Steps 4 and 5. | |

# 1 Organisation

| | |
|---|---|
| 10 | Monitor your progress as you use your organisation. Observe objectively: You could use TEMPLATE: B3 - COMPARE EXPECTATIONS AND REALITY.<br>An organisation system is likely to evolve as you use it; you won't necessarily find the best one immediately. |
| 11 | Maintain your confidence by knowing you are developing a system that suits you. Notice how you benefit from the changes you make and enjoy your progress. |

 p 283: objectively

TEMPLATES

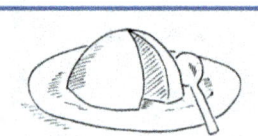

## 5.6 Satisfaction: 'The proof of the pudding is in the eating'

I think the criteria for a good system of organisation are:
- Are the objectives achieved?
- Is the system working well for me and for others involved?
- Does the system feel satisfactory?
- Is it fail-safe[5]?

Figure 1.7
Proof of the pudding

### Examples: Criteria for good solutions

I know I have a good system to deal with paperwork when:

- incoming matters will be noted for action or reading and can be filed until required
- I will be able to find information when needed
- nothing will be forgotten accidentally
- there will be no piles and no ancient papers
- the system will be one that feels easy to use and fluent to operate.

---

[5]'Fail-safe' means that if your system is going to fail it will do so safely; there won't be a disaster. For example, if you fail to operate your system for tax paperwork, you want your fail-safe situation to ensure you pay on time and are not fined. One way to move towards a fail-safe system, in this case, would be never to put important papers away until you've noted the need for action and your note is such that you will notice in time.

# Organisation 1

For good time management:
- I will not be rushing to do something just before a deadline.

### Exercise: Criteria for good organisation

What are your criteria for a good system of organisation?

Think about something you organise well:
- What objectives are achieved? How do you decide?
- How well does the organisation work? How do you know?
- Does it feel satisfactory? Why do you say yes or no?

You may devise a system which works, but which doesn't give you a good sense of achievement.
- Brainstorm your reaction to the system and how it works to find out as clearly as possible what it is that is causing your negative reactions.

Then modify the system until you have one that works well for you. By adopting a constructive approach like this, you can gain satisfaction even from systems that don't initially work.

## 6  Learning to be organised

Being able to organise is a skill that can be extremely useful.  It comes naturally to some people; some dyslexic/ SpLDs become very good at it, as mentioned in ULTRA ORGANISED; others are driven by organisation to a point that is beyond helpful.  You need to reflect whether you have the skills and model you want and whether you are using them to assist you.  At the end of the day, one reason for being organised is that it frees you to do other things that you want to do.

ULTRA ORGANISED: p 49

Ⓖ p 280: descriptions of the 4 most recognised SpLDs

There are some differences in the ways in which organisation is significant for people with different SpLDs.

# 1 Organisation

## 6.1 Dyslexia

Being organised can often really help dyslexic people achieve what they want to do.

You need to be aware of your own THINKING PREFERENCES while sorting out your organisation. Using them well can significantly improve any system you devise.
If you don't know what your thinking preferences are, do the EXERCISE: REALISE YOUR PRESENT ORGANISATIONAL SKILLS and compare the strengths you identify to those summarised in THINKING PREFERENCES.

THINKING PREFERENCES: p 270

EXERCISE: REALISE YOUR PRESENT ORGANISATIONAL SKILLS: p 60

You also need to pay attention to your dyslexic PITFALLS, as they could sabotage an otherwise useful system.

PITFALLS: p 69

It may be that an idea from someone else sounds really good, but it just won't work for you. Understanding why it won't work can be useful.

**Story: Remembering the PIN number for a bank card**

At one meeting, a lad described how he used the long number of his bank card to remember the PIN number. He chose the PIN number to be the first number of each group of 4 on the long number:
long number 6509-4572-8530-5521   PIN 6485.

One of the others in the group decided to do the same. The next time the group met he told us what happened:
 His long number was 3408-5732-8935-2743
 and PIN number 5832  which almost worked.
 He decided to call the long number l...-m...-n...-o...
 and remember his PIN as mnlo.

# Organisation 1

This worked for a few times, but then he got stuck and couldn't make a purchase.

When he got home and worked out what had happened, he realised he'd forgotten the alphabet. He was trying to work with m...-n...-l...-o... to get the PIN from the card number, and of course that didn't work.

It made him realise that trying to use the alphabet to memorise anything was likely to let him down, which was useful to know.

## 6.2 Dyspraxia

How to organise anything, including ideas, is a major problem for most dyspraxic people; it is almost a perpetual obstacle for them. Unless you also have problems that overlap with dyslexia, you may not need to be aware of any thinking preferences.

Once you have a system that works for one type of organisation, it may not be any easier to work out the organisation for the next set of tasks or events. It can be very difficult to see how two tasks are similar and can be organised in the same way, or how to alter one way of organising a task so that it is useful for another.

It is also difficult to remember that organising a task needs to be done.

It is important to see which parts of organisation present significant problems.

**Insight: Organisation of the whole, an overview needed**

I have known one dyspraxic scientist who has well worked-out systems to deal with organisation in general. However, she doesn't manage to have a balanced organisation for her subjects.

 # 1 Organisation

She only values the latest results and she doesn't value the knowledge that went before, although she understands it. She produces essays which state the great new understandings, but which have no backing argument or facts to substantiate her evaluations. Therefore her essays are not a good reflection of her intellectual capacity.

What is lacking is an appreciation of the full organisation of the subjects and the relationships between different subtopics, including the older knowledge.

Although organisation is useful, it is quite important not to become rigid about it.

### Story: Rigid organisation

One student worked out his revision timetable and found a pattern he thought he would be able to stick to. He filled in the details down to every half hour. He had no flexibility built in.

He gradually found that his plan didn't quite work. He was so determined to make it work that he got very tense, he didn't revise well, and he got progressively further from his timetable.

He could not let go of the original plan and work to something that would help him more. His exam results suffered.

You may always need help with organisation. I think it is worth finding someone who is able to listen to your ideas about organisation, who won't do it for you but will allow you to sort out what you need to do and who will do it for you when you really can't.

## 6.3  AD(H)D

Organisation can be useful to help you maintain your attention and use your mind better. Often your motivation, or main interest, is the key into any organisation system generated for you, whether by you or by someone else. Monitor your progress, looking for anything that helps with the attention span as well as with organising a particular task.

*DYSLEXIA:* p 74

The comments written about DYSLEXIA can be applicable to AD(H)D people. Exploring THINKING PREFERENCES as well as the mind techniques is worth doing. See USING THE MIND WELL for mind techniques.

*THINKING PREFERENCES:* p 270

*USING THE MIND WELL:* p 267

## 6.4  Dyscalculia and maths difficulties

Organisation can be extremely helpful in dealing with maths difficulties, whatever the source of the difficulty. In particular the maths itself can be much easier to deal with, to work through and to understand.
Some useful observations can be made using the following questions:

- How are you setting out the maths?
- Does good use of space on the page help you keep track of the processes involved?
- How methodical are you when going from one line of a mathematical argument to the next?
- How do you relate the items you have to learn to the processes you use?
- Are there any pieces of maths knowledge that you need to know but don't?
- Do you understand the maths?

(This isn't an exhaustive list.)

Having observed how you work, you can then assess where difficulties are occurring and you can look for organisation that will help resolve them. Sometimes, good organisation is a fundamental part of understanding the mathematics being learnt.

THINKING PREFERENCES can also be used to bring understanding to the maths issues.

*THINKING PREFERENCES:* p 270

Ask someone you feel comfortable with to watch you work.

# 1 Organisation

**Insight: Watching maths calculations**

As a support tutor, I find it really useful to watch how someone is doing her maths problems. Then I can see what is happening and ask the right questions. When the student describes what she does, she doesn't tell me everything I need to know, because she hasn't seen it for herself.

**Examples: Organisation resolving maths problems**

Problem: Squashing maths work up so that as much as possible can be completed before turning over the page. The work can become so squashed it is difficult to follow.
Solution: To use only one side of the page so that all the steps can be seen simultaneously and easily.

Problem: One student was losing her enthusiasm for maths and finding it difficult to keep working.
Solution: She used her visual strength to good effect to colour-code the different elements of maths:

    red was for definitions

    orange for proofs

    yellow for examples

    green for lemmas

    blue for propositions

    purple for theorems

    pink for remarks and corollaries

She used coloured boxes round sections of her notes. She would highlight significant words during lectures. These methods kept her engaged with her subject in a new way.

MARGIN NOTE: Lemmas and corollaries are mathematical concepts.

## 6.5 Non-dyslexic/ SpLD

The practical ideas in this chapter should be useful to people who have no dyslexia/ SpLD. You may describe problems, especially of time and space, place & direction, that are the same as those for dyslexic/ SpLD people but you won't have the language, organisation or attention problems of dyslexic/ SpLD people.

You won't have to deliberately use your preferred ways of thinking, nor will you need to avoid the pitfalls of dyslexia/ SpLD, but there may be ways that thinking of personal strengths and pitfalls means that organisation becomes easier or more pleasurable for you.

You may find there are some MATERIALS AND METHODS that work better for you than others; you may find some you haven't tried before.

MATERIALS AND METHODS: p 56

## 7  General problem-solving

The MODEL FOR DEVELOPING ORGANISATION is a good format for dealing with many different problems. Among the various dictionary definitions of 'problem' is:

- a matter that exercises the mind.

MODEL FOR DEVELOPING ORGANISATION: p 57

Much of this series is dealing with the impact of dyslexic/ SpLD problems on the lives of the people concerned. Organisation is a fairly common area of difficulty for these groups of people, which is why this book focuses on it.

The ideas in the MODEL FOR DEVELOPING ORGANISATION can easily be extended to apply to other situations or tasks, which could well have no dyslexia/ SpLD issues within them: they still can be classed as 'exercising the mind' and therefore constitute a problem. They are ordinary tasks and situations that occur in most people's everyday life or work.

# 1   Organisation

WORKING ON A GENERAL PROBLEM (below) adapts the model to apply to any situation or task that needs to be thought about.
The aim will vary, for example:

- to increase understanding
- to plan how a task can go forward
- to see the influences working in a situation.

FINDING THE ROOT CAUSE OF A PROBLEM focuses on finding what lies behind any particular problem.  The aim will be better understanding of any underlying causes of the problem.

*FINDING THE ROOT CAUSE OF A PROBLEM: p 82*

## 7.1   Working on a general problem

In many respects the MODEL FOR DEVELOPING ORGANISATION is a special example of a general approach to thinking about or reflecting on any situation or task or set of ideas.

*MODEL FOR DEVELOPING ORGANISATION: p 57*

The table below lists different steps that can be used to work on any general problem.

*TEMPLATES*

You are unlikely to need them all for every problem; you may use them in a different order.

If you monitor your progress with solving problems using TEMPLATE: B3 - COMPARE EXPECTATIONS AND REALITY, you should develop good skills for problem solving.

| 1 | Using the MATERIALS AND METHODS that suit you best plays an important part in the ease of thinking about any problem. |
|---|---|
| 2 | Decide on some key words or phrases to use as the centre of a mind map or as the main heading of a list, i.e. to act as a title for the general problem you want to think about.  Use your title instead of 'general problem' in what follows. |
| 3 | When you've got quite a long title, it often helps to split it into component parts. |

*MATERIALS AND METHODS: p 56*

80

## Organisation 1

| | | |
|---|---|---|
| 4 | Put down what you know about the general problem. If you can, cluster together any ideas that are related; but if clustering distracts you during the brainstorming, don't do it. | |
| 5 | Having a set of USEFUL QUESTIONS that apply to the general problem often helps you gain clarity. | USEFUL QUESTIONS: p 61 |
| 6 | At some stage, see if clustering the ideas together will bring a better understanding of the general problem. | |
| 7 | Set out the present state of the general problem and what you want the outcome to be. Compare the two and see if that helps you to decide what is needed to achieve the outcome. | |
| 8 | Are there strengths that would help? Consider THINKING PREFERENCES, strategies or motivations. | THINKING PREFERENCES: p 270 |
| 9 | Are there any obstacles or hazards, of whatever nature, that need to be considered? | HAZARDS AND OBSTACLES: p 66 |
| 10 | Is there anything missing from your thinking? | |
| 11 | Consider what you have gathered so far. Does it cover all aspects of the general problem? | |
| 12 | Does anything need to happen as the next stage of working on the general problem? If yes, can you make a plan of action? | |

Monitor the different stages suggested here and modify any that don't suit your way of working.

As life evolves after you have worked on a general problem keep noticing what happens and decide whether the general problem needs additional attention.

# 1 Organisation

## 7.2 Finding the root cause of a problem

Quite often, students come with a problem that is causing a lot of disruption in their lives. When I start to make suggestions, I find they have got ways of dealing with it, but that something else is getting in the way. We have to get to the root cause of the problem and tackle that.

**Story: Spelling develop**

One child could not spell develop or development; he always put an 'e' after the 'p'. We talked it through and he realised the 'velop' of develop and envelope were coming together in his mind, so he didn't know which word had the 'e'; he didn't hear the difference in the sound of the two words. Once he knew what he was confusing, he could get it right, though he still had to think about it.

None of his spelling practice before had resolved the problem.

See also: STORY: INSUPERABLE OBSTACLE CHANGED TO HAZARD: p 64

The suggestions here focus on uncovering the root cause of a problem, using some parts of the MODEL FOR DEVELOPING ORGANISATION.

You will probably start by working on a general problem or on the organisation of something. You will have decided on the key words or phrases to use as a title for the problem. There will come a point when you realise there is some issue behind the problem and that it is blocking progress. You then turn your attention onto the root cause of the problem. Use the problem and substitute it in the green text below.

| 1 | Using the MATERIALS AND METHODS that suit you best plays an important part in the ease of finding the root cause of a problem. If you are not already using them, do so as you start to uncover the root cause. |
|---|---|

## Organisation 1

| | | |
|---|---|---|
| 2 | Start a new mind map, table or list to capture ideas. The title will change to 'root cause of problem'. | TEMPLATES <br><br>Use:<br>ROOT CAUSE OF A PROBLEM:<br>F7 - MIND MAP or<br>F8 - SPATIAL or<br>F9 - LINEAR |
| 3 | The emphasis will be to find out<br><ul><li>what is happening in detail</li><li>at what point does something go wrong with dealing with the problem</li><li>what are the pressures on you</li><li>what is happening to your usual ways of dealing with the problem.</li></ul>Explore your ideas as widely as possible. It can be something quite unconnected with the problem that is the root cause of the present difficulty.<br><br>This stage of processing is a combination of OBJECTIVE OBSERVATION and USEFUL QUESTIONS. You may find descriptions of other people's experiences help you to be clear about your own. Use the INDEX and STORY, INSIGHT and EXAMPLE BOXES to find useful descriptions. | ⓖ p 283: objective<br><br>OBJECTIVE OBSERVATION: p 268<br><br>USEFUL QUESTIONS: p 61 |
| 4 | When you have found the root cause of the problem,<br><ul><li>there may be an obvious solution to it</li><li>knowing what it is may mean the problem doesn't disrupt life any more</li><li>or there may be other issues to deal with.</li></ul>As always, monitor what happens to make sure the real root cause has been identified, use TEMPLATE: B3 - COMPARE EXPECTATIONS AND REALITY. | TEMPLATES  |

## References

Miles, Tim, 1993, *Dyslexia: the Pattern of Difficulties,* Whurr, London
Stacey, Ginny, 2020, *Development of Dyslexia and other SpLDs,* Routledge, London

## Website information

Series website: www.routledge.com/cw/stacey

# 2 Time and Time Management

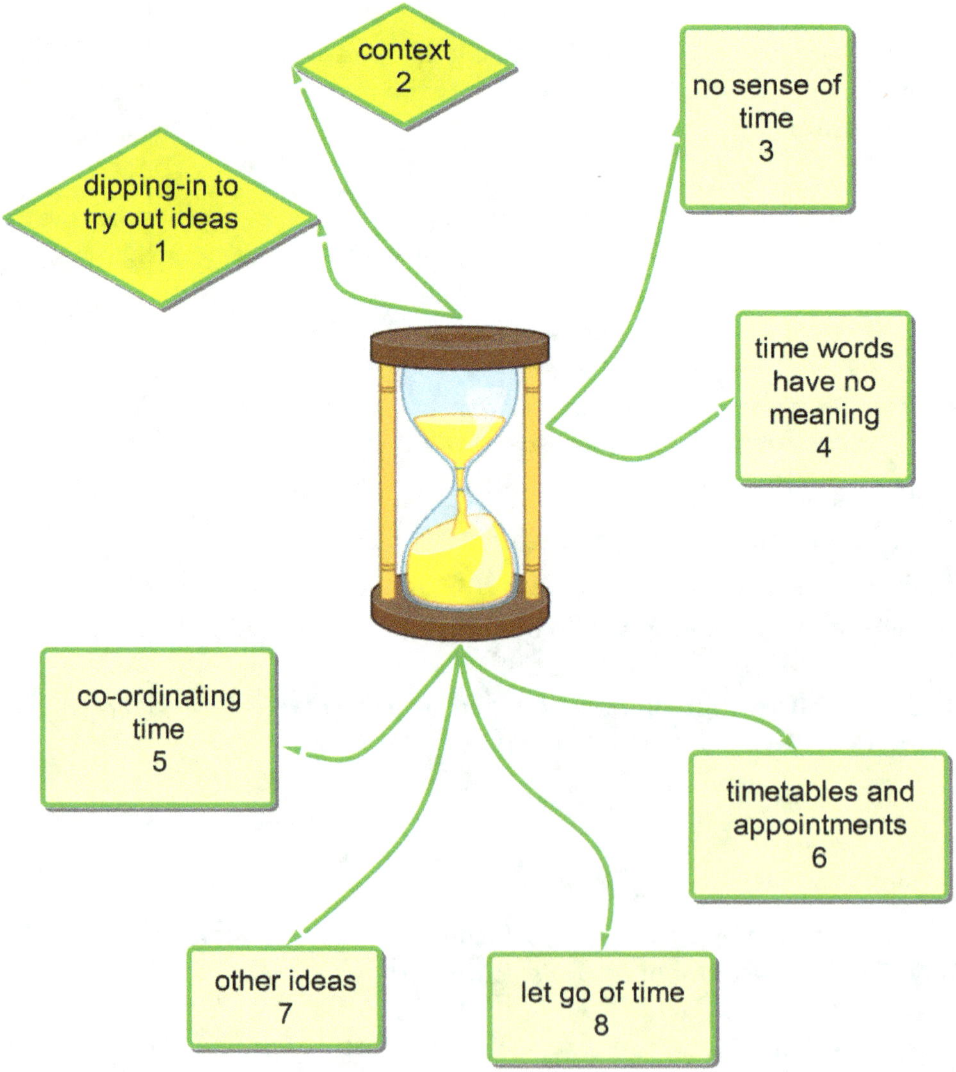

- dipping-in to try out ideas  1
- context  2
- no sense of time  3
- time words have no meaning  4
- co-ordinating time  5
- timetables and appointments  6
- other ideas  7
- let go of time  8

## Contents

| | |
|---|---|
| Vital for dyslexic/ SpLDs, good practice for all ... 85 | 3 No sense of time ... 88 |
| Working with the chapter ... 85 | 4 Time words have no meaning ... 91 |
| Templates on the website ... 86 | 5 Co-ordinating time ... 92 |
| Appendix 1, 2 and 3 ... 86 | 6 Timetables and appointments ... 94 |
| 1 Dipping-in to try out ideas ... 87 | 7 Other ideas about time management ... 98 |
| 2 Context ... 87 | 8 Let go of time ... 100 |
| | References and website information ... 103 |

### Vital for dyslexic/ SpLDs, good practice for all

It is vital for dyslexic/ SpLD people to find solutions for managing time, since mis-management can make all problems relating to dyslexia/ SpLD so much worse.

Dealing with time well is good practice for all.

## Working with the chapter

### Key ideas

- An internal clock  Yes/No
- Time words insecure
- Mis-managing time can make dyslexia/ SpLD problems worse.

Observe what happens to you when you have to deal with time and time management.
Find out what is at the heart of any problem.
Collect your stories, insights and solutions.
Become as autonomous as you can.
Ask for support or accommodations that you need.

Ⓖ p 283: autonomous

85

#  2  Time and Time Management

## Templates on the website

A1   JOTTING DOWN AS YOU SCAN
A4   JOTTING DOWN AS YOU READ
B1   COLLECTING IDEAS THAT RELATE TO YOU

Other useful templates for building accurate knowledge about time are:

F10   UNDERSTANDING TIME OR PLACE PROBLEMS
F11   EXPLORING TIME
B3    COMPARE EXPECTATIONS AND REALITY.

The last one can be used for monitoring purposes.

Useful templates for organising time are:

F12      WEEK WITH HOURS
F13      CALENDAR MONTH – 5 WEEKS
F14-18   HALF A YEAR – 27 WEEKS

Useful templates for problem solving are:

F4   PROBLEM SOLVING - MIND MAP
F5   PROBLEM SOLVING - SPATIAL
F6   PROBLEM SOLVING - LINEAR

Templates

## Appendix 1  Resources

This appendix will help you collect information and make progress as you learn to manage time well.

APPENDIX 1: p 232

## Appendix 2  Individual, Personal Profile of Dyslexia/ SpLD and Regime for Managing Dyslexia/ SpLD

APPENDIX 2: p 246

   Tip: TIME AND TIME MANAGEMENT and building your profile and regime

You can learn about all parts of your profile and regime while organising your time.

# Time and Time Management 2

## Appendix 3 Key Concepts

APPENDIX 3: p 262

This appendix has a summary of the key ideas I cover when doing an audit of skills and knowledge with a dyslexic/ SpLD student. It shows which of the 4 books in the series covers each idea in full.

>
> **Tip: The skills and knowledge you can gain from this series**
>
> APPENDIX 3: KEY CONCEPTS has a list of the main skills and knowledge that you can gain from this series of books. They fall into the categories of:
> THINKING CLEARLY
> USING THE MIND WELL
> YOUR THINKING PREFERENCES
> USEFUL APPROACHES
> ASPECTS OF DYSLEXIA/ SPLD

THINKING PREFERENCES are highlighted in orange in this chapter.

## 1  Dipping-in to try out ideas

Read the section headings, stories and examples.
Notice:
- anything that you recognise as being similar to your experience
- solutions you already use
- anything that seems like a good idea.

Try the good ideas and monitor your progress.

## 2  Context

A lot of modern life is governed by time. For example:
- we have to do something in a certain amount of time
- we have to meet a deadline
- we have to be somewhere at a specific time.

## 2 Time and Time Management

Not everyone finds time easy to deal with. The problems encountered may be the same for dyslexic/ SpLD people and those with no dyslexia/ SpLD. The interaction between dyslexia/ SpLD and time management may make either time management or dyslexia/ SpLD or both worse.

Various aspects of time and time management are difficult for dyslexic/ SpLD people. The following sections describe ways people have told me time goes wrong for them. Some sections have stories and examples; all have possible solutions.

As you work with this chapter, identify any experiences that are relevant to you. Make sure you record them so that you can use the information again. As you try solutions, record any modifications you make and the reasons you make them.

TEMPLATES
Use:
F10 - UNDERSTANDING TIME OR PLACE PROBLEMS

## 3 No sense of time

**Problem**

Some people have no internal clock. They have no way of knowing the time instinctively. They have no way of assessing the passage of time. All their experiences do not build into a data bank of how long it takes to do various tasks. Their attempts to manage time don't work until they deliberately take notice of time.

Other people seem to have a mechanism in their heads that is aware of the passage of time. They can tell what the time of day is quite easily and quite accurately for several hours after the last time they looked at a watch or clock. They are aware how much time has elapsed since they started doing something. They are able to build up a data bank, based on their own experience, which allows them to assess reasonably well how long tasks will take to do.

The mechanism used varies between people, as Richard Feynman (1965 Nobel Laureate for Physics) found. He discovered that he was monitoring time by running a measuring tape visually through his head while a colleague was able to do it verbally by counting.

Feynman (1988)

Whether you have an internal clock or not is not part of dyslexia/ SpLD. Dyslexia/ SpLD can cause problems with time and time management whether you have an internal clock or you don't.

## Time and Time Management 2

**Solutions**

Use:

1. countdown timers: kitchen ones can work with hours & minutes or minutes & seconds; I have several of both
2. countdown function on watches, mobile phones or other electronic devices.

Set the timer to go off when you have to do something.

**Example: Using a countdown timer**

You need to go out at 11.30 am; it takes 10 mins to pick up bags, put on outdoor shoes and coats:
  set timer for 11.20 (or 11.10 until you can rely on remembering all the last minute actions).

Consciously record how long tasks take:
  How long does getting breakfast really take?
  How long do you take to get out of bed & dressed?
  How long does it take to put your kit together?
Compare your estimates with the actual time taken.

Universities use term and semester week numbers; some employers use the week of the year
some meetings or gatherings happen on, say, 2nd Tuesday every month.
And diaries work by dates!

So you may have 2 separate systems used to give time information about events: a system-using-repetition and the system of dates.

Use both systems together; it may seem like extra work, but the hassle saved is worth the extra effort.

*TEMPLATES*

Use:
*F11 - EXPLORING TIME*

## 2  Time and Time Management

If there's one system-using-repetition that you use a lot, it could be worth working out the dates for that system for a year, or a couple of months at a time. Then you have the system-using-repetition with the dates added. Put the combined system where you can easily use it.

### Story: Some rubbish bins collected every 3 weeks

There is one authority that collects bins at different intervals.
- Food caddy, every week.
- Household waste, once a fortnight
- Recycling, every 3rd week.

It does promote neighbourhood cohesion – no one gets it right and the whole street has a weekly conversation to agree whether to put the recycling out, or not.

They could make a list of the actual dates for the recycling collection for a whole year at a time, which would mean only sorting the dates out once a year.

### Example:  Dates and other systems for time

If the week of the year is used for company records and you do a specific task on Tuesdays, make a list of week numbers and the dates of Tuesday in each week, see TIP: PULL DOWN DATES. Keep the list where you can easily use it for the task.

# Time and Time Management 2

**Tip: Pull down dates:**

In Excel and other spreadsheets, you enter the first two dates, select them, use the square handle in the bottom right corner to pull down into the cells below as far as you need; see FIGURE 2.1.

For the STORY: SOME RUBBISH BINS COLLECTED EVERY 3 WEEKS, the first two dates would be 3 weeks apart on the day when recycling is collected, then pulling down dates gives you all the dates of that day 3 weeks apart.

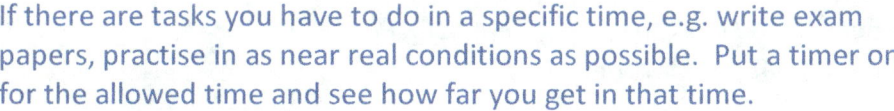
Figure 2. 1
Dates pulled down[1]

If there are tasks you have to do in a specific time, e.g. write exam papers, practise in as near real conditions as possible. Put a timer on for the allowed time and see how far you get in that time.

## 4  Time words have no meaning

**Problem**

You can have a seemingly sensible, accurate conversation about time, but the impression registered by the mind is incomplete because the time words have no meaning attached.

**Story: Time words have no meaning**

One lad kept missing evenings out with friends. They would all agree something like, "See you at 8 o'clock". He would even check that he was free. The connection that was missing was: 8 o'clock was only an hour after dinner time and that the diary entry 'dinner with Matt' meant he was unlikely to be free at 8 o'clock.

Similar but different things kept happening to him. None of the solutions he tried worked until he saw that he was not really thinking about time, even when he was talking sensibly about it.

---

[1] Screenshot of Microsoft Excel 2007

# 2 Time and Time Management

**Solution**

Find some way to attach meaning to the words:

visually see the hands of a clock, or the digital reading on a watch (visual)

see the days or months on a calendar (visual)

attach daily activities to certain times of day (kinaesthetic or Myers-Briggs feeling).

## 5 Co-ordinating time

**Problems**

Find out exactly what goes wrong:

attention is given to the wrong detail

not enough time is allowed for the unexpected

something else: use ideas from FINDING THE ROOT CAUSE OF A PROBLEM to decide what it is that goes wrong.

THINKING PREFERENCES: p 270

FINDING THE ROOT CAUSE OF A PROBLEM: p 82

TEMPLATES
 Use:
B3 - COMPARE EXPECTATIONS AND REALITY

F11 - EXPLORING TIME

PROBLEM SOLVING:
F4 - MIND MAP
F5 - SPATIAL
F6 - LINEAR

See also: PRECISELY WRONG TIME OR PLACE: p 48

---

**Examples: Problems with co-ordinating time**

- People will leave one place at the time they should arrive for a meeting, lecture, etc.: a meeting starts at 10, or the coach to London leaves at 10, and you leave the house at 10.

- Sometimes, it is only as you leave for an event, or just as an event starts, that you remember details and know about another collection of items you should have taken with you.

- You don't remember what you have to do at a useful time; you remember when you can't do anything about it.

---

**Solutions**

You are aiming to get yourself and everything you need to the right place at the right time.

- Add journey time, even from one office to another, to the time that is written in any diary.

# Time and Time Management 2

- For a shopping trip on the way to a class:
    - Work back from the start time of the class, and work out the time you have to leave.
    - Allow time for queues; for the till roll to be replaced; for time to get from one shop to another, be realistic.
    - Take something to do or read with you in case everything goes smoothly and you arrive early.
    - Prioritise what you hope to do so that you can leave out the least important items if time runs out.
    - Reflect afterwards how good your estimates were and adjust future ones.
    - Gradually build up your knowledge of how long it takes you to achieve what you set out to do, see MONITORING PROGRESS.

    This sequence can be adapted to any series of actions.

MONITORING PROGRESS: p 243

- Get everything ready for an outing, or task, in advance. How much in advance will depend on you and the outing. Experiment to find out what is best, but to start with make it at least an hour in advance for relatively uncomplicated outings and tasks.
    - Collect everything you need in one place, possibly in a bag.
    - If there's something you need to pick up at the last minute, put a note where you can't miss or avoid it; see examples below.
    - If there's something you want to use before going out, again put a note that you've removed it from the pile so that you will remember to get it.

    One benefit of preparing in advance is that you give your mind time to bring other items to your attention.

'collect everything', see: OBJECTS NEEDED FOR AN EVENT, TASK OR GENERAL LIVING: p 136

- One benefit of being ready in good time is that you have time for unexpected things to happen.

# 2  Time and Time Management

### Examples:  Possible solutions

- People use countdown timers or alarm clocks, possibly several together.
- Alarms on mobile phones can be used.
- Reminders
    - People with strong visual memory put Post-it notes on the door they go out of.
    - Those who notice what they walk round will leave large notes on the floor (kinaesthetic) or objects they have to walk round.
    - Notes can be clipped to a bag where the hand goes to grab the bag.

Figure 2. 2
Various solutions

## 6  Timetables and appointments

Some dyslexic/ SpLD people find timetables and appointments very difficult to organise.  New timetables may take some weeks to 'get your head round'.  One-off appointments or those that keep changing in some detail (e.g. the time is not fixed) can be almost impossible. Some people must make the timetable their own and use symbols, colour coding, pictures or suitable images to alter the way they react to timetables. See also the related topics in the MARGIN NOTE.

MARGIN NOTE: Related topics:
1) TIMETABLES AND STUDY TIME: p 187
2) MEETING DEADLINES: p 188

### Examples: Some problems with timetables and appointments

- You have to live through the events of a new timetable for a couple of weeks before it, the timetable, takes root in your thinking.
- You are meeting a friend at 6 pm one day.  You are aware of the arrangement in the days before; you think about it during the day in question with pleasurable anticipation.

94

# Time and Time Management 2

> At 5.30 pm, you wonder what to do next and go and do something completely different. No thought of meeting your friend rises in your mind until sometime after, or until your friend asks where you were.
>
> - Having to meet the constraints of timetables increases anxiety.

**Solutions**

- Find the format of a timetable or diary that suits you best.
    - Some people must have the days of the week lined up; they can't use a calendar that has each first of the month lined up.
    - Some people need to see a whole week, month or year visible altogether, without turning over pages.
    - Some people need the day to be broken into hours; to have '2-4 pm' written on the page doesn't show how much time is taken for the activity or how much is left for anything else.

- When you have definite, regular commitments (classes, meetings, evening or weekend activities) it can be very useful to make a timetable with all the regular events. You could stick it in one place in your diary; you could use it as a template; you could put it in a plastic wallet and write extra details on the wallet; you could use it at a definite time to make sure the coming month has all the regular commitments.

- It is often useful to block out time for necessary tasks such as shopping, cooking, dealing with paperwork, checking emails, etc.

- Timetables for specific series of events can be useful, from a list with times noted on it to several weeks or months with details.

Find the best place to put timetables; you want to see them and not avoid them.

TEMPLATES

 Use:

F12 - WEEK WITH HOURS

F13 - CALENDAR MONTH – 5 WEEKS

F14 - HALF A YEAR – 27 WEEKS

 ## 2   Time and Time Management

- Consider electronic diaries; make sure the format is the right one for you before spending too much money.   Especially consider whether the way information is set out makes it easy for you to absorb the information.

- Find the best time to consult your diaries and timetables, whether electronic or paper.  Some people like to look at the coming week on Sunday evening; some people like to look at the next day at a particular time during the evening before.  Use the full functions of the electronic device; take some time to find out what they are.

- Colour coding helps some people (visual): all lectures in a particular series are in one colour; a manager uses one colour for all holiday information; colour is used by others to separate different priorities.  On electronic devices, using categories can be very useful, as can setting alarms.

### Example: To relieve the stress of travel timetables

- You could get everywhere early and have something fun to do in any spare time.
- You could go with the flow, e.g. travel without booking anything in advance, just know your destination.

MARGIN NOTE: see also
LET GO OF TIME: p 100

If a task involves a series of steps that need to happen in a specific order, make a list and put times on it.

### Example:  Using a list to prepare a meal

A list can help you prepare a special meal to be ready at a specified time.

# Time and Time Management 2

- Write out all the steps involved, including lighting the oven and setting the table.
- Show how preparation of one dish overlaps another.
- Allow adequate time for each step.
- Put times on each action.

After the event, assess how accurate your timings were so that you build up your knowledge base about time; use TEMPLATE: F11 - EXPLORING TIME.

TEMPLATES  Use:
F11 - EXPLORING TIME

### Tip:  Everything you need for an appointment

A list, similar to the one for preparing a meal, could be used to get you to appointments with everything you need.

### Example:  Time for revision

Revision timetables can be very useful coming up to exams, especially major ones.
You need a calendar that covers the whole revision period, usually from the day of making the timetable to the end of the exam period.

You need to put in anything that breaks into the time for revision.

I always get students to be as realistic as possible: to put in times for friends' birthday parties including how long it takes to get there and back and recover; to have time off, weekly and on holiday; time for shopping and other household chores; paid or voluntary work during vacations; any other study deadlines; realistic time for dissertations.

We also consider breaks as part of revision; see the next EXAMPLE: TAKING BREAKS DURING REVISION below.

TEMPLATES Use:
F14 - HALF A YEAR – 27 WEEKS

# 2 Time and Time Management

All this information should be considered for the revision timetable. The time left for revision often seems rather too little, but that is often the information that keeps you making progress well in advance of the exams.

### Example: Taking breaks during revision

Break activities are also important components of revision timetables. They need to be personal to you, active, satisfying and probably mentally stimulating.

The length of time needs to be chosen well. Sometimes the activities need to be short, such as BREATHING or RELAXATION exercises, so that they do not take you away from the revision. Sometimes they need to be an hour or so. The choice depends on the way your revision is enhanced by the break.

*Possible break activities: playing musical instrument; gardening; building a complicated model; cooking; sewing.*

*BREATHING: p 265*
*RELAXATION: p A3§1.2*

## 7 Other ideas about time management

**Paperwork**

Part of time management is dealing with paperwork efficiently, which is dealt with in RESPONDING TO THE PAPERWORK.

*RESPONDING TO THE PAPERWORK: p 156*

**Be prepared**

Find your own best way to be prepared in order to reduce hassle and so organise time more effectively.

### Examples: Examples of being prepared

- You mentally regard each day as starting at 6pm the day before, with preparation for all the known events.

- A week might start on Friday evening by checking what has been timetabled for the following week, that time for recreation has been included, that there is enough food to eat, etc.

*The blue is picking out time; red is picking out what is being done or prepared.*

# Time and Time Management 2

### Story: Clothes for the week

One headmistress set out all the clothes she would wear during a week every Sunday, so that choosing what to wear didn't add an extra task to the morning.

### Insight: Benefits from being prepared

- Before settling to a period of concentration, get everything ready for the next activity or outing. This approach can be helpful when you find yourself constantly drawn to thinking about what you have to do next. It is useful to know everything is ready and that all you have to do is scoop it all up and go; you can relax and give your full attention to the task you want to concentrate on.

- Being prepared in advance often allows extra information or ideas to surface in your mind in time to be used to good effect.

These two may seem contradictory, but they can be used together.
As extra information occurs to you, jot it down but continue concentrating.
In the SOLUTIONS for CO-ORDINATING TIME it mentions that being ready in good time allows you to deal with unexpected things. The 'unexpected' includes ideas that come to you while concentrating on another task.
If you have gained time by being prepared, you can deal with these unexpected issues before moving on to the next task.

CO-ORDINATING TIME, SOLUTIONS: p 92

# 2  Time and Time Management

### Stress

Pressure and sickness can make time much more of a problem.  All the things that go wrong are much more likely to do so, and the ways you usually handle your time management disintegrate, as do the ways you handle other effects of having dyslexia/ SpLD.

Deadlines can be useful for some people.  You need to find out the effect they have on you and your work.

---

#### Example:  Varied response to deadlines

Deadlines make some people get going; the buzz of working with just a short time feels really exciting.

Deadlines for others seem to sap all the dyslexia/ SpLD management systems, so that you feel back at McLoughlin's level 2 of compensation, see *4 Levels of Compensation*.

---

*4 Levels of Compensation:* p 276

## 8  Let go of time

It is not always beneficial to be too rigorous about time.

---

#### Examples:  Some jobs and situations can't be predicted

House alteration: you don't know what you will uncover when you start to dismantle a house to make alterations, so you can't always specify the length of time needed.

Journeys: you can't predict traffic flow and many other delays in travel.

Writing a chapter of a book or report: the ideas may not come easily, or you discover that something else needs to be written first.

# Time and Time Management 2

At such times, you have to find out what works best for you.

Do you let go of time, as in the second suggestion in EXAMPLE: TO RELIEVE THE STRESS OF TRAVEL TIMETABLES?

Do you feel comfortable with an estimate of the time?

Do you make an estimate and have a mental allowance for over-run?

EXAMPLE: TO RELIEVE THE STRESS OF TRAVEL TIMETABLES: p 96

### Insight: Good use of over-run time

One writer worked out daily timetables for writing and for other tasks, like emails and shopping.  She decided exactly how far she would get with the writing in a particular time.  When she didn't achieve the goal, she just carried on writing and abandoned her timetable.  She then found herself rushing through the other tasks, never getting anything done properly.  She ended up dissatisfied with life and reluctant to get started on most things.

She needed the timetable to keep her life moving well.  But it wasn't working to put her to-do list into the timetable and she had no evidence of doing extra tasks.

So, she used a note book that was set out with 3 columns on the left-hand page: time, activity, to-do list; this page was the expectations page.  She marked out the day with

- 3 time slots for different tasks
- a significant amount of time for overrun
- a specific time at the end of the day to fill in the right-hand page.

The right-hand page was headed Actual.  She recorded: what she'd done; anything that distracted her; anything she wanted to change; how well the timetable was working for her.  She could also use the right-hand page to capture any ideas that occurred during the day.

# 2  Time and Time Management

> The overrun time allowed her to switch between tasks because she knew she could use it later on the most urgent task. It took stress out of her work and so made it more effective anyway.
>
> Writing down what she'd done allowed her to realise what she had accomplished and to stop feeling that she was getting nowhere.
>
> She commented that it was helpful to see the wider impacts of dyslexia/ SpLD and that she no longer put herself down for many of the things that happen to her.

Some tasks can become more stressful because the time has been specified too tightly and it is better to let go of it. Sometimes being precise, as described in EXAMPLE: USING A LIST TO PREPARE A MEAL, adds too much pressure and takes a sense of creativity or enjoyment out of the task. Again, you need to observe objectively and find out what works best for you.

EXAMPLE: USING A LIST TO PREPARE A MEAL: p 96

## Time and Time Management 2

If you find you can't let go of time, that you are becoming very stressed and quite a lot is not working for you, get help as early as possible.

### Story: Fixation on a timetable

One student worked out a very precise revision regime. She decided to change from one topic to another on the hour or half hour. She left no time for breaks; she didn't have very good strategies for her revision; her revision was not going very well.

I could introduce her to some good techniques, and show her how to build them into her revision plan in such a way that they would not disrupt the flow, e.g. using MIND SET to switch to the new topic. She felt she didn't have time to find out how the techniques would work for her. She could not let go of the change-over moments. In the end, she did not do very well in her exams.

*MIND SET:* p 267

## References

Feynman, Richard, 1988, *What Do You Care What Other People Think?*, Penguin Books, Toronto

Stacey, Ginny, 2020, *Development of Dyslexia and other SpLDs*, Routledge, London

## Website information

Series website: www.routledge.com/cw/stacey

# 3 Space, Place and Direction

- §1 dipping-in to try out ideas
- §2 context — dyspraxia
- no sense of space where you are in:
  - §3 your body
  - §4 your environment
- §5 no sense of place where things are:
  - outside: car or bike parked
  - inside: papers or objects
- §6 no sense of direction
  - get lost going places
  - getting lost in airports
  - shopping
  - way round supermarket
- §7 words for place have no reliable meaning
  - left right
  - top bottom
  - etc
- §8 the impact of the environment
  - need for noise
  - too much noise
  - curiosity about objects around
  - can't see out
  - too untidy
  - too austere
- §9 relating to the space around you

## Contents

Vital for dyslexic/ SpLDs,
        good practice for all .................. 105
Working with the chapter .................. 106
Templates on the website .................. 106
Appendix 1, 2 and 3 .................. 106
1   Dipping-in to try out ideas .................. 107
2   Context .................. 108
    2.1   Dyspraxia                 110
3   No sense of where
        you are in your body .................. 111

4   No sense of where
        you are in your environment .... 113
5   No sense of place .................. 114
6   No sense of direction .................. 115
7   Words for space, place and direction
        have no reliable meaning .................. 117
8   The impact of the environment .................. 118
9   Relating to the space around you .................. 119
References and website information .................. 120

---

**Vital for dyslexic/ SpLDs, good practice for all**

For some dyslexic/ SpLD people, problems with space, place or direction can be serious. The stress then generated makes other problems from dyslexia/ SpLD very much more difficult to manage. It's vital to see exactly what is at the heart of any problem and to recognise anything that is an obstacle rather than a hazard.

Many non-dyslexic/ SpLD people also have similar, significant problems. The work to deal with these problems will be good practice for these people too.

Ⓖ p 283: obstacle, hazard

# 3 Space, Place and Direction

## Working with the chapter

> **Key ideas**
> - Sense of: space, place, direction
>                 yes or no for each one
> - Words for space, place and directions lose their meaning
> - Impact of the world around you

Observe what happens to you when you have to deal with space, place and direction.
Find out what is at the heart of any problem.
Collect your stories, insights and solutions.
Become as autonomous as you can.
Ask for the support or accommodations that you need.

 p 283: autonomous

## Templates on the website

A1    JOTTING DOWN AS YOU SCAN
A4    JOTTING DOWN AS YOU READ
B1    COLLECTING IDEAS THAT RELATE TO YOU

TEMPLATES

Other useful templates for building accurate knowledge about space, place and direction are:
F10   UNDERSTANDING TIME OR PLACE PROBLEMS
B3    COMPARE EXPECTATIONS AND REALITY.
B8    RECORDING TEMPLATE - 4
B3 can be used for monitoring purposes.

## Appendix 1  Resources

APPENDIX 1: p 232

This appendix will help you collect information and make progress as you develop solutions for any problems you have with space, place or direction.

# Space, Place and Direction  3

### Appendix 2  Individual, Personal Profile of Dyslexia/ SpLD and Regime for Managing Dyslexia/ SpLD

APPENDIX 2: p 246

Tip:  SPACE, PLACE AND DIRECTION **and building your profile and regime**

You can learn about your profile and regime while exploring and solving any problems you have with space, place or direction.

### Appendix 3  Key Concepts

APPENDIX 3: p 262

I cover these key concepts when doing an audit of skills and knowledge with a dyslexic/ SpLD student.  The appendix shows which of the 4 books in the series covers each idea in full.

Tip: **The skills and knowledge you can gain from this series**

APPENDIX 3: KEY CONCEPTS has a list of the main skills and knowledge that you can gain from this series of books.  They fall into the categories of
> THINKING CLEARLY
> USING THE MIND WELL
> YOUR THINKING PREFERENCES
> USEFUL APPROACHES
> ASPECTS OF DYSLEXIA/ SPLD

THINKING PREFERENCES are highlighted in orange in this chapter.

### 1   Dipping-in to try out ideas

Read the story, insight and example boxes.

Notice anything that relates to you.

Do the EXERCISE: RELATING TO THE SPACE AROUND YOU.

Use TEMPLATE: F10 - UNDERSTANDING TIME OR PLACE PROBLEMS to find out what happens to you; then use the chapter to develop your best solutions.

EXERCISE: RELATING TO THE SPACE AROUND YOU: p 119

TEMPLATES

107

# 3 Space, Place and Direction

## 2 Context

Some organisation depends on having a good sense of space, place and direction.

By <u>space</u> I mean the three-dimensional physical world, around you or within your body;

<u>place</u> means a position in that physical world and

<u>direction</u> comes from the connections between different places in the physical world.

There is a similarity with organisation relating to time, in that problems can arise

1. from a missing inner sense of space, place and direction
2. when the words for space, place and direction have no reliable meaning.

However, the types of solutions will be different, since it can be quite difficult to set up devices that will help you: for time you can use alarms on clocks and watches and other electronic kit that you can take with you.  Sat Nav can be used for some place related problems, but for many there is no simple kit to help, as yet.

*Sat Nav stands for 'satellite navigation'.*

It is useful to realise the range of skills needed to deal with space, place and direction.

People with a good sense of space

have a good mental map of their body and they relate easily to their surroundings;

those with a good sense of place

know where they are, where other people are and where objects are;

those with a good sense of direction

know in which direction they are moving

can find their way to other places without paying conscious attention

dare to make wrong turnings because they are confident of finding their way back again.

# Space, Place and Direction  3

People who have an internal sense of space, place and direction take in information and process it in the background all the time.

Other people have varying degrees of sense of space, place and direction which can range from moderately good through to not very accurate to non-existent. Even in one person, there can be varying levels of competence in sensing space, place and direction.

Some dyslexic/ SpLD people have a good sense of space, place and direction; others have a poor or non-existent one; some people have inconsistent memories for space, place and direction. The same is true of non-dyslexic/ SpLD people, the difference being that trying to sort out the problems can be made worse by the effects of the dyslexia/ SpLD. Even for those dyslexic/ SpLDs who have a very good sense of space, place and direction, there are some problems that are generated by the dyslexia/ SpLD.

Some dyslexic/ SpLD people are acutely aware of the space around them, and the quality of the environment can have a significant impact on the effectiveness of their thinking, see PROBLEMS AND SOLUTIONS RELATING TO THE ENVIRONMENT.

PROBLEMS AND SOLUTIONS RELATING TO THE ENVIRONMENT: p 118

It can be very interesting to hear how people's minds deal with place, space and direction.

### Story: An inconsistent memory for space and direction

A manager frequently had to direct visitors to the office of the next person the visitor was going to see. The manager's memory for the route depended on the way she was facing. She could remember details of corridors and spaces in the direction that she was facing, but if the route for the visitor turned a corner, she had no memory of what came next unless she turned to face the new direction. But as she turned for the new direction, she lost her memory of the route she'd just described. So to describe a complete route, she had to keep turning herself with every turn of the route.

109

 # 3 Space, Place and Direction

Solutions depend on finding out the underlying cause of the problem and exploring thinking preferences to find out what can improve the situation.

Your confidence and self-esteem can be improved by finding a group of other people with similar experiences.

## 2.1 Dyspraxia

The core problem of dyspraxia is an 'impairment or immaturity in the organisation of movement' (DfES Report, 2005) and the problems caused by space, place and direction are particularly important for dyspraxic people.

The body image of dyspraxic people is not secure and does not provide a stable basis for any skills to develop (Stacey, 2020). *No Sense of Where You Are in Your Body* has further, general discussion about this lack of central core stability.

Whilst I am emphasising the difficulties faced by dyspraxic people, I also want to stress that they can develop skills despite the difficulties.

If your body image is not reliable, then interacting with your environment and the people around you can be fraught with difficulty: you are effectively aiming for a moving target the whole time because nothing becomes stable in relation to where you are.

Ⓖ p 283: confidence, self-esteem

Ⓖ p 280 dyspraxia

DfES Report (2005)

Stacey (2020)

*No Sense of Where You Are in Your Body:* p 111

---

### Story: Not driving on the pavement

One middle-aged dyspraxic man wanted to learn to drive. He enrolled for 20 lessons. When he was asked how he was doing after 10, he said, "I've stopped driving up on to the pavement any more." He eventually abandoned the idea of driving.

## Space, Place and Direction 3

The physical problems of dyspraxia are supported by physiotherapists. It is worth finding out what is known and what you can do to make your life less hazardous.

The lack of a good body image can have an impact on everything you try to do or learn.

One of the difficulties about dyspraxia, as with the other SpLDs, is that the problems are not unknown to people who don't have the attendant learning difficulties. The rest of this chapter is about all those who have any problems with place, space or direction, whether or not they have the learning difficulty that accompanies dyspraxia.

### 3   No sense of where you are in your body

Some people do not have a sense of where they are in their bodies; they may have no central core stability.

- They need to be moving continually, as if that movement outlines their body for them.
- Their body image is not organised, and as a result it seems that nothing else gets organised.

Solutions for this physical need belong in the realm of occupational therapy and are outside the scope of this book.

Someone who is moving around more than expected can disturb those around them, including others who are similarly needing to move around.
These other people need to be aware of the reason for the perpetual motion; they should avoid interpreting it as lack of interest or a failure to concentrate.
If possible, it is best to ignore the movement and carry on as if it were not happening.
If necessary, talk about it. What doesn't help is making the person moving feel as if they are a nuisance or as if they are distracting others.

# 3  Space, Place and Direction

If you experience any problems relating to where you are in your body, the way signals from your body to your brain are used may create problems.  It is worth observing exactly what happens to you.

### Story:  Use of body memory

My left hand is the dominant movement when I'm playing the guitar; it selects the notes.  The right hand just follows and plays.  If a piece of music has an open string, which requires no movement of the left hand, I have great difficulty in remembering to play the note.  There is no signal from the left hand and the right hand has nothing to follow.  On difficult pieces of music, I have to make some gesture in the air with my left hand in order to mark the place of the open string.

**Possible solutions**

Doing Brain Gym exercises may usefully combine your need to move with movements that can assist thinking (Dennison and Dennison, 1986; Stacey, 2019).

Dennison and Dennison (1986)
Stacey (2019)

Being aware of balance and the flow of energy can bring enjoyment and benefit in any kind of physical exercise that you do.

### Insight:  One earring

A single earring gave a 9-year-old lad a sense of where his body was.  A lot of things settled for him after he got the earring.

# Space, Place and Direction 3

Deliberately focus on some item that distinguishes the right and left side of your body – a wedding ring, a watch, the pocket with your pens – or look at your hands and say: "I write with my right."

Consciously think about your body, and label the different parts while feeling the sensations from each, or while moving each part. Focus on moving your fingers independently.

Build a structure so that you can trace a shape on a piece of paper without directly seeing your hand. Use a mirror to see your hand. Trace different shapes, and concentrate on feeling the movement of your hand and arm.

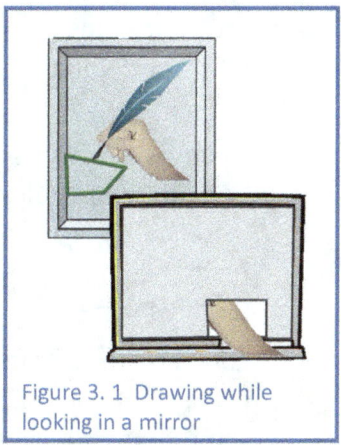

Figure 3. 1 Drawing while looking in a mirror

### Accommodations

Organisation of the space around you needs to accommodate your constant motion, for example:

- chairs should be strong enough
- there should be room for you to move around
- delicate objects should be moved out of your way
- possibly some object which you can play with should be accessible.

Just doodling on paper may give you enough physical sensation to satisfy the need for feedback from your body.

As the person with a need to move most of the time, you could experiment with explaining the situation to others. How well you succeed will depend on your level of confidence and the other people's openness.

## 4  No sense of where you are in your environment

Some people may have a sense of where they are within their body, but no sense of where their body is in relation to the space around them. They can't avoid bumping into objects.

One good solution is to keep the space as clear as possible, putting away anything that might clutter the place as fast as possible.

# 3 Space, Place and Direction

You can see if it helps to invent games to improve your knowledge of the space around you:

a   Walking along the street notice a building that you are walking towards; see more and more details as you get near; when it is behind you, recall it to mind and think of it receding into the distance as you walk away from it – being conscious of its height will increase the awareness that the world has three dimensions.

b   Look at a map before a car journey, then on the journey remember the road as it was on the map and compare it with the road as you see it; be aware of the hills and other physical features and relate them to the symbols on the map.

## 5  No sense of place

People with no sense of place can park cars or bikes and have no sense of where they have left them.  They spend a lot of time looking for them.

With modern electronic devices, you can adopt various strategies for this. You can photograph the place and put the time and date on the photos.  You can use a recording device to describe where you are; your description needs to be clear.  You have to make sure that you always record where the car, bike, etc. is before you leave it.

When inside buildings, people can put objects down and have no sense of where they are.

- You can resign yourself to the time spent looking for them; it often turns up other objects that you'd forgotten about.
- You can have specific places where things belong and be very disciplined about putting things back.  When you reap the reward of such discipline, enjoy the freedom.
- You can have a place where you note the places you have put things, see REMEMBERING DECISIONS for suggestions.
- You can label objects with where they belong, or you can colour code them.  Even within my office, the pens and pencils are colour coded for the computer area and the desk area.  By this method, objects migrate back to where they belong.

REMEMBERING DECISIONS: p 140

## Space, Place and Direction 3

### 6  No sense of direction

Some people have no sense of direction, of how one place relates to another.  They can get lost very easily on any journey, short or long, or in any situation which involves finding their way around.  They get lost on foot as well as in a vehicle.  They can have problems:

- with getting between two places
- finding their way round their local shopping area or their usual supermarket
- navigating big complexes such as airports.

Familiar places can be as difficult as unfamiliar ones.

---

**Insight:  Strategy for directions needs updating**

A dyspraxic student at school had a gang of friends who naturally took her places, around the school and out of it.  She had no resources for getting about on her own and didn't even realise there was a problem.  Then she was taken to university by her parents, and they left after they had settled her into her room.

She could see the dining hall and some shops from her windows.  For the first few weeks of term, these were the only places she went to.  Eventually, it was noticed that she wasn't handing in any work.  The problem was investigated and it was discovered that she hadn't known how to get anywhere.

The solution was that others in her year collected her to take her to lectures.  She could eventually manage most lectures, from college to lecture building (A) and straight back.

One lecture route remained too complicated for her as it involved another building, B; she always had to have a guide to go from college to lecture building A, then on to B and finally back to college.

#  3 Space, Place and Direction

One important part of any solution is to leave enough time to get lost and to ask the way. It's also important to be clear about the destination, so that those you ask can give you the right directions. Sat Nav is useful; it is worth getting a good one as some direct you through ploughed fields.

Sat Nav stands for 'satellite navigation'.

In taking directions from other people, use your THINKING PREFERENCES:

**Verbally**: rehearse the instructions
**visually**: get a map or drawing of the directions
**kinaesthetically**: physically face the way you will be going,
  turn right or left,
  move your hand: for 'take third right', mark 1, 2 with your right hand and then on 3 move your hand off to the right

THINKING PREFERENCES: p 270

ⓖ p 283: kinaesthetic

Use any method that you can invent using different THINKING PREFERENCES and see which one(s) help you.

Some people can work their way from one place to another by quite a roundabout way. They can retrace their tracks exactly, but they can't take a short cut back to the original position.

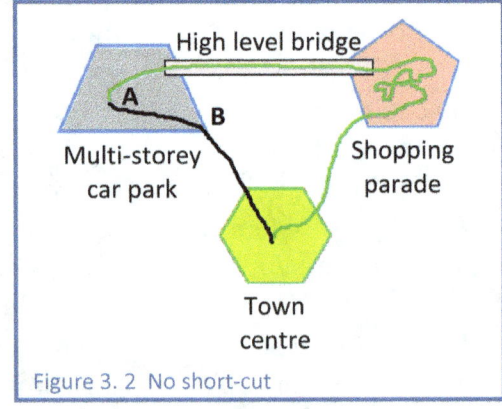

Figure 3. 2 No short-cut

### Insight: No short cut

The car was parked, at A in FIGURE 3.2, in a multi-storied car park which connected directly to a shopping parade and to the ground level of the pedestrian precinct. Having meandered through the shops to get to the town centre, the route back had to be through exactly the same shops. It was impossible to look at the car park entrance at B in FIGURE 3.2 and think: "The car's on the second level, we'll go in at the bottom and up the stairs."

Space, Place and Direction  3

There is also the story at the beginning of this section, AN INCONSISTENT MEMORY FOR SPACE AND DIRECTION. The most useful thing is to be aware of how your mind works with directions, and not to expect it to work in a way that it clearly doesn't. Look at the new devices that come on the market and work out which ones will help you. Borrow someone's device before spending too much money: what works for another person may not work at all for you.

AN INCONSISTENT MEMORY FOR SPACE AND DIRECTION: p 109

## 7   Words for space, place and direction have no reliable meaning

Some people have a good non-verbal sense of space, place or direction, but words used in conversation about the concepts may have no meaning, i.e. you know the direction you are thinking about, but you won't reliably say 'left' or 'right'.

The words used may represent different mental images of space or direction.

In FIGURE 3.3, do you go down the High Street or down the hill?

There needs to be a comparison of how different people are interpreting the words.

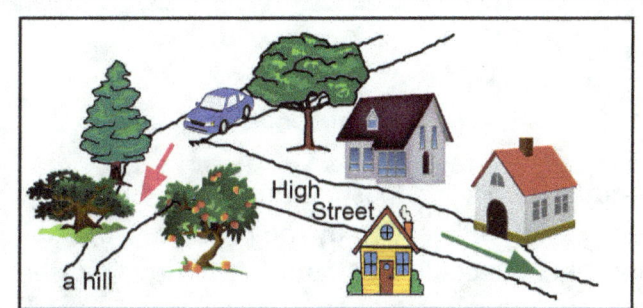

"Come to the top of the High Street and carry on down."

Figure 3.3  Two different interpretations

### Insight:  Can't tell left from right

When giving or receiving directions in a car, many people cannot say 'turn left' or 'turn right' reliably. But they can say 'this way' or 'that way', meaning 'turn towards my side' or 'turn towards your side' respectively, or can wave the appropriate hand to give reliable visual clues.

117

# 3 Space, Place and Direction

Left and right are the most common words that cause problems. *Figure 3.3* shows how 'top' and 'down' also caused problems. The way to resolve the problem is to compare inner mental interpretations and uncover the source of the problem. Then you can work out how to resolve the situation, even if that means avoiding some part that is seen as an insuperable obstacle, see *Hazards and Obstacles*. The inability to tell left from right, etc., should be managed properly.

*Hazards and Obstacles: p 66*

## 8   The impact of the environment

For some people the effects of their dyslexia/ SpLD are worsened when they don't feel comfortable in their environment. They can get to a point where they are unable to function at all well because of the discomfort.

**Examples: Problems and solutions relating to the environment**

A student writing a Masters thesis could not make any progress because he felt trapped by the room he worked in. He worked well when he could look out of a window and see the world beyond. But the windows in his room were too high to look out of when he was seated. However, he was able to turn the desk so that he could see the view beyond the open door, which solved his problem.

Many dyslexia/ SpLD people cannot function when there is a lot of environmental noise, whether from roads, other people gathering nearby, or general building noises. Some use noise mufflers to deal with the sounds; some can use music; and some have to find quiet places to work.

By way of contrast, others find they work better in a place that has a fair bit of noise; it is as if the attention to shut out the noise makes concentration easier.

## Space, Place and Direction 3

### Solutions in general

It is important to identify why an environment feels uncomfortable, and to recognise what is good about beneficial environments; see the exercise below, *RELATING TO THE SPACE AROUND YOU*. Then you have to use these insights to adapt your space so that you can work well in it. You may need to try different adaptations until you get the right one, but each time you will be learning something useful about the way you think and do things well. The eventual progress should justify the adaptations.

### 9   Relating to the space around you

**Exercise:  Relating to the space around you**

On a scale of 1 - 5 (bad to good) remember a place where the environment made you feel uncomfortable at about level 2
Remember how you felt .....
What do you see? .... See any colours, see any movement
Are there any sounds? ... Really hear them
Notice how your body feels....
Notice how you feel about yourself ...
Notice what you feel about the place ...
What's missing from this place for you?

Repeat the exercise whilst remembering a place that made you feel comfortable at about level 4.  Change the last question to:
What is it about this place that makes you feel comfortable?

To help you, you could use *B8 - RECORDING TEMPLATE - 4*, with headings:
A = Date ;    B = Place;        C = What was happening;
D = How and why you felt uncomfortable;
E = Any underlying issues

*MARGIN NOTE:* record the instructions, with gaps at the dots. Use the recording to lead you through the exercise.

*TEMPLATES*

You can repeat the exercise as often as you like with different places to get a full picture of how you relate to the space around you.

119

# 3 Space, Place and Direction

Sometimes you will be able to change the environment so that it suits you better. Sometimes that may not be completely possible, but knowing when the environment is affecting you, and how, stops you using energy and time solving the wrong problem.

## References

Dennison, Paul and Dennison, Gail, 1986, *Brain Gym,* Edu-Kinesthetics, Ventura, CA

Stacey, Ginny, 2019, *Finding Your Voice with Dyslexia and other SpLDs,* Routledge, London

Stacey, Ginny, 2020, *Development of Dyslexia and other SpLDs,* Routledge, London

## Website information

DfES Report, 2005, https://www.patoss-dyslexia.org/Resources/DSA-Working-Guidelines  Accessed 10 June 2020

Series website:  www.routledge.com/cw/stacey

# Space, Place and Direction  3

# 4    Everyday Life

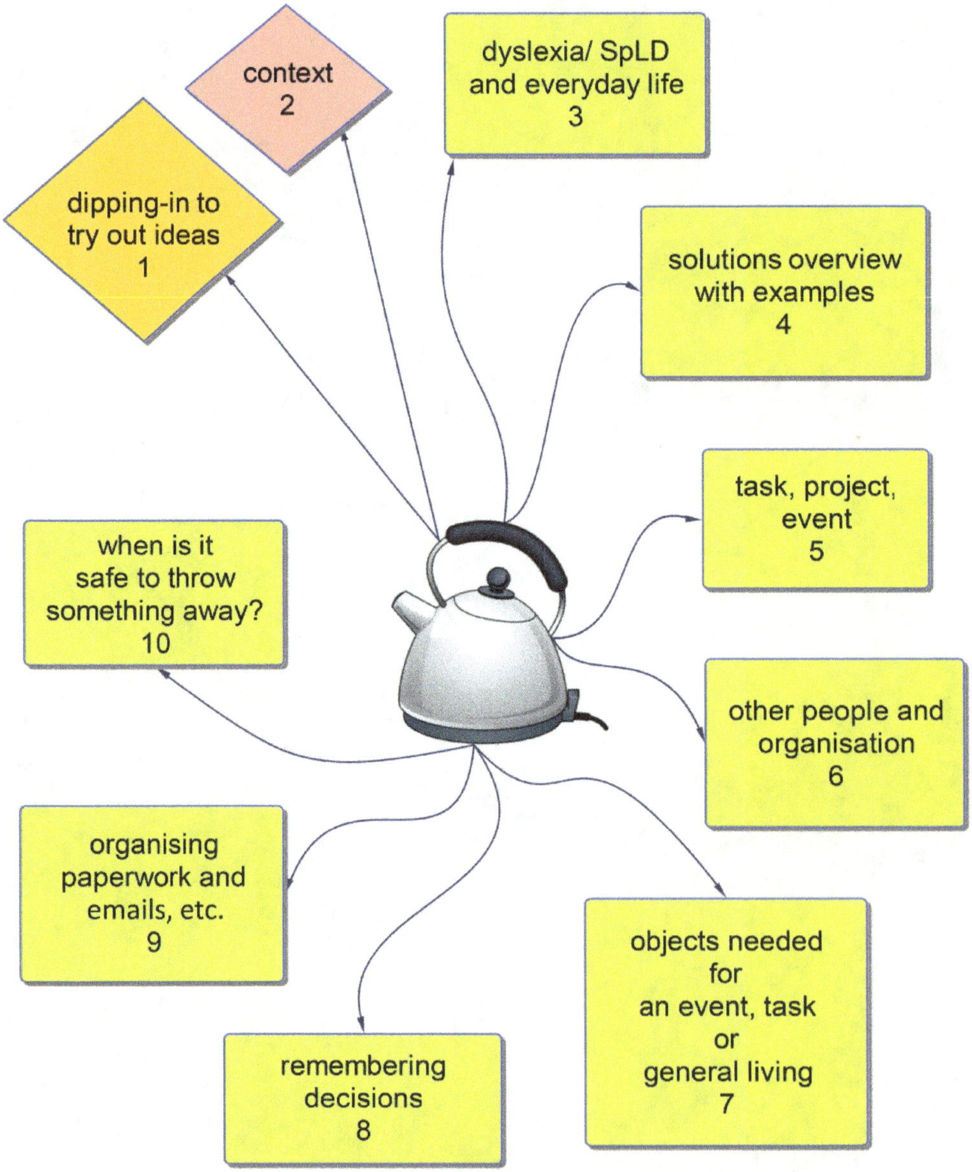

- dipping-in to try out ideas — 1
- context — 2
- dyslexia/ SpLD and everyday life — 3
- solutions overview with examples — 4
- task, project, event — 5
- other people and organisation — 6
- objects needed for an event, task or general living — 7
- remembering decisions — 8
- organising paperwork and emails, etc. — 9
- when is it safe to throw something away? — 10

# Contents

| | |
|---|---|
| Vital for dyslexic/ SpLDs, good practice for all | 123 |
| Working with the chapter | 124 |
| Templates on the website | 124 |
| Appendix 1, 2 and 3 | 124 |
| 1  Dipping-in to try out ideas | 126 |
| 2  Context | 126 |
| 3  Dyslexia/ SpLD and everyday life | 127 |
|    3.1  Maintaining confidence | 129 |
| 4  Solutions overview with examples | 130 |
| 5  Task, project, event | 132 |
| 6  Other people, organisation and everyday life | 133 |
| 7  Objects needed for an event, task or general living | 136 |
| 8  Remembering decisions | 140 |
| 9  Organising paperwork, emails, etc. | 144 |
|    9.1  The flow of paperwork | 146 |
|    9.2  Gathering strengths to deal with paperwork, etc. | 148 |
|    9.3  Assessing hazards and insuperable obstacles in paperwork, etc. | 149 |
|    9.4  People you correspond with | 150 |
|    9.5  Describe the paperwork, etc., to be organised | 150 |
|    9.6  Attractive, constructive organisation of paperwork, etc. | 151 |
|    9.7  Filing | 152 |
|    9.8  Responding to the paperwork | 156 |
| 10  When is it safe to throw something away? | 159 |
|    10.1  Objects | 160 |
|    10.2  Paperwork | 161 |
|    10.3  Computers, emails, and electronic devices – deleting | 165 |
| References and website information | 167 |

---

### Vital for dyslexic/ SpLDs, good practice for all

Being dyslexic/ SpLD is so intertwined with everything that you do in life that it is difficult to separate out specific dyslexic/ SpLD effects.  The approach that is vital for dyslexic/ SpLDs is to stop and look objectively at what is happening.  Finding solutions usually doesn't happen subliminally while engaged with everyday life.

Stopping and looking objectively at what is happening in life can be good practice for all.

Ⓖ p 283: objective, subliminal learning

# 4 Everyday Life

## Working with the chapter

> **Key ideas**
> - Dyslexia/ SpLD affects the whole of life.
> - Everyday life has more options when you are organised to the level that suits you.
> - How you organise yourself is very individual.
> - A main purpose of organisation is to set you free for what you want to do.

Reflect on the situations and stories described and notice any parallels with your own life.

Think about any solutions or systems you already have.

List any situations that you would like to change for the better. Choose the easiest and look for ideas in the whole book to help you make the changes you want.

Use EXERCISE: TO BE CLEAR ABOUT A PITFALL to help you assess the situations you want to change. Adapt the exercise to apply to solutions too.

Build the insights you gain about yourself into your PROFILE and REGIME.

Make sure you keep positive about yourself, see MAINTAINING CONFIDENCE.

EXERCISE: TO BE CLEAR ABOUT A PITFALL: p 68

INDIVIDUAL, PERSONAL PROFILE OF DYSLEXIA/ SpLD: p 248

REGIME FOR MANAGING DYSLEXIA/ SpLD: p 248

MAINTAINING CONFIDENCE: p 128

## Templates on the website

| | |
|---|---|
| A1 | JOTTING DOWN AS YOU SCAN |
| A2 | BOOKMARK – PURPOSE |
| A4 | JOTTING DOWN AS YOU READ |
| B1 | COLLECTING IDEAS THAT RELATE TO YOU |
| B7 | RECORDING TEMPLATE - 3 |
| B8 | RECORDING TEMPLATE - 4 |

TEMPLATES:

## Appendix 1  Resources

APPENDIX 1: p 232

This appendix will help you collect information and make progress as you find out how your dyslexia/ SpLD impacts on your everyday life.

Everyday Life 4

## Appendix 2  Individual, Personal Profile of Dyslexia/ SpLD and Regime for Managing Dyslexia/ SpLD

APPENDIX 2: p 246

**Tip:** EVERYDAY LIFE **and building your profile and regime**

You can learn about your profile and regime:
  while objectively observing your everyday life and how you
    approach it
  by seeing what you like to do differently
    how you make changes
    how you establish the changes into your everyday life.

OBJECTIVE OBSERVATION: p 268

## Appendix 3  Key Concepts

APPENDIX 3: p 262

I cover these key concepts when doing an audit of skills and knowledge with a dyslexic/ SpLD student.  The appendix shows which of the 4 books in the series covers each idea in full.

**Tip: The skills and knowledge you can gain from this series**

APPENDIX 3: KEY CONCEPTS has a list of the main skills and knowledge that you can gain from this series of books.  They fall into the categories of
  THINKING CLEARLY
  USING THE MIND WELL
  YOUR THINKING PREFERENCES
  USEFUL APPROACHES
  ASPECTS OF DYSLEXIA/ SPLD

THINKING PREFERENCES are highlighted in orange in this chapter.

# 4 Everyday Life

## 1 Dipping-in to try out ideas

Look at the tables: WHAT'S TO BE ORGANISED and DIFFERENT STYLES FOR ORGANISING.

Read the story, insight and example boxes.

Decide on some situation you would like to organise better. Then work with the most appropriate sections of the chapter and book.

WHAT'S TO BE ORGANISED: p 130

DIFFERENT STYLES FOR ORGANISING: p 131

## 2 Context

There are many situations and things that need organising in daily life: family life; social life; personal living; household chores: shopping, washing; paperwork; and emails. Some things become part of regular routines, or are done often enough that they are familiar. Others never settle to any particular pattern. Others are new for a while, before becoming well established.

Anything that needs organising will have elements from the 5 categories included in this chapter:

> task, event, project
>
> people
>
> objects
>
> remembering decisions
>
> paperwork/ emails.

Knowing the general principles that work for you will allow you to adapt systems that suit you to anything new that comes your way.

One major point is to recognise early enough that something would be better looked after with a bit of thoughtful organisation.

In the general principles that work for you, you can include recognising when being un-organised is the best way to approach a situation.

The discussion in this chapter is relevant to many situations in study peripherals and employment. In both STUDY PERIPHERALS and EMPLOYMENT, there is a general reminder to use this chapter as well as some specific references to individual subsections.

STUDY PERIPHERALS: p 168

EMPLOYMENT: p 206

# Everyday Life 4

Dealing with relationships with other people is very much part of everyday life. The main discussion is in HANDLING PEOPLE RELATIONSHIPS WELL as part of the chapter on EMPLOYMENT, since people relationships can be an important part of employment.

HANDLING PEOPLE RELATIONSHIPS WELL: p 223

## 3 Dyslexia/ SpLD and everyday life

Dyslexia/ SpLD can govern the way your mind thinks about anything, as can your THINKING PREFERENCES. Therefore, the way you do, or think about, anything in life is likely to be different from the way the non-dyslexic/ SpLD group operates. When the difference is acknowledged, and accommodated, life can run smoothly and you may even find you have a valuable approach to bring to various situations; see STORY: OTHERS USING A SYSTEM ESSENTIAL TO A DYSLEXIC.

THINKING PREFERENCES: p 270

STORY: OTHERS USING A SYSTEM ESSENTIAL TO A DYSLEXIC: p 51

### Examples: Problems in everyday life

You go out to get petrol and decide to do a few other things as well; you come back having done most of the other things but you haven't got the petrol.

You don't leave the house in one go; you go back inside several times as you remember items that you should be taking with you.

You daren't rely on your memory to prompt you when something needs doing, e.g. putting out the bins, leaving to meet a friend.

Working out the key action for the boot of a new car never happens subliminally; you have to consciously stop and register what is different from the old action.

You offer people a cup of tea and frequently forget to give it to them.

# 4  Everyday Life

Everyday life can be disrupted by other people not realising the full impact of dyslexia/ SpLD on everyday living.

### Insight:  Problems with recall from memory

Many dyslexic people's thinking is triggered by their immediate surroundings; if there is nothing in the surroundings that relates to what they need to think about, they may not recall anything useful.

### Story:  Seriously ill with intermittent pain

One dyslexic/ dyspraxic man who is also severely disabled has a very difficult time with many of the medical profession.  He gets sent to hospital for checkups and investigation and fails to make any progress with sorting out his life.  If his pain is not present while the consultant asks questions, her questions will not trigger any memory of the pain.  The man has a very happy disposition in the absence of pain, so when he does remember his pain and problems it gives the impression of someone trying to take advantage of the welfare system.

The same thing has happened to me.  It was only the puzzled look on the consultant's face as he got to the end of his questions that shocked me into thinking: Why am I here? Most of my answers had to be revised.

People, especially those in positions of authority, communicating with dyslexic/ SpLD people need to be aware of the underlying problems and how they impact on so many areas of life.

Everyday Life  4

### 3.1 Maintaining confidence

It may come as a surprise just how much your dyslexia/ SpLD affects your everyday life.  There are many different stories and reactions as people realise how far-reaching the impacts are.  Some people have positive reactions, such as those listed in INSIGHT: CONFIDENCE IS VALUABLE.

Other people have a hard time adjusting to the new insights and would like their dyslexia/ SpLD to go away.  One way of getting that to happen is to learn what you can do to manage your dyslexia/ SpLD so that you can maximise your potential.

---

#### Insight:  Confidence is valuable

The most important thing is to maintain confidence and to see understanding your dyslexia/ SpLD as an opportunity.

Understanding might
- make sense of what happens to you
- give you possibilities to make changes that you want
- help you achieve more
- stop you belittling yourself
- improve conversations with others
- allow others to be more supportive of how you are
- help in an 'other' way:  this is an incomplete list

What is your reaction to how much your dyslexia/ SpLD affects your everyday life?

In all of these possibilities, if you let yourself move forward with confidence, the dyslexia/ SpLD will have less restricting influence on your life.

If you find you struggle to keep positive, seek professional help from someone who also understands the wider impacts of dyslexia/ SpLD.

---

Ⓖ p 283: confidence, self-esteem

Ⓖ p 283: other

# 4 Everyday Life

Whichever way you react, maintaining confidence is worth the effort. The *Exercises: Breathing* and *Physical Relaxation* will help you to keep positive. Ideas around confidence and self-esteem are covered in *Finding Your Voice with Dyslexia and other SpLDs* (Stacey, 2019 ).

*Exercise: Breathing:* p 266
*Exercise: Physical Relaxation:* p 267

Stacey (2019 )

## 4 Solutions overview with examples

The steps referred to here are from the *Model for Developing Organisation*.

*Model for Developing Organisation:* p 57

Solutions will depend on:

- what needs organising (step 3)
- what the desired outcome (step 5) is
- the best way (step 1) of managing your dyslexia/ SpLD (step 2)
- the best way of minimising the effects of the things that can go wrong (steps 1, 2 and 4).

*Time and Time Management:* p 84

Ideas from *Time and Time Management* and *Space, Place and Directions* may also help with organising everyday life.

*Space, Place and Directions:* p 104

| What's to be organised: | Examples |
|---|---|
| task, project, event | going away for the weekend; joining a sports match |
| other people | getting the family out of the house, into the car, with everything needed to go swimming |
| objects needed | enough food; right equipment for a sport |
| remembering decisions or actions | how to work new processes; cups of tea given to people |
| paperwork/ emails | paperwork; paying bills |

*Task, Project, Event:* p 132

*Other People, Organisation and Everyday Life:* p 133

*Objects Needed for an Event, Task or General Living:* p 136

*Remembering Decisions:* p 140

*Organising Paperwork, Emails,K etc.:* p 144

# Everyday Life 4

| when it is safe to throw something away, or not re-visit it | papers; emails; old music disks |
|---|---|

*When Is It Safe To Throw Something Away?*: p 159

The following table has a number of different ways that you could organise getting all the things you need for an event. Choosing the method that suits you can make the difference between success and failure.

*Different styles for organising*

| | |
|---|---|
| **linear** thinker | making a list |
| **doing (kinaesthetic)** person | a doing person can also make a list and then leave it behind because making it will often be sufficient |
| **verbal** person | reciting the items; making up a mnemonic |
| **visual** person | making a mental picture containing all the items |
| Myers-Briggs **feeling** person | associating another person or animal with the items |
| **doing** or **visualising** person | imagining yourself at all the places where you will collect the items and making a story to link them together |

The highlighted words indicate different *Thinking Preferences*: p 270

Ⓖ p 283: mnemonic

You can learn about your *Thinking Preferences* and the *Pitfalls* of your dyslexia/ SpLD as you work on organising something.

*Thinking Preferences*: p 270

*Pitfalls*: p 69

The discussion in this chapter will not cover every possibility, but it should allow you to work out how you will best deal with organisation.

131

 4   Everyday Life

## 5   Task, project, event

It is easier to have something definite to discuss: 'going away for a weekend' is quite a good project to use.  See the *Exercise: To Work Out What Is Needed for an Activity* for a method of making an event become as alive as possible.

*Exercise: To Work Out What Is Needed for an Activity:* p 136

Following the general ideas set out in *Working on Organisation*

- choose the *Materials and Methods* you want to use
- use the *Useful Questions*  to think about 'going away for a weekend'

*Working on Organisation:* p 55

*Materials and Methods:* p 56

*Useful Questions:* p 61

- adapt the questions to be more specific to 'going away for a weekend':

    e.g. 'Do you use your resources of time and energy well?' could lead to questions such as:
    - When do we need to book our travel or accommodation?
    - Who will be able to do it easiest?
    - What can we do alongside normal living to make preparation easier for us: washing, shopping, getting information from internet or library?
    - What time management is needed?
    - How will progress be monitored?

- think whether there are any other aspects you need to consider

- look at the table *What's To Be Organised* and decide what you need to think about and organise.

*What's To Be Organised:* p 130

If this is an activity that you do fairly often, consider making a master plan for the organisation so that you can modify it to meet the differing circumstances of each weekend away.

Big projects need breaking down into manageable sections. *Study Peripherals* and *Employment* are both broken into subtopics, but they could both be regarded as single projects.

*Study Peripherals:* p 168

*Employment:* p 206

Everyday Life 4

**Example: Organisation for going away for the weekend**

Materials and method: old envelopes for several lists; everything filed in holiday wallet in filing cabinet, except actions-now list.

What needs to be organised:
  actions-now, booking; put next action & date in diary
  actions before going: clean clothes, money, fuel in car
    ideas for weekend
    packing, when and what
    shopping.

Find master packing lists, including hobby or travel ones.

## 6 Other people, organisation and everyday life

Most situations involve other people and they will have an impact on what you need to do about organisation.

Informal situations include:
- you and members of your family leaving the house with everything needed
- members of a choir arriving on time for rehearsals
- going away on holiday
- friends meeting up for an evening
- book group meeting for discussion.

Formal situations include:
- organising the date of a meeting to suit colleagues
- reminding people to come for appointments
- a school letting parents know what to bring for the school fête and by when
- children at school having the right equipment for a swimming trip
- a student organising a group of students doing a project together.

Relationships with other people are discussed in HANDLING PEOPLE RELATIONSHIPS WELL: p 223

# 4  Everyday Life

Dyslexia/ SpLD will impact on these situations in many different ways. Possible issues and solutions are set out in the table below. For any situation you are dealing with, you can use the MODEL FOR DEVELOPING ORGANISATION to see what your goals are; what you want to do to achieve them; and what you can do to achieve them.

MODEL FOR DEVELOPING ORGANISATION: p 57

| Situation | Possible issues | Possible solution |
| --- | --- | --- |
| family going out | you can't pay attention to yourself while dealing with others | deal with your needs either first or last, but not at the same time |
| choir on time | any dyslexic/ SpLD members may find it difficult to be on time | someone organises a pick up system – this may happen spontaneously or it may be by deliberate action |
| going on holiday | any dyslexic/ SpLD people on the trip may have difficulty getting everything together, or may find it impossible | someone capable does a very detailed plan including precise times and places; the plan can be emailed or given to every person included and then the trip is run to that plan |
| friends meeting for an evening | any dyslexic/ SpLD people could well be late; they can be seen as unintelligent; it can make agreeing times to meet frustrating | if that's you, it helps to be open about it and why you can't get to the right places on time; if it's someone else and no one wants to nag, you have to be flexible and focus on the reasons why that person is good to include |
| book group meeting | the group don't know when to start if someone is late | as a group you need to come to a good way of responding; everyone being there is not as important for a book group as it is for a choir |
| date for a meeting with colleagues | when some people don't respond, decision making becomes slow and inconvenient, with people holding too many dates in reserve | give a deadline for responses; make communication succinct, with spaces so that reading is easy; say what will happen after the deadline in the face of no responses |

# Everyday Life 4

| Situation | Possible issues | Possible solution |
|---|---|---|
| reminding about appointments 1 | dyslexic/ SpLD students can miss appointments simply because it is part of what they are struggling with | 1-1 support is the opportunity to develop a) strategies to deal with the problems, and b) some kind of reminder system that acknowledges the problems and uses the strategies |
| reminding about appointments 2 | as above; other people find it a burden to send out reminders | you have to find the best possible way of dealing with all your issues around being in the right place at the right time, with all the right preparation done, which is what this book is about! |
| school fête information | no one way of giving out the information will reach all the parents; dyslexic/ SpLD parents of dyslexic/ SpLD children just adds to the difficulties | these happen at sufficiently long intervals that it is worth using every possible means of communication: website, emails, texting, letters home, posters, direct conversations; and then recognising that there is not much more you can do |
| school swimming trip | it doesn't help to nag either parents or children; again dyslexic/ SpLD parents of dyslexic/ SpLD children can add to the difficulties | have enough spare towels and costumes to cover likely shortfall |
| student project | as the dyslexic/ SpLD person in a group, you may need to be organised ahead of the others; you may not be able to get on with your part because someone else has to do something first | you may end up organising meetings and schedules of work in order to do anything yourself |

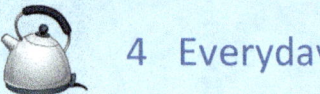 4  Everyday Life

## 7  Objects needed for an event, task or general living

You have to work out what's needed, gather everything together and then take it all with you or use it at the appropriate moment.

Gathering objects together may be spread over a length of time.

---

**Exercise: To work out what is needed for an activity**

- Use imagination (visualisation) deliberately to put yourself into the action
- use vision, hearing and kinaesthetic senses to make the action as vibrant as possible
- then notice what equipment you have, or are using, and what you need to have in reserve
- let the scene evolve from beginning to end so that you register what objects you need to take with you
- use methods from MATERIALS AND METHODS to capture what you discover.

MATERIALS AND METHODS: p 56

---

Later, monitor the effectiveness of what you did, see MONITORING PROGRESS.

MONITORING PROGRESS: p 243

### As you collect items[1]:

- you can tick them off on a list or diagram
- you can list the items as you collect them
- you can leave your main list or diagram in one place and have another list of 'still to do' or 'extras'.

You may need to use some objects after you have started gathering them all together. Make a list, or use another memory device, so that you remember the ones you are still using and gather them up at the last minute.

---

[1] Collecting items: For the time aspect of collecting objects, see 3rd bullet under SOLUTIONS in CO-ORDINATING TIME.
The paragraph starts: 'Get everything ready for an outing, or task, in advance' p 93

# Everyday Life  4

Don't assume you will remember anything (until experience shows what you can rely on remembering). Give yourself the opportunity to catch useful thoughts as they arise in your mind.

**Examples: Different ways of organising objects**

Collecting together sports gear:
imagine yourself arriving at the sports area (visualisation)

- see yourself changing and what you need
- see yourself playing
- see yourself showering and changing back again
- see yourself relaxing with others at the end

at each stage notice what you need and add it to your list of gear to take.

Making sure you have your keys:

- put them with something you know you will take; some people put them in the fridge with their lunch
- create an obstacle that will make you take them; some lock their bike in the garage, so that they can't go off without the keys.

Shopping:

- have a place where you can add to a shopping list at any time
- it may help to have lists for shops that are in different places, say a supermarket shopping list and one for the local shops
- when you run out of something that's used regularly, don't throw the wrapping away until the item is added to the current shopping list(s)
- you could have a list or collage or drawing that you consult before going shopping

## 4  Everyday Life

Shopping continued:

- it is useful to be able to pick up the shopping list at short notice when a suitable time to go shopping suddenly occurs
- note the items you haven't been able to get and make sure they are transferred somehow to the next list
- give yourself time to think through or imagine the coming week or days so that you will remember almost everything you need.

Dealing with other people in relation to paperwork:

- think what they may need you to have at hand
- collect everything you need, including documents
- keep bank information together so that you can work with it
- imagine the other person and try to work out what they need from you, then make sure you have it to hand.

If you go out to many different events that require the same group of items, keep them together.
For example, meetings when you are likely to use pens, pencils, etc.:

- have a special pencil case that holds a small collection that will do for most needs
- don't use anything from this pencil case while at home
- keep it in a particular place so that you can always find it.

While getting used to where it is kept:

- put a note in the pencil case to remind you to put it away in the chosen place
- put a note up on a notice board or in the front of your diary or on your electronic device, so that you know where to find it again.

Everyday Life 4

To make sure you take your diary, especially when you have to use it up to the last minute:

- have a piece of card in your diary with 'diary' on it
- put this card beside the pile of objects you will be taking, or with your keys, or clipped to your coat, or some other place you know you can't miss.

The card needs to be positioned so that you will not ignore it at the last minute! You only put the card back in the diary as you add the diary to your collection of objects, even moving your note just one minute before you go out can mean you leave the diary behind.

### Story: System disrupted

Take care that your system does not get interrupted. A colleague has a very well used method for making sure she takes everything; she can rely on putting papers on a table where she will see them, having the mental thought, 'put papers in'.

However, if a friend rings to check she has remembered the papers, in telling him everything is under control, she mentally ticks the box 'papers done' and leaves them behind.

In telling her friend that the papers were under control, she needed to use language that acknowledged the final actions still needed to be done.

These are examples of dealing with objects. They are not expected to be exhaustive. As with most of managing dyslexia/ SpLD, it is always important to notice 'other' aspects of managing the objects needed.

## 4 Everyday Life

### 8 Remembering decisions

It is quite frustrating when you know you have made a very sensible decision about how to do something, where to keep something, when to do something, etc. and you cannot remember what the decision was.

**Examples: Problems in Remembering Decisions**

- Where you put your decisions for organising a task, project or event
- where you put the information that you need in order to talk to your internet provider, or bank
- where you put the Christmas presents that you bought during the summer and what they are
- where you put items that you need later the same day, week or month
- what you decided needs to be done as a result of an email or letter
- what method you are going to follow to file a collection of papers (hard copies) or organise computer documents or emails (soft copies)
- where you have moved something to, especially when it has been at the old place for a while.

Everyday Life  4

**Solutions**

Possibly one of the hardest things is to remember that you forget rather too easily and that you have to do something so that you will remember your decisions.

You will probably need to know something about your THINKING PREFERENCES in order to find the solutions that work for you.
Probably no one solution will work for all the times you need to remember decisions; you may need different solutions depending on the nature of the event or task.
How you manage your time will also have an impact on the way you deal with remembering.

THINKING PREFERENCES: p 270

TIME AND TIME MANAGEMENT: p 84

**Examples:  Prompts and ideas for remembering decisions**

These are a few examples that work for me.  You need to use the MODEL FOR DEVELOPING ORGANISATION to find out what will work for you.

MODEL FOR DEVELOPING ORGANISATION: p 57

"What am I likely to be thinking about when I need this again?"
   Answer: The person or organisation I need to talk to, say internet provider.
   Action:  I put anything I need to remember in a group under 'Internet provider'.

"When do I need this again?"
   Answer:  In a couple of days' time.
   Action:  I make a note in my diary and I add where the information is filed, or object stored.  I always use angle brackets <to show where I have put something>.

For seasonal items, Christmas or birthdays:
I have a place where presents always gather and if anything is too big, or needs keeping in the freezer, I put a note about it (on a coloured old envelope so that it's visible) in the place with everything else.
I put a note in my diary about any birthday presents about a week before the birthday.  I put a note in my diary about the middle of November to check Christmas presents.

**4   Everyday Life**

**Decisions from post, emails, phone calls or conversations**

Items to record:   any decisions
  questions that need raising
  place for filing
  additional notes and thoughts
  where any action is listed in your diary, or notebook
  other information, including cross referencing

They are recorded on:
  incoming letters
  printed emails
  scrap paper, A4, A5 or A6 that can be filed, for conversations or unprinted emails.

 **Example:  Keeping track of deadlines and tasks to be done**

In a diary, notebook or electronic device, write:

- any action with a deadline: a note on the day of the deadline, a day before and a week before

- urgent actions but with no specific deadline: a note on the day that's the earliest you think you might expect to carry out the action

- anything else, a note on the day or the week that it arrives, so that it gains priority by how long it has been waiting to be attended to.

Some diaries have spaces for notes.  Near the day for action on a particular task, write KEY WORDS and <where any information is filed>.

It's probably important to have only one place where this information is recorded.

KEY WORDS: p 274

This example will not suit everyone.  You can analyse what is being achieved with it and compare that to what you want to achieve.  You can think about the style of diary, note book or electronic device you want to use.

Everyday Life  4

**Decisions about organisation:**

You need instant access to your decisions and that's what determines where you will put the information.

    Have a folder on your computer, C:\...\organisation\, where you can save:
- mind maps of organisation
- lists
- storage places around the office, house and attic.

Put any system where you will need to refer to it, e.g.:
- details of organisation using spread sheets could be put on the first tab of the spread sheet
- decisions about filing papers could go inside the appropriate folder
- any notation that you use could go inside your diary, e.g. <filing or storage>, {cross references} or [diary, lists].

**Example: Remembering the system for the family accounts**

The steps include getting statements on-line for all accounts; utility bills; other documents; using Excel spreadsheets

Over the years I have developed an efficient system, using advanced features of Excel.

There's a hard copy of the whole system in the main ring binder. It's a print out of the first tab in the Excel spreadsheet, named 'steps'. 'Steps' covers everything in the process, ending with fixing the date for the next batch of work.

 **4  Everyday Life**

You need to know where you have put items that you need later:
add the place where papers or other items are being kept to whatever method you are using to organise yourself, which might be:
a list for the day or week
your diary for future days, weeks or months
your electronic organiser.

To remember where you have moved an item or a section of filing, make a note somehow in the old place.

**Example: To do list for a weekend**

*List:*                                    Where I will find what I need
Ring team member of EDA group    <A-Z / E> (EDA just stands for the group name.)
Tax form                           <Ring Binder: Financial Correspondence / Tax>
Garden/ sow seeds                  <kitchen window sills>

*Comments:*
The EDA page will have the phone number of the team member and the items for discussion.
The Tax section will have everything you need for the next stage of the work.
When you want the seeds, you won't have to look for them.

## 9  Organising paperwork, emails, etc.

The purpose of organising paperwork is to ensure that dealing with official matters or correspondence is as easy as possible and you don't generate extra paperwork by neglecting something.

This section on organising paperwork is not about the thinking that deals with the subject of the paperwork, but how the mechanics of handling the paperwork can be as efficient (painless?) as possible. It includes assessing how you need to think about any other person involved in a correspondence.

Electronic devices are more and more used to deal with paperwork. To make them effective, you still have to be organised in the way you use them. For example, to make the best use of electronic searches,

# Everyday Life 4

you need to be consistent in your terminology and you need to remember what it is. The electronic scene is changing all the time. The principles behind organising paperwork and emails should be adaptable to future electronic developments.

Dealing with paperwork can involve all the steps in the *Model for Developing Organising*. In *Figure 4.1*, the mind map of the model has been extended to refer to household paperwork.

*Model for Developing Organising:* p 57

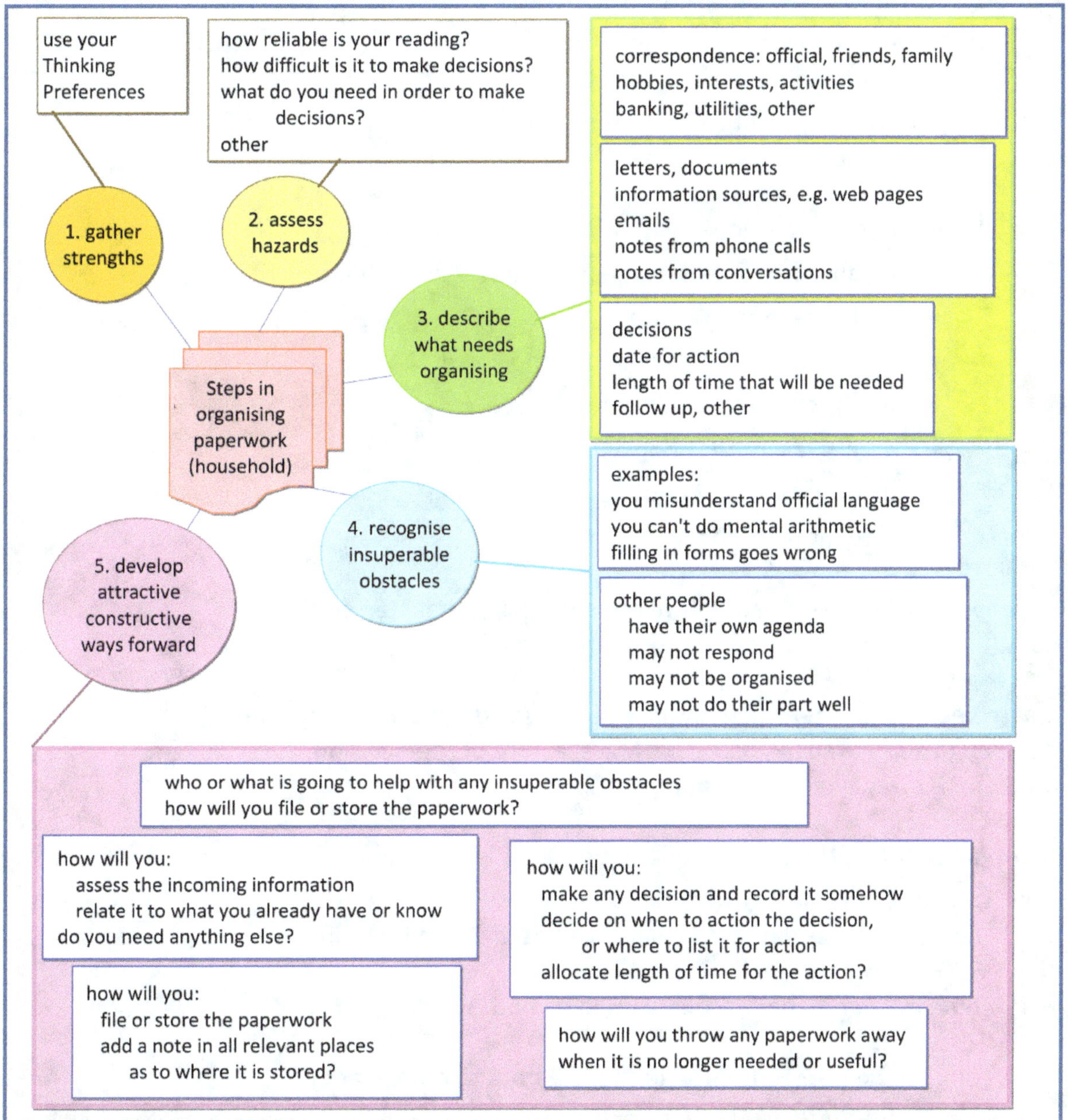

### Steps in organising paperwork (household)

**1. gather strengths**
- use your Thinking Preferences

**2. assess hazards**
- how reliable is your reading?
- how difficult is it to make decisions?
- what do you need in order to make decisions?
- other

**3. describe what needs organising**
- correspondence: official, friends, family
- hobbies, interests, activities
- banking, utilities, other
- letters, documents
- information sources, e.g. web pages
- emails
- notes from phone calls
- notes from conversations
- decisions
- date for action
- length of time that will be needed
- follow up, other

**4. recognise insuperable obstacles**
- examples:
  - you misunderstand official language
  - you can't do mental arithmetic
  - filling in forms goes wrong
- other people
  - have their own agenda
  - may not respond
  - may not be organised
  - may not do their part well

**5. develop attractive constructive ways forward**
- who or what is going to help with any insuperable obstacles
- how will you file or store the paperwork?
- how will you:
  - assess the incoming information
  - relate it to what you already have or know
  - do you need anything else?
- how will you:
  - make any decision and record it somehow
  - decide on when to action the decision, or where to list it for action
  - allocate length of time for the action?
- how will you:
  - file or store the paperwork
  - add a note in all relevant places as to where it is stored?
- how will you throw any paperwork away when it is no longer needed or useful?

Figure 4.1 Steps in organising paperwork

145

 **4  Everyday Life**

### 9.1  The flow of paperwork

(part of Step 1 in MODEL FOR DEVELOPING ORGANISATION)

*STEP 1: GATHER STRENGTHS:* p 60

Something starts a chain of paperwork: a holiday, a utility contract, ... namely, 'the subject of the paperwork'.

1. You send out a letter or email or other (e.g. speak to someone):
    - make a note of the action and any dialogue;
    - you may want to be able to chase it up if necessary (e.g. if there's no response)
    - you may want to find your records when there's a response.

2. When there is a response you need to:
    - be able to remember the previous state of affairs
    - understand the response
    - know whether it is complete and correct
    - think about the other person involved
    - gather any other information
    - make a decision about your next action.

Make sure you take note of 'the small print'.

These two stages are repeated until the something that started the chain ('the subject of the paperwork') is finished.

At some point while dealing with the paperwork, decide how long you will need to keep it, see PAPERWORK. Make a note of the decision somewhere prominent on the paperwork.

*PAPERWORK:* p 161 in *WHEN IS IT SAFE TO THROW SOMETHING AWAY?*

The organisation of the two stages can be simplified as follows:

Stage 1/action   (after dialogue or action, or as part of Stage 2):
    notes or copies dated and filed, so that they can be found again when required
    time marker made for follow up (e.g. a note in diary for follow up)
    time marker for further action (e.g. a note to do research on the web)

Everyday Life 4

Stage 2/ receiving (after receipt of something):
>on the paperwork, write the date you receive it; or note the date using whatever system works for you
>understand enough to decide whether to deal with it now or later; especially note any time constraints
>deal with now
>>understand what's come
>>make decision
>>back to stage 1
>deal with later
>>do you need further information or to contact someone?
>>make time marker for action needed
>>back to stage 1

| | *Use ideas from:* | | |
|---|---|---|---|
| §7 | OBJECTS NEEDED FOR AN EVENT, TASK OR GENERAL LIVING | to work on the materials (objects) that you need to assemble as part of the stages 1 (action) & 2 (receiving) | §7: p 136 |
| §8 | REMEMBERING DECISIONS | to organise recording your decisions | §8: p 140 |
| | NO SENSE OF TIME | to allocate sufficient time | NO SENSE OF TIME: p 88 |
| §9.8 | RESPONDING TO THE PAPERWORK | to organise time markers and allocation of time | §9.8: p 156 |
| §9.3 | ASSESSING HAZARDS AND INSUPERABLE OBSTACLES | to identify anything that is hampering your progress | §9.3: p 149 |

### 4   Everyday Life

### 9.2   Gathering strengths to deal with paperwork, etc.

(Step 1 in MODEL FOR DEVELOPING ORGANISATION)

Gathering strengths is especially important for those dyslexic/ SpLD people who do not like dealing with paperwork. Deciding on the MATERIALS AND METHODS you will use will also depend on your THINKING PREFERENCES and how you need to avoid the PITFALLS of your dyslexia/ SpLD. Paperwork exacerbates most of the problems of dyslexia/ SpLD, therefore using your THINKING PREFERENCES and avoiding your own particular PITFALLS are both essential for organising it; it is also important to be very conscious of how you will benefit.

STEP 1: GATHER STRENGTHS: p 60

MATERIALS AND METHODS: p 56

THINKING PREFERENCES: p 270

PITFALLS: p 69

**Exercise:  How will you benefit?**

What are you going to gain by being able to organise your paperwork?

- A sense of calmness that nothing urgent is going to come out of the woodwork unexpectedly
- Time
- Money
- A sense of achievement
- Less frustration in your life

How will you use the time to your benefit?

Make sure you allow the various benefits to happen.

Many non-dyslexic/ SpLD people also don't like paperwork and there is far too much in modern living.

Everyday Life  4

## 9.3  Assessing hazards and insuperable obstacles in paperwork, etc.

(Steps 2 & 4 in *Model for Developing Organisation*)

There will probably be two categories of hazards and obstacles, some more to do with the task of organising, others to do with your dyslexia/ SpLD.  As always, to find an effective solution you need to get to the source of the problem and it may take several trial solutions before you find that source.  Make sure you record what you are trying and why; there's not much fun in repeating solutions that have let you down before.

*Step 2: Assess Hazards:* p 60
*Step 4: Recognise Insuperable Obstacles:* p 64

*Margin Note:* See the *Index* for further discussion and examples of hazards and obstacles

### Exercise: To resolve problems in your paperwork system

To find the source of a problem in your paperwork system you need to:

- use your favourite *Materials and Methods*
- observe with an open mind
- reflect on your system and decide what is causing it not to work
- then decide whether the cause is a hazard you can alter, or whether it is an insuperable obstacle that you need to avoid
- decide how you will work with the hazard
- decide how you will get round the obstacle
- modify your system to include your decision
- test your modified system.

You may need to repeat this cycle until you find an organisational system that works well for you.

*Materials and Methods:* p 56

One very prevalent hazard is the unreliable short-term memory of many dyslexic/ SpLDs: you may not remember decisions or discussions even 2 minutes later, therefore making understandable notes about paperwork is a major part of organising it all.

149

 **4 Everyday Life**

## 9.4 People you correspond with

(Step 4 in MODEL FOR DEVELOPING ORGANISATION)

STEP 4: RECOGNISE INSUPERABLE OBSTACLES: p 64

Some people are the best help you can ever come across and they don't realise that they are being special.

Other people can be insuperable obstacles in your paperwork organisation because they are not under your control:

> their response may be incomplete or incorrect
>
> they may not respond
>
> they may be incompetent and/ or disorganised
>
> they may have their own agenda
>
> their way of thinking about any situation may be different from yours
>
> they may be super efficient and answer questions you haven't thought about.

You need to prepare carefully:

> Use techniques from THINKING CLEARLY to keep focused, calm and confident.
>
> Review the correspondence or the situation, before starting a new dialogue.
>
> What are the issues? What questions do you have? Are you clear about them? Do you need to check that you haven't overlooked something?
>
> A useful question is:
>> If I were the other person what would I want me to know/ do/ bring/ have to hand?

THINKING CLEARLY: p 264

## 9.5 Describe the paperwork, etc., to be organised

(Step 3 in MODEL FOR DEVELOPING ORGANISATION)

STEP 3: DESCRIBE WHAT NEEDS ORGANISING: p 61

To describe what needs organising, you need to think of:

- what categories you want to use for the paperwork (see MARGIN NOTE)
- what type of paperwork is involved
- what types of actions are involved and the time factors: 'how long?' and 'when?'

MARGIN NOTE: examples of categories for travel:
Information about place(s)
Passports
Tickets, other bookings
Health documents
Travel insurance
Packing lists
Hobby information

Everyday Life  4

Look at the mind map in *Figure 4.1, Steps in Organising Paperwork,* are there any categories that need including?

You could spread out a pile of paperwork and ask yourself: What belongs together? What will I want together when I use it?

*Figure 4.1 Steps in Organising Paperwork:* p 145

**Tip: A sense of the ridiculous used in organising paperwork**

Many dyslexic/ SpLDs have difficulty in deciding what goes together, so start with ridiculous groups and gradually work towards useful ones:
  putting the tax paperwork with gardening information is unlikely to be helpful, even for a professional gardener.

## 9.6  Attractive, constructive organisation of paperwork, etc.

(Part of Step 5 in *Model for Developing Organisation*)

To develop attractive, constructive ways forward, you need to think about
- how the insuperable obstacles will be dealt with, see §9.3
- how you are going to store the paperwork, see §9.7
- responding to the paperwork
- managing decisions, and follow up action
- filing or storing the paperwork (actually doing it)

all of which relate to both *Stage 1/ Action* and *Stage 2/ Receiving* of the *Flow of Paperwork.*

*Step 5: Develop Constructive Ways Forward:* p 65

*§9.3 Assessing Hazards and Insuperable Obstacles:* p 149

*§9.7 Filing:* p 152

*Stage 1:* p 146
*Stage 2:* p 147

**Tip: Enjoy the benefits**

Remember: energy and time to enjoy other pastimes are intended benefits of organised paperwork.

 **4 Everyday Life**

The USEFUL QUESTIONS in Step 3 of MODEL FOR DEVELOPING ORGANISATION will help to assess your progress, as will SATISFACTION: THE PROOF OF THE PUDDING IS IN THE EATING.

USEFUL QUESTIONS: p 61

SATISFACTION: THE PROOF OF THE PUDDING IS IN THE EATING: p 72

**Tip: Any system must work for you**

It is really important that any organisation works for you, rather than anyone else. If it doesn't, you will probably not use it and that will be further demoralising.

For some people, it is very important that the containers for paperwork look attractive, or there is something else about the system that appeals to an aesthetic sense. If something like colour allows you to engage with the system, then don't let yourself be talked out of using it.

Electronic equivalents: fun backgrounds and sounds that make you smile

The organisation system should enhance your life and let you be free to enjoy yourself; if you find you are feeling discouraged by it, you should probably change something.

### 9.7 Filing

STEP 5: DEVELOP CONSTRUCTIVE WAYS FORWARD: p 65

(Part of Step 5 in MODEL FOR DEVELOPING ORGANISATION)

It is important to categorise your paperwork in a way that makes it easy to access and use. Notice whether it helps to be leafing through a lot of other material when looking for one page, or do you want to go straight to it? Either might be right for you, and which is right may be different for different areas of your life.

The two main options for categories are alphabetical or in topic areas, such as household, hobbies, family, friends. These can be subdivided as many times as you find easy to use, again either using topic areas or an alphabet system or topics alphabetically arranged.

The volume of paper relating to any particular person or area of work will probably determine how you categorise the areas.

# Everyday Life 4

### Example: Categorising paperwork

You may find that correspondence with family and friends and about most of your hobbies will fit in one A4 ring binder over a year, but you may have a major role for one of your hobbies and the correspondence for that has its own ring binder with divisions for several projects, minutes of meetings and general correspondence.

Which helps most:

- having all the family letters building up together in a date ordered sequence or
- having them grouped by person first and then by date?

In the first you get a picture of the whole family when you search for one letter; in the second you recall details specific to one particular person.

You have to observe yourself to know which is most useful to you. It is questioning like this that will help you decide what categories suit you best.

You must keep copies of letters, make notes of phone conversations and print off important emails, especially official ones.

### Tip: Dates and numbering on pages

Make sure dates are written on all the pages and the notes. Put page numbers on when there are several pages. There is nothing worse than having to read several pages just to work out the order in which to file them – most dyslexic/ SpLDs can't just glance at them to do this job.

# 4  Everyday Life

The options for storing paperwork are:

- ring binders, lever arch files, box files, etc.
- wallets, card or plastic
- filing cabinets
- in, out, pending trays
- heaps
- drawers
- card index systems
- dividers where they will help, especially within folders.

**Insight:  Pretty defeats boredom**

The more an area of paperwork bores me, the prettier the ring binders have to be.

My visual thinking preference then allows me to engage with the paperwork.

If your memory is such that you easily know where something is in a heap, then heaps are doing a good job and you should resist all attempts to organise you into a different way.  If other people have to access the same material, you may need to negotiate a reasonable compromise.  If heaps result in matters not being dealt with, they are not a good idea.

**Story:  Evolution of organisation system**

I find I usually let a system evolve.

I start with something that is too chaotic for me to handle and I make five to ten groups of similar papers (I will do the same with materials for a project too); they have to be spread out on a large surface and I often make a temporary label for each group, just to deal with my short-term memory.

I work in such a way that if I run out of time I can put dividers between the groups and gather them all up quickly; then I can just spread them out again when I next work with them.

154

# Everyday Life 4

Questions you can use to help you organise your paperwork:

- What will you be thinking about when you want this again?
- What does this have in common with the other papers you've put here?
- Can you colour code this in any way to make it easy to find?
- How can you keep together papers that belong together?
- What type and size of container do you need?
- Where will you keep the container?
- Where will you record useful details of the system?
- Will you ever want this again? is also important, see WHEN IS IT SAFE TO THROW SOMETHING AWAY?

WHEN IS IT SAFE TO THROW SOMETHING AWAY?: p 159

### Example: Filing systems

Some of my systems and thinking:

**ring binders** hold paperwork that I need fairly regularly or that are relevant to the current year:

- finance accounts; finance letters; utilities; gardening has a ring binder of its own; odd jobs, long term shopping, and hobbies share a ring binder

within a ring binder there may be:

- a complete A-Z, as for general correspondence
- sections in alphabetic order, e.g. utilities: council tax, electricity, gas, telephone, TV, water, etc., with one major section for bills and another for letters
- subsections can be useful: a piece of card that sticks up above the A4 pages rather than to the side can be used to mark a place, e.g. where a particular frequent correspondent is found in the A-Z, see FIGURE 4.2

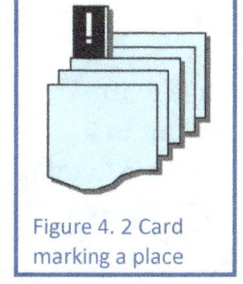

Figure 4. 2 Card marking a place

155

# 4 Everyday Life

lever arch files are slightly more difficult to handle, so I tend not to use too many of them; they are more tedious to open at any place depending on need, but they do hold more

filing cabinet: useful, I find, for collections of papers that need to be kept together e.g. car documents, holiday information, work we've had done to the house

box files: useful for objects and papers of different sizes

decisions about the categories, and why I came to those decisions, are kept with the papers: in the front of ring binders or lever arch files; on a coloured card in the front of a filing cabinet wallet. Even temporary decisions are kept somewhere useful.

Some paperwork doesn't need action nor to be kept long term but you want to keep it for a while because you might want to refer to it again; how to deal with it is discussed in WHEN IS IT SAFE TO THROW SOMETHING AWAY?

WHEN IS IT SAFE TO THROW SOMETHING AWAY?: p 159

**Tip: Filing or storing the paperwork (actually doing it)**

It is worth treating yourself by actually doing the filing, with the result that you can find something when you want it again. It saves a lot of frustration and time when you no longer spend your valuable energy looking for something.

## 9.8 Responding to the paperwork

You make a decision at the end of STAGE 2/ RECEIVING, in THE FLOW OF PAPERWORK. The decision may be that you need to take action, possibly to respond or to get further information. This section deals with the organisation of your actions.

STAGE 2/ RECEIVING: p 147

Everyday Life 4

The important aspects are:
- remembering that you need to take action
- timetabling enough time into your life to take it
- making sure that no hazard or obstacle is preventing your action, see ASSESSING HAZARDS AND INSUPERABLE OBSTACLES.

THE FLOW OF PAPERWORK covered annotating your paperwork so that you have a record of progress and decisions.

ASSESSING HAZARDS AND INSUPERABLE OBSTACLES: p 149

THE FLOW OF PAPERWORK: p 146

### Reminders

If your memory doesn't prompt you to action you have to do something deliberate, which is the situation for most dyslexic/ SpLD people, even when they don't have a lot to do.

Non-dyslexic/ SpLD are often able to remember what they need to do, but when they are very busy they may also need to use reminders.

People use diaries, electronic devices, notebooks, and lists of various forms as the means for managing their reminders.

You need to find the format that is going to work reliably for you and give you a sense of achievement; it shouldn't be a system that increases your anxiety because you come across the same reminder many times when you can't actually deal with it.

#### Insight:  Dealing with reminders

I try to limit the number of places where I have reminders.

I recognise that I'm unlikely to remember without any system.

Out of sight is truly out of mind (my insuperable obstacle).

I try not to overload myself with many reminders of the same thing:
   I can get to a point where I don't register any of them.

HAZARDS AND OBSTACLES: p 66

# 4 Everyday Life

**Setting reminders**

Date all papers, especially when official ones arrive (as part of STAGE 2/ RECEIVING in THE FLOW OF PAPERWORK)

STAGE 2/ RECEIVING: p 147

**Tip: Date papers as you receive them**

If you're using a notebook or some other system that doesn't have dates on it, make sure you record the date the papers were received with your notes.

How you set your reminders (see MARGIN NOTE) will depend on whether the matter is urgent, has a deadline sometime in the future, or needs a response at some time:

- if urgent: make a note in your *diary* for immediate attention
- if there is a deadline: note the deadline in your *diary* and on the paperwork; also make a note in your *diary* for action about a week before the deadline
- if the response is needed at some time: make a note in your *diary* for attention; put the note on or near the date when you received the incoming paperwork so that the date can remind you how much time has elapsed without action.

MARGIN NOTE: for simplicity I will refer to a *diary* for managing reminders and I will write it in *green italics* so that it represents all the other devices, e.g. electronic devices, notebooks, and lists of various forms.

When you send something off to someone, make a note to follow it up[2]; I put this in my *diary* at a few days beyond when I expect the reply.

**Recording, especially where you've put something**

- In your *diary*, record where you have filed the papers.
- On the papers, note when you have put your reminder in your *diary*.
- As you read the paperwork, or have a conversation, write any decisions or thoughts that occur to you on the paper or on a separate piece of paper which you file with the paperwork.

---

[2] To 'follow up' means to check whether there has been a response, and if there hasn't, to do something else to get one.

Everyday Life  4

**Checking reminders**

Once a week, I check my paperwork notes and prioritise what I will attend to during the next week, depending on importance, deadline and length of time since the need for action was noted.

Some people need to check once a day. You need to find a rhythm for checking paperwork notes so that dealing with it is as easy as possible and so that you don't make matters worse by forgetting anything.

**Setting aside time**

You need to allow yourself adequate time to deal with paperwork.

> NO SENSE OF TIME deals with finding out how long tasks take to do
>
> TIMETABLES AND APPOINTMENTS deals with making time for necessary tasks such as paperwork
>
> INSIGHT: GOOD USE OF OVER-RUN TIME describes one way of putting overrun time into a schedule.

NO SENSE OF TIME: p 88

TIMETABLES AND APPOINTMENTS: p 94

INSIGHT: GOOD USE OF OVER-RUN TIME: p 101

## 10   When is it safe to throw something away?

Throwing away involves decisions about objects and paperwork or clearing out computer files and emails. Any system is going to be highly individual, because it will involve the INDIVIDUAL, PERSONAL PROFILE OF DYSLEXIA/ SPLD.

INDIVIDUAL, PERSONAL PROFILE OF DYSLEXIA/ SPLD: p 248

A routine for clearing out objects and paperwork that are no longer needed can be very useful. You may eventually find that 'ease of clearing out' is an integral part of your organisation systems.

One decision to make is how you will dispose of anything.
- Objects you might sell, give away, re-cycle, take to the tip, or put in the rubbish bin.
- Some paperwork might have to be destroyed because of confidentiality or the possibilities of identity fraud; some could be recycled; some might have to go to landfill.

Electronic information also has to be considered in terms of possible confidentiality issues or identity fraud.

# 4 Everyday Life

## 10.1 Objects

Sometimes small living spaces, e.g. living on a houseboat, dictate that almost everything must be thrown away fairly rapidly and the priority is to decide what has to be kept.  Sometimes, you have accumulated so many objects that there is no room for your current hobbies and occupations.


**Some questions to assist decision making:**

Are the objects gathering dust and taking space for no good purpose?

Are you restricted in what you can do because too many objects take up too much space?

If you had wanted something, could you find it?

Might it be useful at some unspecified time?  If so, would you find it?

Do you want to keep some things for a while and then get rid of them?

You could use TEMPLATE: B7 - RECORDING TEMPLATE - 3 to collect your answers and ideas together, with headings:

    A: Importance to you

    B: Object's name

    C: Comments: description/ where it came from/ what it's for/

    D: Reason to keep or throw away

    E: Action

Another column that might be useful is: where the object is currently kept.

TEMPLATES

The answers might make you treasure what you have more so that you are happy with the continued presence of the objects.

You might be able to select some things to give or throw away or sell.

You might look at how you are organising the objects, how you are recording where they are so that you can find them easily.

You might decide on a system of storage and labelling such that after a year (say) 'anything in this box can go'.

Everyday Life  4

### 10.2  Paperwork

Throwing paperwork away involves several decisions and requires a fair degree of confidence.

**Example:  Insurance renewal papers**

When any insurance is renewed the necessary papers tend to come with a collection of other papers: the policy update, advertising for other products, information about the firm sending you the renewal, etc. You could:

1   keep it all and over the years build up a large collection

2   keep all of this year's collection and throw away most of last year's, see below ¥ and ✦

3   keep only this year's cover note and any policy changes, and throw everything else away.

Modifications to 2:
¥ you may need to keep some of the documents as evidence of insurance; for example, you don't want to lose no claims bonuses on car insurance.  Check with an insurance provider or someone else knowledgeable as to exactly what needs keeping and for how long.

✦ when you check the insurance to make sure it is all OK, you could write on it [cover note/ keep], [policy/ keep], [extras/ ditch next year]; you are recording the decision when the content of each is alive in your mind; when throwing away a year later, you can simply follow the decisions you recorded without worry.

In the example of insurance renewal papers:

Approach 1:   You don't take many decisions; you accumulate a lot of papers, many unnecessarily; you probably don't store them in a way that makes it easy to find what you want at some future date.  This approach doesn't take a lot of confidence, just a lot of space!

# 4  Everyday Life

Approach 2:    You would be taking decisions about last year's papers, which probably requires less confidence than Approach 3. You need the same amount of space from one year to the next. You should have everything you want and be able to find anything you want.

Approach 3:    You need to be really confident of your decisions about this year's papers; so you need to be confident that you have understood them all. This approach uses the least space. With the right decisions, you will have everything that's necessary and you will be able to find what you need.

Modifications to Approach 2: You need to be able to assess the importance of the documents in order to come to a decision. You need less confidence in your decisions than for Approach 3 because you are not throwing anything away for a year. In a year's time you won't have to read it all again, which is a benefit.

The following discussion should help you design and use the system you feel most comfortable with.

**Insight:  Throwing away paperwork without re-reading**

When the time has come to throw away paperwork, I don't particularly want to spend time and energy re-reading the documents. I want to be able to gather up a collection and dispose of it, being confident that nothing of importance is going too. Noting when something can be thrown away is an integral part of my paperwork organisation.

Some paperwork has to be kept for legally specified lengths of time, or indefinitely.

Some needs to be kept for a short time, but how long is unknown.

Some might be interesting to read or refer to, but may be unimportant.

Some should be passed on when an object is passed on.

Everyday Life  4

Some needs to be destroyed rather than put in the recycling.

There are other possibilities; this is not an exhaustive set of options.

There are suggestions below to cover these possibilities. I have also included some thoughts about knowing when pages of a diary or note book are finished with, from the point of view of organisation. I find throwing away systems evolve until they work well and they are often part of a complete organisation system.

You could use TEMPLATE: B8 - RECORDING TEMPLATE - 4 to collect your answers and ideas together, with headings:

    A: name for paperwork

    B: where it's filed

    C: reason for keeping it

    D: specific time

    E: could be divided into narrow columns that are ticked as appropriate:

        short time

        long time/ indefinite

        until a related object is thrown away.

TEMPLATES

The first decision is the category to which any piece of paperwork belongs. It was suggested in THE FLOW OF PAPERWORK that, when you are initially working on some paperwork, you should decide how long it will need to be kept. The decision will probably be easiest to make towards the end of dealing with an issue. If you have written your decision on the paperwork, it should be fairly easy to decide on the time category for your paperwork.

THE FLOW OF PAPERWORK: p 146

### Keeping papers for a specified time

You could store papers together that can be thrown away together, e.g. all documents for a given tax year and the relevant tax return; it is useful if the bundle has the date when it is no longer required on it. You could make it part of the change of the tax year that one collection of papers is thrown away.

# 4  Everyday Life

### Keeping papers for at least a year

Correspondence and information that you might need to refer to over a few months can be organised in a 2-year rotation of ring binders or lever arch files.  This year's collection would be on easily accessible shelves.  Last year's collection could be on higher shelves that need some effort to reach.  A Post-it flag can be used to mark any paper that needs to be considered before it is thrown away, see FIGURE 4.3.  At the change of the appropriate year, calendar, financial or academic, everything in last year's collection is at least a year old and you can just remove it all, only looking at tagged pages as you do so.

Figure 4. 3 Post-it flag on important page

### Destroying as opposed to recycling

You should destroy paperwork which is confidential or has personal details that could be used for identity fraud.  If there are one or two such pages, they could be flagged with the Post-it tag, as above.  Or you could have a system of writing on pages, as in EXAMPLE: INSURANCE RENEWAL PAPERS.

EXAMPLE: INSURANCE RENEWAL PAPERS: p 161

A guiding question for finding the right system is: How will I look at this page(s) again without having to read everything around it?

### Keeping papers in batches of three months

There are various collections of papers or magazines which you might want to keep for a short time, but not indefinitely.

#### Story:  Magazines kept for a few months

Some hobby magazines I want to keep for a while, but not more than a year.  They accumulate in magazine racks.  I have colourful card or other dividers with three months on them.  Once every three months I throw away the oldest group and put the divider back to the beginning of the collection.  Again, I can tag anything that I don't want to throw away without further thought.

# Everyday Life 4

**Diary or notebook pages**

Often diaries come with bookmarks or perforations that allow you to remove corners so that you go immediately to the present week.

If you use your diary for notes as well, you need to know when you have dealt with all the notes on a double page spread, so that you are confident you need not look at those pages again.

You could use the corner that doesn't have the perforations; you can cut it off when you have dealt with all the notes or transferred the information somewhere else.

You can do the same with any notebook that you use for any kind of project. It just saves having to read or process the pages many times over.

## 10.3  Computers, emails, and electronic devices – deleting

Storage and having enough memory for the device to work fast are often the reasons why computers and electronic devices need to be cleared of old material.

Sometimes, you need to clear the desk top or your folders so that you can work more easily. You might be sorting out files and emails because you are updating your software or changing to a new computer.

Whatever the reason for clearing out old materials, you have to make decisions about what can or should go, and what you might want in time to come.

If you might want something in the future, it is also helpful to think how you might find it again.

It is worth thinking about how you will archive, or delete, folders and files, emails, or bookmarks while you are evolving your whole system of organising the electronic equivalent of paperwork.

 **4 Everyday Life**

You don't want to open files or emails just to decide what can be deleted safely, any more than you want to re-read hard copy paperwork.

It is worth thinking about the organisation of files and emails so that they can be deleted, or moved, in batches without undue thought. Again how you do it will depend on your INDIVIDUAL, PERSONAL PROFILE OF DYSLEXIA/ SPLD.

INDIVIDUAL, PERSONAL PROFILE OF DYSLEXIA/ SPLD: p 248

### Computer files

I archive rather than delete. I don't like my computer or working folders to be too cluttered up, but I have found it useful to be able to go back many years and still find files.

I store files on DVDs, memory sticks or an external hard drive.

Often I use separate DVDs for a specific category of activity e.g. work; I write the date and category on the DVDs; I store them in one place, but sorted by categories.

Having archived my files off the computer, I then have to trust my decisions and confidently prune the folders and files to just those I need.

### Emails

On a regular basis, it is worth going through the inbox and outbox (sent folder) and moving every email into a suitable folder, except the most recent or those you must work on.

At suitable times during the year, have a system of deleting any email more than a year old in the folders; many email programmes allow you to tag anything you want to keep for longer.

### Bookmarks

Web browsers, and some other software, allow you to use bookmarks. If these are going to be useful, they need organising as they are made and then removing when they no longer are useful to you.

Everyday Life 4

**Using the cloud**

The cloud is used by many people to store electronic material. You usually have a quota, some of which is free. Sometimes, you pay for extra when you have run out of space.

Good use of the cloud includes the ideas about organisation in this chapter, especially being able to find something again using search facilities, and preserving your time and energy for anything you want to do.

## References

Stacey, Ginny, 2019 , *Finding Your Voice with Dyslexia and other SpLDs*, Routledge, London

## Website information

Series website: www.routledge.com/cw/stacey

# 5  Study Peripherals

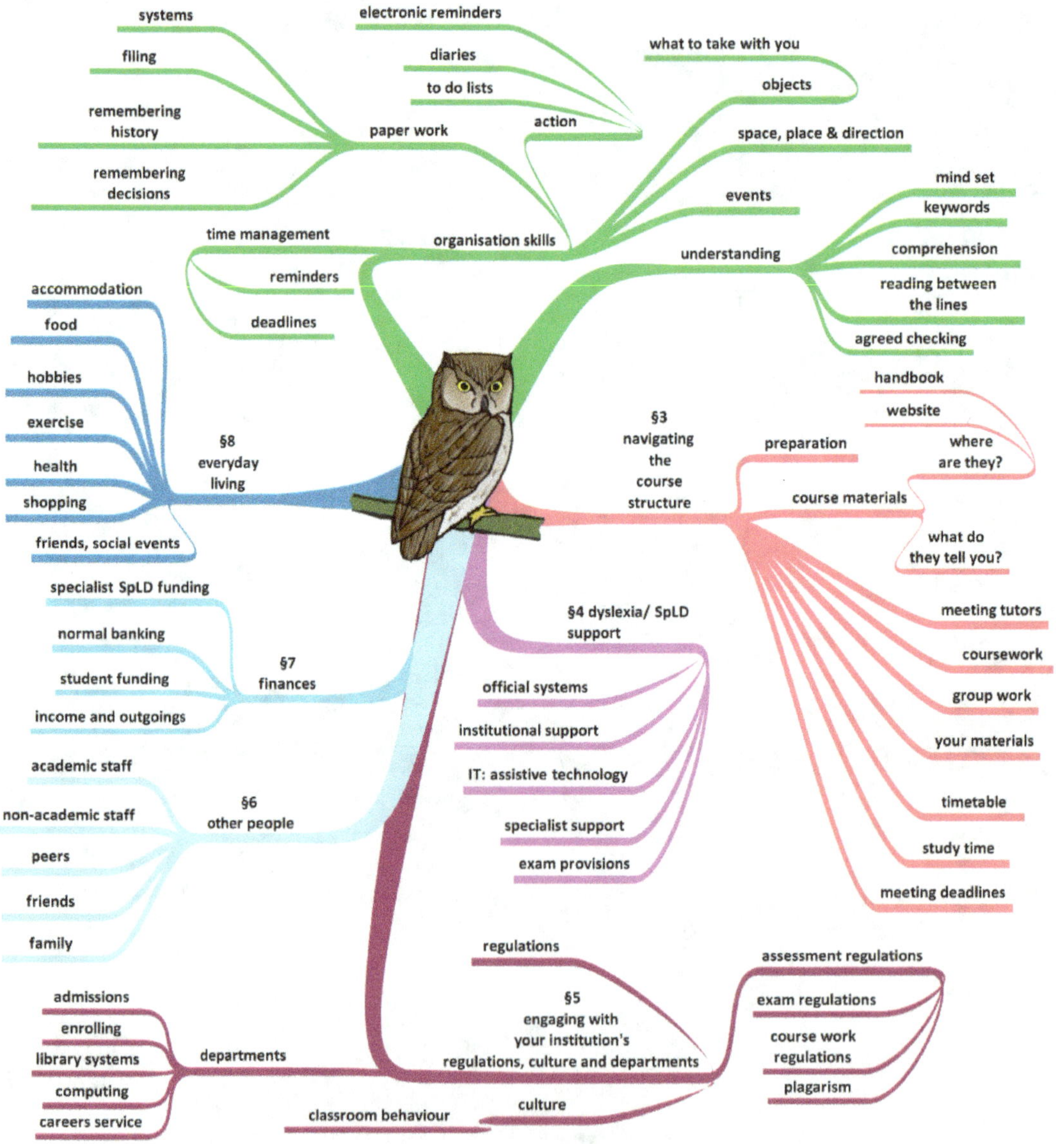

- organisation skills
  - paper work
    - systems
    - filing
    - remembering history
    - remembering decisions
    - electronic reminders
    - diaries
    - to do lists
  - action
    - what to take with you
    - objects
    - space, place & direction
  - events
  - understanding
    - mind set
    - keywords
    - comprehension
    - reading between the lines
    - agreed checking
  - time management
    - reminders
    - deadlines

- §3 navigating the course structure
  - preparation
    - handbook
    - website
    - where are they?
  - course materials
    - what do they tell you?
    - meeting tutors
    - coursework
    - group work
    - your materials
    - timetable
    - study time
    - meeting deadlines

- §8 everyday living
  - accommodation
  - food
  - hobbies
  - exercise
  - health
  - shopping
  - friends, social events

- §7 finances
  - specialist SpLD funding
  - normal banking
  - student funding
  - income and outgoings

- §4 dyslexia/ SpLD support
  - official systems
  - institutional support
  - IT: assistive technology
  - specialist support
  - exam provisions

- §6 other people
  - academic staff
  - non-academic staff
  - peers
  - friends
  - family

- §5 engaging with your institution's regulations, culture and departments
  - regulations
    - assessment regulations
    - exam regulations
    - course work regulations
    - plagarism
  - culture
    - classroom behaviour
  - departments
    - admissions
    - enrolling
    - library systems
    - computing
    - careers service

> The green branches are general skills
> that will be used to organise the areas
> on the other branches, which are the peripherals of study.

# Contents

Vital for dyslexic/ SpLDs, good practice for all ... 169
Working with the chapter ... 170
Templates on the website ... 170
Appendix 1, 2 and 3 ... 170
1 Dipping-in to try out ideas ... 171
2 Context ... 172
3 Navigating the course structure (worked example) ... 175
   3.1 Preparation ... 176
      3.1.1 Step 1: gather strengths ... 176
      3.1.2 Step 2: assess hazards ... 177
      3.1.3 Step 3: describe what needs organising ... 180
      3.1.4 Step 4: recognise insuperable obstacles ... 181
      3.1.5 Step 5: develop constructive ways forward ... 181
   3.2 Course materials ... 181
   3.3 Meeting tutors ... 183
   3.4 Coursework ... 184
   3.5 Group work ... 185
   3.6 Your materials ... 186
   3.7 Timetable and study time ... 187
   3.8 Meeting deadlines ... 188
4 Dyslexia/ SpLD support ... 189
   4.1 IT: assistive technology ... 190
   4.2 Specialist 1:1 support ... 191
   4.3 Exam provisions (worked example) ... 194
5 Engaging with your institution's regulations, culture and departments ... 199
6 Other people ... 204
7 Finances ... 204
8 Everyday living ... 205
References and website information ... 205

---

### Vital for dyslexic/ SpLDs, good practice for all

Study is hard for most dyslexic/ SpLD people. It is vital for you to keep on top of the organisation that goes with it. If you don't, you are likely to have extra work to sort out anything that goes wrong.

Keeping up with the systems around study is good practice for all.

# 5  Study Peripherals

## Working with the chapter

> **Key ideas**
>
> - Study peripherals are the network of systems supporting and enabling anyone to study.
> - It is better to keep on top of using and organising the systems.
>
> You need to know:
> - what you have to do
> - when you have to do it
> - who can help you.

Keeping up with study peripherals is very important.  You could waste time and energy if you don't.  Make sure you have a system for anything you need to PRIORITISE.

PRIORITISE: p 236

## Templates on the website

TEMPLATES

| | |
|---|---|
| A1 | JOTTING DOWN AS YOU SCAN |
| A2 | BOOKMARK – PURPOSE |
| A4 | JOTTING DOWN AS YOU READ |
| B1 | COLLECTING IDEAS THAT RELATE TO YOU |
| B3 | COMPARE EXPECTATIONS AND REALITY |
| F1 - F3 | DEVELOPING ORGANISATION |
| F14 | HALF A YEAR – 27 WEEKS |

## Appendix 1  Resources

APPENDIX 1: p 232

This appendix will help you collect information and make progress as you deal with study peripherals.

# Study Peripherals 5

## Appendix 2  Individual, Personal Profile of Dyslexia/ SpLD and Regime for Managing Dyslexia/ SpLD

APPENDIX 2: p 246

**Tip:** STUDY PERIPHERALS and building your profile and regime

You can learn about your profile and regime while organising your study peripherals.

## Appendix 3  Key Concepts

APPENDIX 3: p 262

I cover these key concepts when doing an audit of skills and knowledge with a dyslexic/ SpLD student.  The appendix shows which of the 4 books in the series covers each idea in full.

**Tip:** The skills and knowledge you can gain from this series

APPENDIX 3: KEY CONCEPTS has a list of the main skills and knowledge that you can gain from this series of books.  They fall into the categories of
>    THINKING CLEARLY
>    USING THE MIND WELL
>    YOUR THINKING PREFERENCES
>    USEFUL APPROACHES
>    ASPECTS OF DYSLEXIA/ SPLD

## 1  Dipping-in to try out ideas

CONTEXT: p 172

Look at the bullet points in the CONTEXT.

Look at the section headings in NAVIGATING THE COURSE STRUCTURE.

NAVIGATING THE COURSE STRUCTURE: p 175

Do the EXERCISE: WHAT ARE STUDY PERIPHERALS?

Scan the chapter to notice anything relevant to you immediately and where information is.

EXERCISE: WHAT ARE STUDY PERIPHERALS?: p 180

Work through NAVIGATING THE COURSE STRUCTURE applying the ideas to your own course.

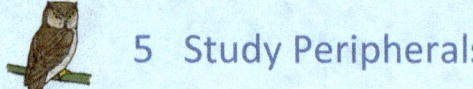
# 5 Study Peripherals

## 2 Context

Study is about acquiring new knowledge, understanding, skills, and ways of thinking:
- you are following someone else's curriculum in order to achieve certain goals
- you will probably be aiming to gain a qualification.

You shouldn't be surprised if it is a continual source of difficulties and that these difficulties are often changing.

### Study

To study, you need to know how you work best in order to:
- understand the subject
- produce the work required.

### Study Peripherals

In order to study, you need to find out
- what you are to study
- what teaching is available and when
- what resources are available and how
- when you have to complete work
- what form is required for the final work.

You need to construct a timetable of events (lectures, seminars, etc.) and of deadlines
you need to decide a pattern of study work.

You can see there is some organisation that needs to be done to enable you to study and there is the organisation of studying itself.

STUDY PERIPHERALS, this chapter, is about the organisation that enables you to study.

*Gaining Knowledge and Skills with Dyslexia and other SpLDs* (Stacey, 2021) covers the processes involved in study.  Stacey (2021)

# Study Peripherals 5

The lists below show many of the study peripherals that need organising and skills useful for organising.

Study peripherals will include:
- navigating the course structure
- dyslexia/ SpLD support
- engaging with the institution's regulations and culture
- other people
- organising finances
- everyday living.

These will involve:
paperwork    events
time and time management
space, place and direction
objects    actions
understanding.

Skills to use will include:
remembering decisions
remembering history
how to file
how to organise
using time reminders
meeting time deadlines

comprehension
mind set
key words
reading between the lines

organising what to take with you on a day-to-day basis.

General organisational skills will be involved in each area and many of the situations discussed in TIME AND TIME MANAGEMENT, SPACE, PLACE AND DIRECTION, and EVERYDAY LIFE will be similar to those encountered while navigating through a course and during study itself.

TIME AND TIME MANAGEMENT: p 84

SPACE, PLACE AND DIRECTION: p 104

EVERYDAY LIFE: p 122

**Insight: General skills and immediate relevance**

Dyslexic/ SpLD people rarely find it possible to learn the general skills either in an abstract way or on a topic that has no immediate importance to them.

It is not that they are unwilling to learn the skills in a general way, but simply that their minds don't hold anything in short-term memory long enough for it to make sense and become useful.

# 5 Study Peripherals

> If you recognise that this lack of learning happens for you:
> - you aren't alone
> - you need to find out how your mind learns
> - you need to respect your own way of learning
> - you need to use your way of learning, and not try to fit in with others.

My preferred way of teaching is to discuss with my students what they are struggling with and which problems seem most urgent to work on. We deal with the urgent problems and develop skills through that work; how to navigate study peripherals is also useful for students to learn the skills for managing dyslexia/ SpLD.

NAVIGATING THE COURSE STRUCTURE and EXAM PROVISIONS are essentially worked examples.

NAVIGATING THE COURSE STRUCTURE: p 175

EXAM PROVISIONS: p 194

### Insight: Worked example

A worked example is annotated in some way so that it is obvious what processes are being used. The worked examples should give you a pattern to adapt for other areas you need to organise.

In NAVIGATING THE COURSE STRUCTURE, key elements are highlighted. To apply the example to another situation, these elements will need replacing as appropriate. EXAM PROVISIONS has ADAPTING THE EXAMPLE notes that tell you how to apply it to another situation.

A worked example cannot be completely prescriptive because each dyslexic/ SpLD person will have their own innate THINKING PREFERENCES and PITFALLS.

You may need several attempts to find the best methods; anything that goes wrong should be regarded as an opportunity to find out more about the way you process information and the way you think well. I would suggest you only get other people to do things for you when there is no way that you can avoid a problem.

THINKING PREFERENCES : p 270

PITFALLS: p 69

Study Peripherals  5

NAVIGATING EMPLOYMENT STRUCTURES is based on NAVIGATING THE COURSE STRUCTURE and has a table showing how to replace the key elements. The course terminology is highlighted in blue in this chapter and the replacement employment terminology is listed in the TABLE: STUDY - EMPLOYMENT.  For other situations, use the TABLE: STUDY - EMPLOYMENT to help you make an appropriate list of the key elements.

The terminology to change is not highlighted every time; it is highlighted the first time and if it hasn't been mentioned for a few paragraphs.

    The icon of parchment, quill and ink[1] is used to indicate that terminology can be altered to make the section apply to employment.  For any other purpose you need to work out what the appropriate terminology would be.

NAVIGATING EMPLOYMENT STRUCTURES: p 219

NAVIGATING THE COURSE STRUCTURE: p 175

TABLE: STUDY - EMPLOYMENT: p 220

### 3   Navigating the course structure

(worked example)

Most degrees and other adult qualifications are made up of several individual courses.  You may have to develop a slightly different navigation process for each one, and for the qualification as a whole.  You may find the people involved with your course, the secretary, librarian or tutor, change from one term/ semester to another.  Their way of communicating may be different and that may have an impact on the system you need in order to maintain your organisation.  You need to monitor progress each new term/ semester to make sure organisation is helping you and lack of it is not moving you into crisis.

> **Tip:  Others are disorganised**
>
> If your tutor is disorganised, you may experience difficulty that is not of your making: don't think everything is your fault.

---

[1] Parchment, quill and ink belong to the electronic age since they are made of electrons and other fundamental particles.  When first in use, they were as important as the electronic devices used today.

# 5  Study Peripherals

## 3.1  Preparation

Most of the ideas discussed in earlier chapters are relevant to navigating the course structure.

The steps for the MODEL FOR DEVELOPING ORGANISATION are used to look at the processes involved, see FIGURE 5.1.

MODEL FOR DEVELOPING ORGANISATION: p 57

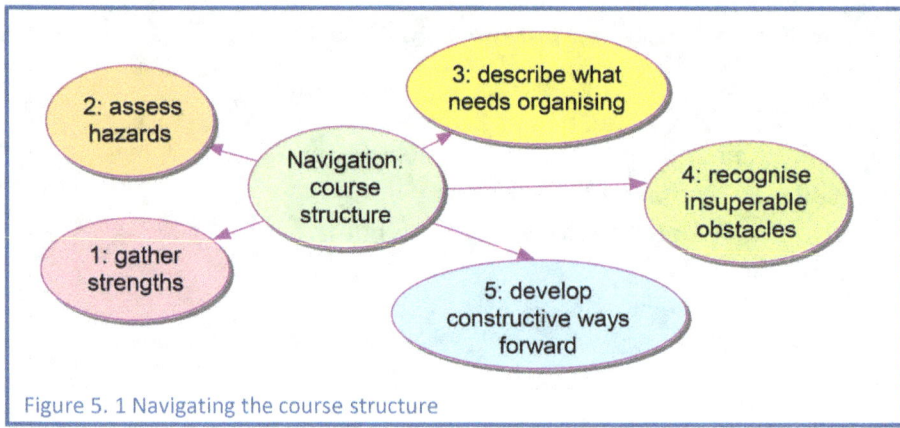

Figure 5.1 Navigating the course structure

## 3.1.1  Step 1: gather strengths

- Think how you like to gather information for working on organisation, see MATERIALS AND METHODS, and THINKING PREFERENCES.
- Have a system for ORGANISING PAPERWORK, EMAILS, ETC.
- Have a system for organising anything to do with TIME AND TIME MANAGEMENT
- Have a system for organising anything to do with SPACE, PLACE AND DIRECTION

You are either gathering your innate strengths, or checking that you have good strategies in place.

If necessary, develop your organisation strategies as you navigate the course structure; don't forget to record the changes in your systems as you make them.

MATERIALS AND METHODS: p 56

THINKING PREFERENCES: p 270

ORGANISING PAPERWORK, EMAILS, ETC: p 144

TIME AND TIME MANAGEMENT: p 84

SPACE, PLACE AND DIRECTION: p 104

# Study Peripherals 5

### 3.1.2 Step 2: assess hazards

What are the hazards your peers face in common with you?

What are the difficulties[2] of your dyslexia/ SpLD?

Who knows you have dyslexia/ SpLD?

How willing are they to help?

<sup>G</sup> p 283: hazard

OTHER PEOPLE has a list of people who might be important to you on your course.

OTHER PEOPLE: p 204

**Hazard: what are the hazards your peers face in common with you?**

It is worth noticing the hazards that are faced by all students on a course. You can feel worse about a situation if you think you are the only one who is struggling. The impact on you may be different from the impact on your peers; you may find the questions and problems you voice help a lot of other people as well, which is similar to the example given in STORY: OTHERS USING A SYSTEM ESSENTIAL TO A DYSLEXIC.

STORY: OTHERS USING A SYSTEM ESSENTIAL TO A DYSLEXIC:
p 51

**Hazard: what are the difficulties of your dyslexia/ SpLD?**

Knowing the PITFALLS of your dyslexia/ SpLD can help you to assess the hazards on a particular course. As you get better at dealing with them in general situations you will probably find they cause you less anxiety when you have to deal with them while navigating the course structure.

PITFALLS : p 69

Make a list of your known PITFALLS and your usual ways of dealing with them.

- Which ones can you manage on your own by adopting strategies?
- For which ones do you need to negotiate some accommodation?
    - Who do you need to negotiate with?
    - What accommodation do you need?
    - If asked, could you explain why you need the accommodation, or could you produce evidence that shows the accommodation works for you?

Keep a record of discussions and progress, and lack of progress, so that you can build on your experiences.

---

[2] PITFALLS, p 69, can help you explore the difficulties of your dyslexia/ SpLD

# 5  Study Peripherals

**Hazard: choices**

One difficulty many dyslexic/ SpLDs encounter is how to make choices.

 CHOICES, p 210, can be an important issue in employment.

### Insight: Choice as a hazard

Students can often choose which particular modules to study and sometimes you feel like saying, "Could I just do the course first to see what it is like? Then, I will know how to make a choice".

Many dyslexic/ SpLD people find making choices difficult because:
- they feel they haven't got all the information that could be helpful
- they don't build their past experiences into a memory bank that would help them decide
- they can't predict how they will feel in the future.

You may have other reasons why you find choices difficult; list them.

Suggestions for resolving issues about choices:
- Use METACOGNITION to be as accurately aware as possible of anything that is preventing you from making choices.

- Using Dilts levels from NLP (Stacey, 2019) might help you to clarify your goals and capabilities, and thus enable you to make a good choice.

- Sometimes using a chance device, such as flipping a coin or throwing dice, will help you to be clear about choices. If the coin toss produces a choice that you subconsciously don't want to take, your instinctive reaction can show you what you're feeling about that choice.

METACOGNITION: p 268

 p 283: NLP

Stacey (2019)

Study Peripherals  5

**Insight: Good choices**

It is better to make a choice based on what you are interested in, rather than to make a choice based on avoiding dyslexic/ SpLD problems.

Your interest is likely to diminish the problems, while choosing a subject that is not interesting is likely to increase them.

The probable impact of making good employment choices is spelt out in CHOICES; the impact of good choices on the way you progress through your course is likely to be very similar.

CHOICES: p 210,

**Hazard: who knows you have dyslexia/ SpLD?**
Find out who knows you are dyslexic/ SpLD; their attitude towards helping you can reduce or increase your hazards.

I would suggest you are looking for someone:
- who is able to give you correct information,
    o in a style that suits you
    o when you need it
    o with the level of detail that you need
and someone with whom you feel comfortable to ask questions.

If you're not feeling comfortable, you may find some of the suggestions in THINKING CLEARLY help you deal with the discomfort.

THINKING CLEARLY: p 264

You may need to discuss the situation with them (the people you are not comfortable with but who are the ones giving you the information) and try to show them it is more work for them when things go wrong for you.

# 5  Study Peripherals

### 3.1.3  Step 3: describe what needs organising

**Exercise:  What are study peripherals?**

Brainstorm the issues that you think belong to the study peripherals of your course; don't include study itself.

- Use your preferred method for brainstorming.
- Allow yourself time to think about a wide range of issues.
- Pause for a few moments to make sure no other ideas occur to you.
- Then compare your ideas with either the chapter mind map arm 'navigating the course structure' or compare them with the list below.

Does anything else occur to you from the topics I've suggested below?

ⓖ p 283: brainstorm

Navigating the course structure includes:
   knowing where to find information
   meeting tutors
   finding out what you have to do, overview of the course
   organising your materials
   seminars and group discussions, and deadlines
   setting your own study time
   meeting deadlines
   'other', note any other issues that need organising.

It is probably worth keeping a copy of your brainstorming for future use, so make sure you can find it again.  You may want to tidy it up, or you may want to use it as it is.  You will probably find you add to it as you progress through the course, or from one course to another.

Each area of navigating the course structure needs organising well.

# Study Peripherals 5

Some of the methods you use will apply to several different areas; but you may find you use a variety of different techniques over the whole range of navigating your course structure.

### 3.1.4 Step 4: recognise insuperable obstacles

As you organise navigating your course, you may find some of the hazards you identified are, in this situation, insuperable obstacles. You may come across other issues that are insuperable. The important thing is to recognise them; to understand why they are insuperable; to think how they could be avoided; and then find the right people to negotiate your way round each obstacle. If you have prepared your evidence well, you are more likely to be able to negotiate effectively.

ᴳ p 283: obstacle

### 3.1.5 Step 5: develop constructive ways forward

Navigating the course structure has been divided into seven different topics in order to discuss constructive ways forward. The comments arise out of working with many different students studying different courses, mostly at my two local universities, but not always. The comments are a mixture of:

- indications of what needs to be organised
- the benefits to be gained from the organisation
- suggestions about organisation
- insights about dyslexia/ SpLD
- warnings of possible problems.

There is no single pattern of comments that applies to all the different topics.

As you work with the ideas in this section, keep a record of your progress and of the things that don't quite work for you. Both the progress and the non-progress are useful in modifying how you construct your way forward.

Use MONITORING PROGRESS: p 243

## 3.2 Course materials

Your course materials are the instructions and information that you need in order to succeed on a course; they have the information that allows you to navigate your way through the course. They are likely to be on a website for your institution; you may get

Course materials include:
course handbook
lecture lists
reading lists

 # 5 Study Peripherals

handed a hard copy of a course handbook.  You need to make sure that you can consult the course materials whenever necessary.  You need to know whether you will be getting extra information as the course progresses.  When well presented, they are a very useful resource.

You need to get an overview of your course materials right at the beginning of any course you undertake.  It is a good idea to apply skills from USING THE MIND WELL.  Other reading skills can be found in *Gaining Knowledge and Skills with Dyslexia and other SpLDs* (Stacey, 2021).

Survey the course materials to find out what kind of information is included.

Where are the main themes and details of the subject matter given?

Where are the skills necessary for the course given?  Are they assumed to be known or will they be taught?

What are the regulations governing your course?

Where can you find your deadlines?

Where are instructions about assignments given?

Are any marking criteria given?

Make sure you pay attention to the themes of the course and skills necessary for the course, see next paragraph.  You should register any deadlines and anything that needs dealing with straight away.  For the rest of the material, you probably don't need to read and understand all the details, you just need to know where they are so that you can consult them easily when you need them later.

 **Overview of your course**

Use your course materials to give you an overview of the course:

- Is the course divided into modules or different parts?
- What are the subtopics of the modules?
- Do any of the modules build on earlier modules in the course?

Create a list or flow diagram of the course.

---

syllabus and synopsis of course
past exam papers

USING THE MIND WELL: p 267

Stacey (2021)

# Study Peripherals 5

It is probably more useful to make the list or flow diagram of the subtopics just before each module or section so that the details are fresh in your mind at the start of the module.

What skills are involved?
- Is it assumed that you have them? Do you? To the standard necessary?
- Are there any that you could strengthen before the course?
- What skills are being taught?

Make a list of the skills.
Being conscious of the skills helps you use and develop them.

To study effectively, you will need to put the overview of your course together with skills and techniques for study (*Gaining Knowledge and Skills with Dyslexia and other SpLDs* (Stacey, 2021)).

Stacey (2021)

## 3.3 Meeting tutors

Lecturers, tutors and other members of the academic staff usually have a role to play in helping you through the course. Students are often assigned to one particular member of staff. Either information on the website or in the course handbook will tell you what your tutors do and how to contact them. You need to find out the situation as early as possible during your course.

| Issues that arise in communications with tutors include: | Useful concepts in the series |
|---|---|
| Knowing what they are there for and how they operate | COMPREHENSION and READING (Stacey, 2021) |
| Making appointments, keeping them | TIME AND TIME MANAGEMENT: p 84 |
| Preparing for discussions | TALKING (Stacey, 2021) |
| Understanding instructions and implications | COMPREHENSION and READING (Stacey, 2021) |
| Remembering what's been said | LISTENING (Stacey, 2021) |

183

# 5   Study Peripherals

| *Issues that arise in communications with* tutors *include:* | Useful concepts in the series |
|---|---|
| Feeling comfortable enough to ask questions | THINKING CLEARLY: p 264<br>KNOW YOUR GOAL: p 275 |
| Knowing how they can help you manage your dyslexia/ SpLD. | INDIVIDUAL, PERSONAL PROFILE OF DYSLEXIA/ SPLD: p 248 |

Keeping good relations with your tutors is helpful (see HANDLING PEOPLE RELATIONSHIPS WELL) and maintaining a reasonable level of organisation in your dealings with them is worth the effort involved.

HANDLING PEOPLE RELATIONSHIPS WELL: p 223

## 3.4   Coursework

Many dyslexic/ SpLD students choose modules that only have coursework in order to avoid taking exams. As suggested previously when thinking about GOOD CHOICES, choosing modules that you are interested in may help you deal with dyslexic/ SpLD problems more easily than choosing modules that have no exams. Navigating the course may also be easier when the course is one you are interested in.

INSIGHT: GOOD CHOICES: p 179

Coursework may be required weekly, at different times through the term/semester or at the end of term. Your organisation is likely to be different depending on how frequently coursework is to be done. For instance, when coursework is to be done weekly you can get into an established rhythm, which is usually easier for dyslexic/ SpLD people to maintain. Use suggestions from TIME AND TIME MANAGEMENT and MEETING DEADLINES to organise the time aspects of coursework.

TIME AND TIME MANAGEMENT: p 84
MEETING DEADLINES: p 188

Other suggestions about navigating through your coursework include:
- find out in advance what's involved and what you need to organise, see YOUR MATERIALS
- decide what you don't understand and ask questions in advance.

YOUR MATERIALS: p 186

Study Peripherals  5

> 💡
>
> **Insight: Asking questions in advance**
>
> It is not always easy to ask questions in advance because many times something does not make sense until you are actually using the information.
>
> However, you are likely to need to organise your materials and your time before you start work on a piece of coursework.
>
> Keep a record of your individual experience as you try to organise something in advance; this way you will learn what the particular HAZARDS AND OBSTACLES are for you and you will have a better understanding of how to manage the situation.
>
> It may be worth explaining your predicament and what you are trying to do about it to your tutor or another person in charge.

HAZARDS AND OBSTACLES: p 66

 **3.5  Group work**

Group work is often part of the assessment process for a course. It can be good practice for the teamwork involved in employment. Organisation will include:

- negotiating with others, see OTHER PEOPLE for a list of people
- helping a group to gel and work well together
- having to work on your part when you need material from someone else who is slow to produce it
- organisation of the group, who will do what, and when to meet
- getting on with individual members
- not being stuck in your dyslexia/ SpLD because of others in the group
- the work, presentations, write-up.

The precise issues will vary from one piece of group work to another and from one group to another. The processes recommended throughout this book – of objective observation and of finding out the

OTHER PEOPLE: p 204

Ⓖ p 283: *objective*

185

### 5  Study Peripherals

heart of any problem – are likely to help you resolve any difficulties. Be as accurate and as factual as you can, then use the pattern shown in CONFLICT RESOLUTION.

CONFLICT RESOLUTION: p 228

Group work is found in many courses.  It has both benefits and difficulties.  One benefit is the opportunity to find out how to work with colleagues on a project; in most areas of employment important skills include being able to work well with your colleagues and relate well to a manager.

#### 3.6  Your materials

The issues tend to be:
1. knowing what you want/ need
2. getting them to hand for when you need them
3. finding them when you need them
4. not taking everything possible, just in case you need it.

The problems and solutions are the same as those in OBJECTS NEEDED FOR AN EVENT, TASK OR GENERAL LIVING.  There is nothing to add that is specific to study and courses, except 1) how you will find out what you need, for which see COURSE MATERIALS; and 2) that your peers and tutors may also be helpful when you want to check you have everything covered.

OBJECTS NEEDED FOR AN EVENT, TASK OR GENERAL LIVING: p 136

COURSE MATERIALS: p 181

**Tip: Organising your course materials.**

It is worth emphasising that there is a flow to these 4 issues in organising your materials.

You can benefit by looking beyond the immediate.  If you're working on a piece of coursework: think through the whole process, what you will need at each stage, and what you will need to take with you going to different places; thus you will know what needs to be got together at different times (issues 1 and 2).

At this early stage, you can also make a note of where anything is and whether you will have to take action to get anything; this allows you time to organise to do so – all of which covers issue 3.

# Study Peripherals 5

> By thinking through your materials this carefully, you should be more confident of your choices and be able to leave some things at home (issue 4).

 **3.7 Timetable and study time**

TIMETABLES AND APPOINTMENTS discusses the problems and suggests solutions for dealing with timetables and appointments. It can be very important to mark all the fixed activities (lectures, seminars, group discussions, etc.) into your timetable for a week; to give time for meals; to put in your leisure activities and some time off; and then work out how much time is left for study and to write in the length of each period of study. You need to prioritise your activities and make sure you are not cutting your study time too short, see PRIORITISING.

TIMETABLES AND APPOINTMENTS: p 94

PRIORITISING: p 236

You often find that there are short periods when nothing is written into the diary/ timetable and you need to think how you are going to use these times effectively. They could be used for:
- relaxation
- catching up with emails or other paperwork that needs doing
- preparation for a longer period of study.

If you don't decide how to use the short periods, you might find life getting uncomfortably disorganised.

Many of the techniques for study result in time being used more effectively, for example MIND SET.

MIND SET: p 267

You need to assess where you would like there to be improvements in how you organise your timetable or your study time. You could use COLLECTING INFORMATION TOGETHER to help you assess your time accurately for a couple of situations involving your study time. You could use WORKING ON A GENERAL PROBLEM to understand the study peripherals; you might see changes that you can make that will help you. Then use the relevant parts of the series *Living Confidently with Specific Learning Difficulties (SpLDs)* (Stacey, 2019, 2020, 2021) to help you make the changes you want, including managing timetables and study time as well as you can.

COLLECTING INFORMATION TOGETHER: p 234

WORKING ON A GENERAL PROBLEM: p 80

Stacey (2019, 2020, 2021)

# 5   Study Peripherals

## 3.8   Meeting deadlines

For most people, it is important to realise how much time there is before a deadline and whether several deadlines all occur very close together.  Just writing a list of the deadlines, and what they are for, doesn't convey enough information about the elapse of time.

One technique that I use over and again for students, and for myself, is to use a spreadsheet that has the days of the week as columns and enough rows to represent all the weeks from now until the furthest deadline.  All the deadlines are written in on the correct days, with the time of day included.  We then number the weeks backwards with 1 in the week before the last deadline.  If there are several deadlines involved, colour coding can be used to help separate one topic from another.

We put in holidays, and days when no work will be done for whatever reason; then we work out how much time there is for all the different deadlines to be met.  We divide that time between the deadlines, taking into account how much work is needed for each to be met.

This practice can be particularly important for people who find it very difficult to start work when it sounds as if a deadline is still a long way ahead.

See also:
TIMETABLES AND APPOINTMENTS:
p 94
TIMETABLE AND STUDY TIME: p 187

### Story:  Distant deadlines

One person had three deadlines all in one week which was several months away.

We had a single calendar sheet which went from the present day to the last of the deadlines.  When we put in her lectures, her holidays, some family events and calculated the amount of time she had for each deadline, she found she had just three weeks for each of the deadlines.

Realising how little time she had gave her the motivation to work seriously even though each deadline was several months away.

TEMPLATES

F14-18 - HALF A YEAR – 27 WEEKS

Study Peripherals 5

It is generally recognised that extending deadlines is not very useful when the extended time runs into the next period of activity. This is particularly true in study situations where one piece of work is expected to be finished before work starts for the next piece; for study, one good solution is early preparation.

In everyday life or employment, one needs to be aware of the length of time needed for any particular task and set achievable deadlines.

## 4   Dyslexia/ SpLD support

Finding out the sources of support is very similar to navigating your way through your course.  You need to find out where the information is and how to access support.

It is possible that you don't even know what you're looking for; you don't know what support might be available; which problems you experience that might be recognised as needing support; or which organisations might provide support.  Even to do an Internet search, you need to have the right search phrases (step 5 in CHECK-LIST FOR USING THE MODEL FOR DEVELOPING ORGANISATION).

CHECK-LIST FOR USING THE MODEL FOR DEVELOPING ORGANISATION: p 70

I would suggest you use the MIND SET techniques, in particular surveying any information you have been given, to get some ideas about what is available; then brainstorm from your own experience using what you've found in the survey.  Generally sort the information and your notes into categories that make sense for you; and record what you have done.  Prioritise anything that needs immediate action; note anything that you don't understand and find someone to consult.

MIND SET: p 267
Ⓖ p 283: brainstorm

Don't ignore, or put aside for later, finding information about support; something may be available which you can use early in a course and which will make a lot of difference to the way you progress through a course.  It is better to have no support because you don't need it rather than to have no support through ignorance.

### Official systems and institutional support

There will be official systems, such as financial support from funding bodies, and institutional support, such as exam provisions.  This book isn't the place to list what's available as it will change from place to place and with time.

# 5  Study Peripherals

In many colleges and universities, there are disability service departments that organise support or provide it or do both.  They will be the people who can tell you how you can access support, what documentation has to be in place to have accommodations within the university or to have funding for 1:1 specialist support.  They are likely to be able to help you decide what's best for you.  They should be able to tell you what provisions are made within different departments of the university or college.  It is best if you are in touch with such a department before you start your course.

## 4.1   IT: assistive technology

Information technology (IT) is a very powerful way of dealing with many of the problems of dyslexia/ SpLD.  There are many programs that have been written by dyslexic/ SpLD people themselves and made available on the web.  There are firms who specialise in the technology, hardware and software, that is found to be most useful.  The term 'assistive technology' is often used to refer to all that is available.  There are some IT suppliers who specialise in assistive technology.  Technology is an area of support that is always developing.  Current practice that is likely to continue includes:

    customising word processors

    arranging computer desktops to suit you

    customising window colours and fonts

    using:

        voice recognition software

        digital recording devices

        mind mapping programmes

        dyslexia/ SpLD friendly spellcheckers and proof-readers

        2 monitors

        laptops, tablet computers, smartphones.

It is very useful to try any IT before purchase, especially to try it on a task that you are currently working on.  Some devices sound very good until you come to use them and find that there is some way they don't fit with your dyslexia/ SpLD.

# Study Peripherals 5

UK students who have been professionally identified as being dyslexic/ SpLD may be eligible for *Disabled Students' Allowances*. Within the allowances, there is funding to pay for assistive technology and training to use it properly.

## 4.2 Specialist 1:1 support

The following list of typical problems faced by adults with dyslexia/ SpLD has been re-organised from DfES Report, 2005.

DfES Report, (2005)

**Processing**

- noticeable inconsistency between what can be achieved on 'good' and 'bad' days
- difficulty becoming fluent in a new skill to the point where it becomes automatic, for example reading, writing and driving a car
- poor short-term memory for carrying out instructions or copying from the board and remembering what has just been read and/or said
- poor attention span and concentration
- difficulty retaining the visual image of words, signs, symbols, formulae, musical notation

MARGIN NOTE: the DfES descriptions do not use the phrase 'working-memory'. Many practitioners regard poor working-memory as a key issue for those with dyslexia/ SpLD.

**Confidence and stress**

- lack of confidence
- particular susceptibility to stress, which may be associated with deadlines or examinations or meetings

**Organisation**

- poor at organising work and other aspects of life
- taking longer than other students to complete tasks
- a poor sense of passage of time, mixing up dates, times and appointments
- directional confusions, getting easily lost, having problems using maps or finding their way to a new place

LEARNING TO BE ORGANISED: p 73, discusses the way organisation, or the lack of it, affects people with the individual SpLDs.

# 5 Study Peripherals

**Language**
- lack of comprehension, despite appearing to read fluently
- poor reading of text due to visual distortions such as blurring or moving letters
- difficulty sequencing letters in spelling, or numbers and signs in maths, difficulties using dictionaries, encyclopaedias and directories, remembering phone numbers and entering them accurately into a phone
- difficulties taking messages

**Motor control**
- mispronunciations and poor word retrieval when speaking, both caused by motor problems or difficulties in discriminating sounds
- poor motor control resulting in a range of difficulties including handwriting, inaccurate reading and spelling

**Maths**
- sequencing, such as instructions and mathematical procedures, sequencing of numbers or letters

**Support**

The problems are not experienced in the same way by different individuals with the same nominal SpLD, nor are the solutions identical.

Often you will only learn your way through a problem in a practical way, i.e. when you are faced with the problem. Anyone who is going to help you needs to have specialist understanding of what the issues are likely to be. Therefore you often benefit from specialist 1:1 support while at university or while doing any sort of course.

The name of 'specialist 1:1 support' has been the subject of debate and it may change again.

# Study Peripherals 5

The aim of the support is to enable you to learn and demonstrate your learning at a level consistent with your innate potential. Usually support is given individually because the experience of the problems and solutions necessary is particular to you.

You also need to develop your skills in ways different from those used by other dyslexic/ SpLD students.

Group support can also be beneficial because it gives you the opportunity to share your experiences with others who have similar ones. Being in a group can reduce the feeling of isolation.

The length of time over which support is necessary is also very variable.
- You may need very little or no 1-1 specialist support.
- You may just need a few hours of support every time you embark on an enterprise that needs a new level or style of skills or knowledge.
- You may need ongoing support most of the time because
    - you have an intractable difficulty that is effectively an obstacle rather than a hazard, see H AZARDS AND O BSTACLES
    - you need to work out what to do in dialogue with someone who understands the effects of your dyslexia/ SpLD.

*HAZARDS AND OBSTACLES: p 66*

It is worth finding out how specialist study support is provided on your course and what you need to do to access it.

The skills you gain in this way will help you with study and with using the result of that study later on in employment.

Even students who have had very good specialist support at school will benefit from some support at university because the methods of studying have to develop beyond those needed at school.

# 5  Study Peripherals

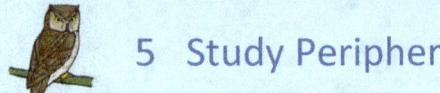

## 4.3  Exam provisions

(worked example, see: INSIGHT: WORKED EXAMPLE)

INSIGHT: WORKED EXAMPLE: p 174

The BOXES: ADAPTING THE EXAMPLE contain suggestions for replacing the bullet points in the example in order to apply the same process to another situation.

This section on exam provisions includes:

- the reasons for exam provisions (ACCOMMODATION)
- applying for them
- assessing the appropriateness of exam provisions, written and non-written
- negotiating different accommodation for dyslexia/ SpLD when the standard provisions don't meet your needs, with examples of other options.

ACCOMMODATION: p 69

### The reasons for exam provisions

The purpose of exam provisions is to level the playing field.  The results of exams should reflect the work, knowledge and skills of the individuals taking the exams, and they should not be affected by dyslexia/ SpLD.

Exam provisions have been the subject of debate for many decades, and no doubt the debate will continue in the future.  There are often constraints of time and resources that need to be taken into account.

Many people worry about giving an unfair advantage to people with dyslexia/ SpLD, and this includes many dyslexic/ SpLD people.  It is often thought that highly intelligent dyslexic/ SpLD people should not have exam provisions because they are already able to achieve good results;

> **Adapting the example:**
> 
> - the circumstances for employment or taking part in hobbies or other social activities may be such that your dyslexia/ SpLD is masking what you could achieve if you were fulfilling your potential
> - establish the reasons for accommodation
> - find out the concerns that people have

Study Peripherals 5

however, since they would achieve even better results without the dyslexia/ SpLD, they are being handicapped if they are denied exam provisions.

**Applying for exam provisions**

Any institution or exam board that runs exams is likely these days to have processes for exam provisions. You need to:

- find out where the information is available
- make sure you have the appropriate documentation to establish need
- apply in good time
- be sure you understand all the processes involved for every exam for which you need exam provisions
- make sure the provisions available will enable you to complete the exam demonstrating the work you have put in, the knowledge you have acquired and the skills that you have
- check whether there are any changes from one course to another.

You should get written confirmation of the provisions put in place for you. You might need to take the confirmation with you if exam provisions are not well established. It would be better to take a photocopy of the confirmation rather than the original, as exams are stressful times and you don't want to lose the original written confirmation while you are at the exam.

**Checking provisions are suitable for written exams**

The most common exams are written ones and the usual provision is extra time, with the use of a computer being granted where appropriate. Extra time allows you to deal with many of the processing difficulties of dyslexia/ SpLD. You need to be sure that the use of the computer within

**Adapting the example:**

- know what resources are available
- find out what you have to do to access them
- find out how consistent your situation is or what changes there are from one time or place to another
- decide how formal the acknowledgement of the arrangements needs to be

**Adapting the example:**

- find out what common practice exists
- you need to be thinking in a very wide ranging way in

# 5  Study Peripherals

time constraints is actually a better way of demonstrating your knowledge and skills than writing by hand; others also need to be sure this is not an unfair advantage when comparing your performance with that of somebody with equal potential.

You should find out any rules and regulations that apply to your exam as part of the process of checking the suitability of the provisions and as part of preparing for the exams.

To assess the suitability of these provisions, you also need to be aware of the details of your exam.
- How long is it?
- What type of questions are set?
- How many do you have to answer?
- How are you expected to answer?
- Do you have rough/scrap paper?
- What sort of paper do you write on, sheets or booklets, etc.?

**Checking provisions are suitable for other types of exam, i.e. not written exams**
*Gaining Knowledge and Skills with Dyslexia and other SpLDs* (Stacey, 2021) has several subsections about different types of exams, including discussions of problems that could be encountered and strategies that could be used to manage them. There will be different styles of exam provisions that have already been put in place for these types of exams; you need to check that the provisions are suitable for you, following the ideas above for written exams.

You need to experience the style of exam in a practice situation in order to know 1) whether the provisions are correct and 2) how to complete the exam. You need to do the practice, e.g. take the

⇧ order to assess whether anything about your circumstances is making the issues of dyslexia/ SpLD worse than need be

**Adapting the example:**
- know the situation well
- check whether the accommodation allows you to fulfil your potential
- if it does, all you have to do is make sure you access it
- if it doesn't, see below WHEN THE EXAM PROVISIONS DON'T MEET YOUR NEEDS

**Adapting the example:**
- as the last two boxes

Stacey (2021)

# Study Peripherals 5

mock exam well in advance of the actual exam, so that if anything needs altering about the way you take the exam there is time for you to learn new techniques or for new arrangements to be made or both.

**When exam provisions don't meet your needs**
It can be very difficult to negotiate different exam provisions.

One difficulty can be that other people will think they know better than you what your needs really are and how they can be met.

- You need to know the circumstances and setting of the exams in detail
- it may help you to keep clearly in mind what knowledge or skills the exam is supposed to be testing, and what is not being tested
- you need to be very clear about the PITFALLS of your dyslexia/ SpLD and how they affect your performance in the exam
- it is good to know what your strengths are and how they could be demonstrated, or used, if more suitable provisions were available
- it helps if you know what provisions would accommodate your needs
- you need to be able to argue your case with evidence from your work
- you may need to find an advocate, a dyslexia/ SpLD professional, who will be able to help you put the case
- it also helps to be aware of the reasons others will be reluctant to agree to the new provisions and what their worries are.

On some occasions when I have been involved with getting the right provisions for a particular dyslexic/ SpLD student, the examiner has

See also NEGOTIATING ACCOMMODATION: p 258

PITFALLS: p 69

**Adapting the example:**

- gather evidence about the situation
- know how your dyslexia/ SpLD masks your performance
- be able to describe how other conditions could improve your performance.

use the ideas for keeping good records in CHOICES: p 210

describe how you manage your dyslexia/ SpLD using your REGIME FOR MANAGING DYSLEXIA/ SPLD: p 248

**Adapting the example:**

Once you have identified suitable accommodation:

- if you are the only person involved, it should be a question of putting it in place
- you may have to recognise any reluctance on your part, see EXAMPLE: INSUPERABLE OBSTACLE CHANGED TO HAZARD: p 64

# 5 Study Peripherals

improved the exam conditions for all students, kept the standards required high and achieved a level playing field.

When considering whether to ask for different provisions, you need to weigh up the amount of time and energy you will have to put into the process and make sure that your end gain will be worth it.

Exams can have a very long term impact on your life, so getting the provisions to suit you is worth quite a bit of effort. In the future you may look back with more acceptance if you try to get the right provisions but they aren't granted than if you just didn't spend the time and energy trying.

**Examples**

Quite often the alteration to the provision is very minor:
- being allowed to take in a coloured ruler to assist reading
- exam papers being written on coloured paper, sometimes a particular colour for one individual
- a maths student providing the exam office with the lined paper that helps him organise his maths answers
- students having rough/ scrap paper when this isn't standard practice
- a student having two copies of the exam paper when questions are on more than one side of a page.

More major accommodations can include:
- amanuensis
- dictating answers to a dictaphone

- if someone else is involved, you will need to negotiate with them to arrange the conditions that will allow you to fulfil your potential
- you may need a process something like the one suggested in RESOLVING INTERPERSONAL ISSUES: p 228

use the ideas for keeping good records in CHOICES: p 210

TEMPLATES  Use:
B3 - COMPARE EXPECTATIONS AND REALITY to collect your experiences together so that you can use them in any discussion.

**Adapting the example:**

- find examples from this book or other resources of cases where accommodation has been successfully put in place
- be able to discuss the benefits in these cases and relate them to your situation

MARGIN NOTE: transcription: your answer is re-written by someone with clearer handwriting, or is typed; both

# Study Peripherals 5

transcription, see MARGIN NOTE

listening to questions on a dictaphone

a calculator for certain maths problems

rest time when the exam is particularly long, often the papers can be taken away during the rest time.

your original and the transcription are sent to the examiner for marking.

Multiple choice exams appropriate provisions:

students being allowed to write the answer they know rather than select one of the options, which are often very close to each other in meaning

students writing the letter of their answer on the exam paper with the examiner filling in the multiple choice matrix.

**Insight: Provision for multiple-choice exam**

One student regularly had difficulty with selecting the right box to mark in her multiple choice exams. The appropriate provision was an invigilator who watched that when she said "The answer is A" she marked the 'A' box.

## 5 Engaging with your institution's regulations, culture and departments

All institutions and societies have formal regulations that govern the processes of the institution and communications within them. Also, there is often a culture which is usually not written down but which governs the behaviour of the people. In a big institution, there will be different departments and the culture can vary from one to another. The regulations, the culture and the departments can all present challenges to dyslexic/ SpLD students.

# 5  Study Peripherals

## Regulations

Dealing with the regulations will be very similar to NAVIGATING THE COURSE STRUCTURE. Some of the regulations will never be relevant to you; some will be immediately important; some will be important in the future. There will be many different levels of importance and relevance; you need skill to deal with the regulations.

There is often a meeting or lecture in which the regulations that affect you are discussed. Probably the best way to deal with such a meeting or lecture is to expect to gain an overview of what is involved, find out where information is available and to find out who can help with any problems. The techniques outlined in USING THE MIND WELL will help you gain the overview. The next priority is to find out what you have to do and any timescale that applies. Use the CHECK-LIST FOR USING THE MODEL FOR DEVELOPING ORGANISATION to work your way through the regulations, replacing the green text what you need to organise with what do I have to do and by when?

If anything needs to be sorted out, it will be your responsibility to make sure it happens, to make sure it doesn't get forgotten and to see it through to the proper conclusion. You will also have to be aware of any deadlines involved. Use the ideas in ORGANISING PAPERWORK, EMAILS, ETC. to create a system that will work for you.

## Assessment regulations

The regulations governing assessment are the ones that determine how you produce the evidence that you have gained knowledge and skills from your course. You need to find out what these regulations are at the beginning of your course, not at the end.

There will also be regulations about plagiarism. Plagiarism is using other people's work as if it were your own; it is a form of cheating. Dyslexic/ SpLD students can accidentally plagiarise other people's work because they don't understand the subtleties involved.

- You need to break down the regulations about plagiarism into sections that make sense to you
- you need to check your understanding carefully with your tutor
- you need to be careful about the way you take notes so that you distinguish between quotes from sources and the ideas of other people, and your own ideas

---

NAVIGATING THE COURSE STRUCTURE: p 175

USING THE MIND WELL: p 267

CHECK-LIST FOR USING THE MODEL FOR DEVELOPING ORGANISATION: p 70

ORGANISING PAPERWORK, EMAILS, ETC: p 144

# Study Peripherals 5

- you need to find out how much of other people's work, in particular quotes, you can include in your work.

Even with all this care there may be something that happens that leads your tutors to suspect you of plagiarising; if you keep all your notes and working, you will have evidence to show how you have worked and that you haven't deliberately plagiarised.  If you can explain what has happened, you should be given extra time to put right whatever has gone wrong.

---

### Story: Two writers or one?

One student was accused of plagiarising because the style of writing changed so much in his assignment.  He was a practical person who always struggled with theoretical regulations.

He was studying a module that involved a new code of practice for which there were few supplementary sources. The student had not understood the reasons for the new procedures nor the details; his writing about the theoretical material was very muddled.

He had done related practical work and could write well about it.

He was accused of using someone else's work for the good parts of his assignment.

He had kept his rough drafts and assignment plans.  He was able to show that both the practical and theoretical parts of his assignment started in a muddle and how he could work on the practical elements to produce good writing.  He could also show his attempts to sort out the theory.

His explanation was accepted.  He was allowed extra time to re-write the theoretical part.

# 5  Study Peripherals

### Culture

The presence of unspoken cultures applies to educational institutions just as much as it does at work, see CULTURE AT WORK. You need to be aware that the culture surrounding you and your fellow students may be subtly different from that which governs your interactions with academic and non-academic staff.

CULTURE AT WORK: p 224

The behaviour patterns between students may depend on the location; the way you interact with each other when out for an evening could be much more relaxed than the way you interact with each other during classes. One of the difficulties for dyslexic/ SpLD students is that so much mental energy is spent understanding the words being used and the systems in place, that there is again no capacity to pick up subtle clues about relationships and the culture.

Working-memory capacity: see Stacey, (2019)

### Departments

There will be some departments that you need to have contact with besides your course department. Some of these deal with the structures and processes of your institution, such as admissions and enrolling; others provide services: the library, computer services, careers services, disability services, etc. Many of these departments will have their own way of supporting dyslexic/ SpLD students. Each one will have its own sources of information, in a similar way to the course handbook. Use the suggestions for dealing with COURSE MATERIAL to find what you need.

COURSE MATERIAL: p 181

At the beginning of a course, you could well feel overloaded with all the information that comes your way. You don't need to understand it all straightaway; much of it you will probably never need; however some of it will be really important immediately. There are two skills that you can gradually acquire through dealing with the study peripherals:

1. being able to discern the important and immediate, and dealing with them
2. not losing the next round of things to do.

They are skills that will stand you in good stead throughout your working life.

# Study Peripherals  5

Don't give yourself a hard time when it is all problematic to start with. Use WORKING ON A GENERAL PROBLEM to sort out how your department functions.  At step 5 your useful questions might be:

- Is there anything I need to do?
- By when?
- How can this department help me?
- Who do I contact about *any particular issue I might have*?  Specify the issue.

The last question can be repeated for different issues.

Also, find a sympathetic person who can help you get answers to your questions.

Be especially cautious with processes like admissions and enrolling.  They involve paperwork and filling in forms; getting details wrong can take a lot of energy, time and sometimes money to put right.

Do make sure that at some stage you understand the services that are available.

For example, careers services often have advisers who have trained in dyslexia/ SpLD issues; it is worth discussing your career with such an adviser early in your course.

What they are able to tell you may well influence choices you make during your course.  You may be in a better position for the career you really want to follow as a result of discussions with careers advisers.

Counselling services will also probably have staff trained in dyslexia/ SpLD issues.  Talking through problems with a professional can mean they are dealt with earlier rather than later, which will benefit your progress.

WORKING ON A GENERAL PROBLEM: p 80

# 5  Study Peripherals

## 6  Other people

The main discussion about people relationships is in HANDLING PEOPLE RELATIONSHIPS WELL.

While studying, the people you will be in contact with are:
- academic staff: including teachers, lecturers and tutors
- non-academic staff: administrators, secretaries, librarians, computer technicians, caretakers, etc.
- your peers: the people on the course with you, especially those doing group work with you
- your friends, who may or may not be on the same course as you
- your family
- others.

Each type of relationship will have its own characteristics and dynamics.  Paying attention to these is likely to benefit you and your study, see HANDLING PEOPLE RELATIONSHIPS WELL.

Non-academic staff may be extremely helpful to you in terms of helping you with the details of your course.

## 7  Finances

Finances seem to be a fixture of life and can be very complicated when they get into a mess.

They can take more time and energy to sort out once they are in a mess, therefore it is worth having a system for them that you work out before starting on a course.  In a perfect world, you would try to have some reserves that you can draw on while you're studying.

Keeping a record of income and outgoings, and checking the balance between the two is worth doing.  You will have your normal banking systems to keep organised.

If you're using student funding, you will also need to engage with the processing systems to ensure that the funding is in place when you want it.  For UK students, as mentioned above in SPECIALIST 1-1 SUPPORT, there are *Disabled Students' Allowances* which fund support for dyslexic/ SpLDs students while at university.

---

HANDLING PEOPLE RELATIONSHIPS WELL: p 6§6

HANDLING PEOPLE RELATIONSHIPS WELL: p 6§6

MARGIN NOTE: keeping your finances organised could be helped by many of the ideas in EVERYDAY LIFE: p 122

Finances are also discussed in *Gaining Knowledge and Skills with Dyslexia and other SpLDs* (Stacey, 2021)

SPECIALIST 1-1 SUPPORT: p 191

Study Peripherals  5

## 8  Everyday living

While you are studying, you are still living and your everyday life needs attention.

*Everyday Life:* p 122

- You need to think about your accommodation and your health
- you will need food to eat which will mean organising shopping or meals in your college/hall of residence
- most students find exercise beneficial
- many engage with others in their hobbies
- there will be friends to meet and social events to go to.

Having a balanced life is as important while studying as it is while working and the many ideas in *Everyday Life* can be used to make sure your everyday life nurtures you.

## References

Series *Living Confidently with Specific Learning Difficulties (SpLDs):*
Stacey, Ginny, 2019, *Finding Your Voice with Dyslexia and other SpLDs*, Routledge, London
Stacey, Ginny, 2020, *Development of Dyslexia and other SpLDs*, Routledge, London
Stacey, Ginny, 2021, *Gaining Knowledge and Skills with Dyslexia and other SpLDs*, Routledge, London

## Website information

DfES Report, 2005, https://www.patoss-dyslexia.org/Resources/DSA-Working-Guidelines  Accessed 10 June 2020
Series website: www.routledge.com/cw/stacey

# 6 Employment

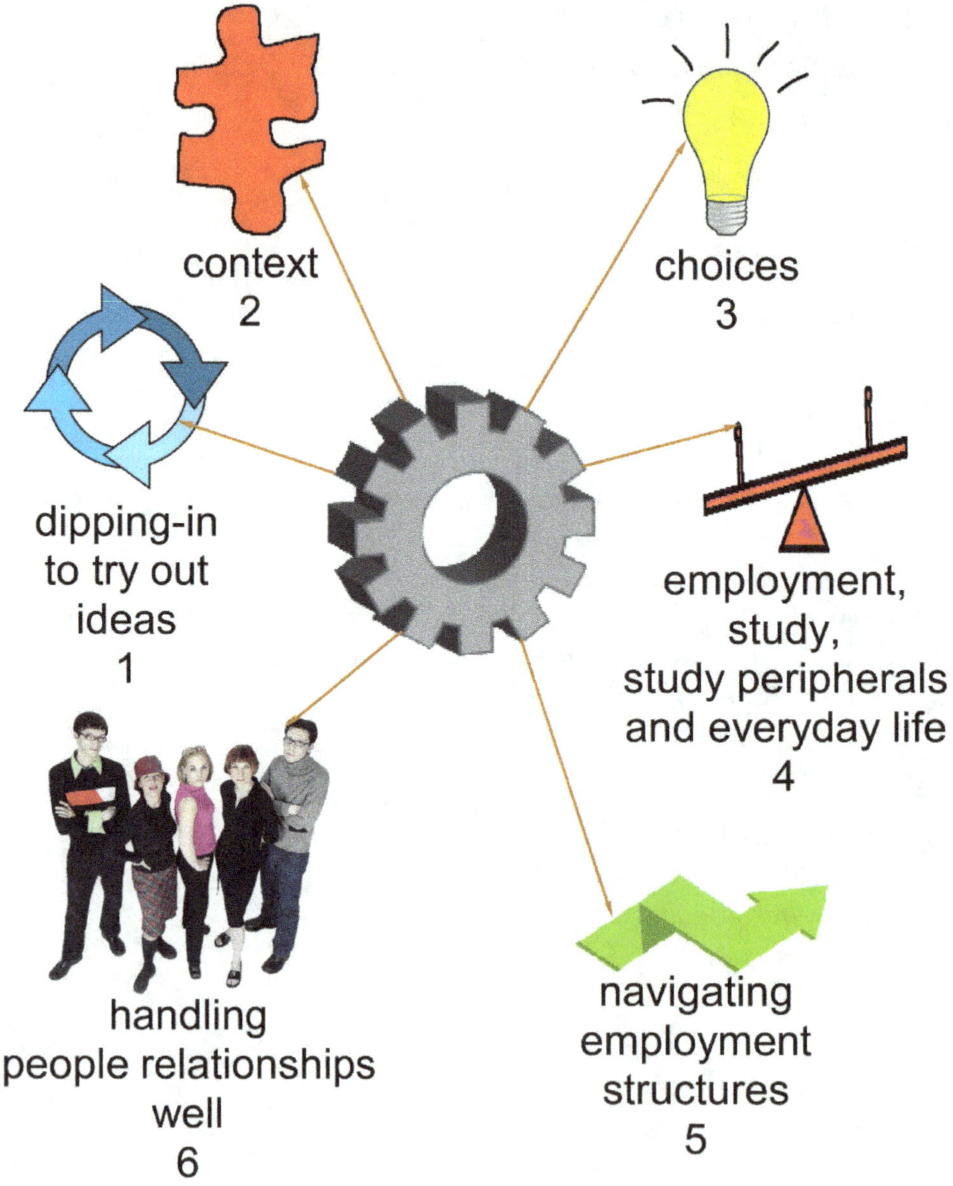

- context 2
- choices 3
- dipping-in to try out ideas 1
- employment, study, study peripherals and everyday life 4
- navigating employment structures 5
- handling people relationships well 6

## Contents

Vital for dyslexic/ SpLDs, good practice for all ... 207
Working with the chapter ... 208
Templates on the website ... 208
Appendix 1, 2 and 3 ... 208
1 Dipping-in to try out ideas ... 210
2 Context ... 210
3 Choices ... 210
   3.1 To declare your dyslexia/ SpLD or not ... 212
   3.2 Choices in employment ... 213
   3.3 Keeping good records of your ideas ... 214
   3.4 Choosing to change jobs ... 214
4 Employment, study, study peripherals and everyday life ... 215
   4.1 Possible problematic issues in employment ... 217
   4.2 Learning new systems ... 218
   4.3 Support at work ... 218
5 Navigating employment structures ... 219
6 Handling people relationships well ... 223
   6.1 Culture at work ... 224
   6.2 Dyslexic/ SpLD differences at work ... 226
   6.3 Resolving interpersonal issues ... 228
   6.4 Dyslexic/ SpLD impossibilities ... 230
References and website information ... 230

---

### Vital for dyslexic/ SpLDs, good practice for all

Having the right job is vital for dyslexic/ SpLD people; in the wrong job all the issues of dyslexia/ SpLD can get worse.

It is good practice for everyone to have a job that suits them well.

# 6 Employment

## Working with the chapter

> **Key ideas**
>
> - Employment builds on everyday life and study.
> - Not recognising the culture of work is similar to not learning subliminally.
> - Making the right choices.
> - People relationships need handling well.

This chapter allows you to look at the situation in your workplace and see whether there are any issues that arise from your dyslexia/ SpLD. You'll find the ways to resolve most issues in earlier chapters of the book.

Making good choices and getting on with other people are discussed in detail in this chapter.

GENERATING USEFUL QUESTIONS : p 238

Use GENERATING USEFUL QUESTIONS and MONITORING PROGRESS to help you.

MONITORING PROGRESS: p 243

## Templates on the website

| A1 | JOTTING DOWN AS YOU SCAN |
| A2 | BOOKMARK – PURPOSE |
| A4 | JOTTING DOWN AS YOU READ |
| B1 | COLLECTING IDEAS THAT RELATE TO YOU |
| B3 | COMPARE EXPECTATIONS AND REALITY |
| B4 | ACTION, RESULT, NEXT STEP |

TEMPLATES

## Appendix 1  Resources

APPENDIX 1: p 232

This appendix will help you collect information and make progress as you manage your dyslexia/ SpLD in the workplace.

Employment 6

## Appendix 2  Individual, Personal Profile of Dyslexia/ SpLD and Regime for Managing Dyslexia/ SpLD

*Appendix 2: p 246*

**Tip:** *Employment* **and building your profile and regime**

You can learn about your profile and regime while reflecting on what happens to you in the workplace.

## Appendix 3  Key Concepts

*Appendix 3: p 262*

I cover these key concepts when doing an audit of skills and knowledge with a dyslexic/ SpLD student.  The appendix shows which of the 4 books in the series covers each idea in full.

**Tip: The skills and knowledge you can gain from this series**

*Appendix 3: Key Concepts* has a list of the main skills and knowledge that you can gain from this series of books.  They fall into the categories of

> *Thinking Clearly*
> *Using The Mind Well*
> *Your Thinking Preferences*
> *Useful Approaches*
> *Aspects of Dyslexia/ SpLD*

209

# 6 Employment

## 1 Dipping-in to try out ideas

Scan through the following sections to see if anything is relevant to you:

- *CHOICES*
- *INSIGHT BOX: REASONS FOR ACCOMMODATION*
- *INSIGHT BOX: UNDERLYING DYSLEXIA/ SPLD ISSUES*

Read the *STORY* and *INSIGHT BOXES*.

Scan the rest of the chapter to see whether anything is relevant to you now.

Take note of what is in the chapter for future use.

*CHOICES:* p 210

*INSIGHT BOX: REASONS FOR ACCOMMODATION:* p 216

*INSIGHT BOX: UNDERLYING DYSLEXIA/ SPLD ISSUES:* p 224

## 2 Context

For the purposes of discussing organisation, employment can be considered as a combination of study, including the study peripherals, and everyday life, all taking place in the special environment of work.

This chapter starts by considering some of the personal choices you need to make in terms of your employment.

It then discusses how the ideas about everyday life, study peripherals, and study relate to employment.

After that is a section on *NAVIGATING EMPLOYMENT STRUCTURES* which includes a table showing you how to change the terminology in *NAVIGATING THE COURSE STRUCTURE* so that you can work with the issues of employment.

The final section deals with people relationships.

*NAVIGATING EMPLOYMENT STRUCTURES:* p 219

*NAVIGATING THE COURSE STRUCTURE:* p 175

## 3 Choices

Several students have discussed their career choices with me wondering how to take into account the difficulties of their dyslexia/ SpLD. Many times they have suggested it would be better to choose a job that is not so interesting but which would not challenge their dyslexia/ SpLD management.

At conferences on dyslexia I have heard people speak about job choices and the way some dyslexic/ SpLD people find a job they like, get promoted to a point where their dyslexia is hampering their work and then they leave the job they like rather than seek to resolve the issues around their dyslexia/ SpLD.

*MARGIN NOTE:* Applying for a job is dealt with in some detail in *Gaining Knowledge and Skills with Dyslexia and other SpLDs* (Stacey, 2021).

# Employment 6

### Example: Promotion in catering

Someone choosing a career in catering might have practical strengths which are satisfied by the work aspect. She might have creative skills which produce new recipes and original presentation.

Promotion to a managerial, or supervisory, role could include more writing, dealing with people and having financial responsibilities. All of these could increase the dyslexia/ SpLD problems.

Making choices in general can be difficult for many dyslexic/ SpLD people; and CHOICE AS A HAZARD is discussed in NAVIGATING THE COURSE STRUCTURE.

CHOICE AS A HAZARD: p 178

### Tip: Go for a job you will like

It is much better to choose a job that interests you, that gives you satisfaction.

Your interest is likely to use your best MOTIVATION and your best ways of thinking so that you are already engaging your dyslexia/ SpLD management strategies; this will probably reduce the effects of your dyslexia/ SpLD.

MOTIVATION : p 271

Your work will probably be better and therefore more valued because you are more enthusiastic.

The managers of your job are likely to be more helpful because they value your work.

You are likely to feel more confident in what you do and therefore much more able to discuss the issues of your dyslexia/ SpLD and work with those around you to find the solutions.

# 6 Employment

## 3.1 To declare your dyslexia/ SpLD or not

It is not a legal requirement to declare your dyslexia/ SpLD. But no employer can help you or be held responsible for supporting you if you haven't told them. You need to work out what you feel comfortable doing.

Some people are worried that they won't be offered a job, or even an interview, if they mention their dyslexia/ SpLD too early.

Some are worried that they will be 'found out' and they would rather let the employer know in advance.

Some feel comfortable talking about their dyslexia/ SpLD once they have been offered a job.

In making your choice you are balancing several issues, one of which is your guess as to how your employer would respond. It is not an easy decision to make.

Remember also, that your employer may see any impact of your dyslexia/ SPLD as mistakes if he doesn't know the underlying cause. He may think you are being careless and that your performance is unsatisfactory.

### Insight: Employer reaction

One dyslexic person was in a job for several months before mentioning that she was dyslexic. She asked her employer whether he would have given her the job if he had known. His reply was: "No, I wouldn't have done, but I am glad that I did."

It is sometimes useful to put the accommodations for dyslexia/ SpLD into perspective by comparing them with different situations, as in the next story.

# Employment 6

>
> **Story: Left-handed accommodation in a coffee shop**
>
> In a coffee shop, you have a team of people doing different parts of the work. In one particular shop, there was a rota so that everybody took a turn at all the jobs. One of the people was left-handed and one of the jobs was slicing the ham.
>
> The slicing station was set up to suit right-handed people and to change it to suit a single left-handed person would have meant rearranging several different workstations. For the left-hander to slice ham in a right-handed way would have been dangerous.
>
> The only safe and economic accommodation was to arrange the rota so that the left-handed person did not slice ham.
>
> In the past, there was as much stigma about being left-handed as there can be now about being dyslexic/ SpLD.

Gradually, management is likely to become more willing to organise accommodations as more dyslexic/ SpLD people are able to be open about the difficulties they face, the way they approach them, and the reasons for the accommodations they need. The focus of attention should shift from the problems to a recognition of the contributions that dyslexic/ SpLD people can make in the workplace.

## 3.2  Choices in employment

The amount of choice you have in your work can vary considerably. In some jobs what you have to do and how you have to do it is laid down by the management very precisely. At the other end of the spectrum, some jobs may have many opportunities for you to make different choices and your own individual contributions. Since many dyslexic/ SpLD people have a tendency to think differently, jobs that require independent thinking should be very suitable. Even in the jobs that are very precisely set out, dyslexic/ SpLD people may see better ways of accomplishing a task, see *Example: Others Using a System Essential to a Dyslexic*.

*Example: Others Using a System Essential to a Dyslexic:* p 51

# 6 Employment

### 3.3 Keeping good records of your ideas

In all situations, you need to find out how management will respond to your suggestions and the choices you want to make.

In some form that you find easy, keep good records of:
- your ideas
- your reasons for them
- any tests you have made to see whether they work
- anything that you think is relevant to the development of your ideas
- how management responds.

By building up your experience around making choices you should be able to make them in a constructive way that will be accepted in your workplace.

*Margin Note:* also see *Handling people relationships well:* p 223

### 3.4 Choosing to change jobs

People have many reasons for choosing to change jobs. It is good to make the choice in an informed way.

You could use several of the ideas in this book to work out
- how far your job is providing you with
    - the financial income you want
    - job satisfaction
    - a good life–work balance
    - the opportunity to negotiate new conditions within the employment you have
- whether it's time to think about finding a job in a completely new setting.

You might discover that there is some other part of your life, i.e. not your job, which you would like to change; in this case changing your job may be the wrong choice.

# Employment 6

It should be obvious that the philosophy of this book is that unresolved dyslexia/ SpLD issues are not a good motive for changing jobs. However, it is also recognised that sometimes you can't get anywhere trying to negotiate accommodations at work and then it is probably a good idea to change jobs.

## 4   Employment, study, study peripherals and everyday life

One main theme of this book is that dyslexia/ SpLD affects all of life from the way you deal with everyday life to the way you study and organise your study, and to the way you organise yourself in employment. As a result, this book on organisation has dealt with many aspects of life in terms of everyday life rather than study or employment.

The chapters on EVERYDAY LIFE and STUDY PERIPHERALS contain many ideas useful during employment.

Finding solutions for employment difficulties should be possible using GENERAL PROBLEM-SOLVING, which includes FINDING THE ROOT CAUSE OF A PROBLEM.

NAVIGATING EMPLOYMENT STRUCTURES builds on NAVIGATING THE COURSE STRUCTURE by replacing key elements as shown in TABLE: STUDY - EMPLOYMENT.

In the worked example EXAM PROVISIONS:

- there are BOXES: ADAPTING THE EXAMPLE
- the second bullet point in the first box is to 'establish the reasons for the accommodation'
- INSIGHT: REASONS FOR ACCOMMODATION shows some possible dyslexic/ SpLD employment issues and how they relate to ideas discussed elsewhere, with cross references to where the discussion can be found
- adapting the rest of the worked example would be one way to find the right solutions.

EVERYDAY LIFE:
p 122

STUDY PERIPHERALS:
p 168

GENERAL PROBLEM-SOLVING:
p 79

FINDING THE ROOT CAUSE OF A PROBLEM: p 82

NAVIGATING EMPLOYMENT STRUCTURES: p 219

TABLE: STUDY - EMPLOYMENT: p 220

EXAM PROVISIONS:
p 194

# 6 Employment

**Insight: Reasons for accommodation**

| *Employment issues* | *Dyslexic/ SpLD issues* | *Where to find further information* |
|---|---|---|
| New processes at the new job | Almost all dyslexic/ SpLD characteristics can affect the way you deal with new processes. | 'NEW' CAN BE PROBLEMATIC: p 52 |
| Work space | Many dyslexic/ SpLD people need to spread out their work. Do you? | EXAM PROVISIONS: p 194<br>TIME AND TIME MANAGEMENT: p 84<br>SPACE, PLACE AND DIRECTION: p 104 |
| Environment | The environment needs to suit your way of working, for example, fluorescent lights, distractions, noise levels. | THE IMPACT OF THE ENVIRONMENT: p 118<br>RELATING TO THE SPACE AROUND YOU: p 119 |
| Hot-desking; dealing with disturbances | An unstable environment can destabilise dyslexia/ SpLD management. | THE IMPACT OF THE ENVIRONMENT: p 118<br>RELATING TO THE SPACE AROUND YOU: p 119 |
| Computer & equipment | The right technology can make a huge difference to the way you deal with dyslexia/ SpLD. | Technology is changing fast. Some is helpful; some causes problems. Using knowledge of your profile should help to establish reasons for accommodation: INDIVIDUAL, PERSONAL PROFILE OF DYSLEXIA/ SpLD: p 248 |

Employment 6

| Employment issues | Dyslexic/ SpLD issues | Where to find further information |
|---|---|---|
| Projects or routine tasks | Knowing exactly what you have to do, and checking that with organisers/managers; organising deadlines. | USING THE MIND WELL: p 267<br>AGREED CHECKING OF DETAILS: p 52 |
| Decisions | Remembering decisions. | REMEMBERING DECISIONS: p 140 |
| Pay, holidays, pensions, and all finances | Uninteresting parts of the job could get ignored which may lead to later chaos, difficulties and stress. | ORGANISING PAPERWORK, EMAILS, ETC.: p 144<br>COURSE MATERIALS: p 181 |
| Report writing, etc. | Reports may be patchy, off the point, wrong length, badly planned. | *Gaining Knowledge and Skills with Dyslexia and other SpLDs* (Stacey, 2021) |

## 4.1 Possible problematic issues in employment

The following are examples of issues that you may encounter with some ideas about dealing with them:

How you deal with emails:
- have set times for reading them
- use folders to organise them
- organise them with categories and tags
- have templates for standard, or near standard, emails and answers
- use text-to-speech software for reading or proof-reading.

Work out your best way of taking notes in meetings:
- mind mapping
- voice recording
- using symbols
- going over your notes soon after a meeting while you still remember what they mean
- asking someone to take notes and circulate.

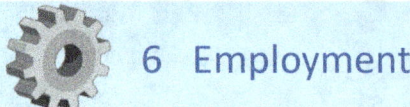

# 6 Employment

Dealing with interruptions:

- if you work in an open plan office, you may be able to book a private room for concentrated work
- work from home
- ask colleagues not to interrupt
- adjust your hours so you can be in the office while it is quiet before others arrive.

## 4.2 Learning new systems

New systems and procedures are part of modern working. Standard training may not suit you. Being in a training group with others who learn differently could cause problems for you. You may need to negotiate to be able to learn in a way that suits you, and with a time schedule that works for you. Negotiating such accommodation is likely to be easier if you have accumulated evidence from your past experiences. You need to be able to show that you learn better and that the employer will feel the benefit of your increased capabilities.

## 4.3 Support at work

You may need 1-1 support from a manager or supervisor. It may be that some simple things will make a significant difference to the way you can work:

- advance warnings of deadlines
- knowing you will not be asked to produce work at short notice
- tasks that use your best strengths
- positive feedback.

Regular constructive conversations on a 1-1 basis may be possible, and very productive.

An employer is legally require to make 'reasonable adjustments' under the Equality Act 2010.

You may be eligible for funding from Access to Work for suitable software and training, equipment, such as a digital voice recorder; and training to develop workplace strategies. Access to Work is a

Access to Work: www.gov.uk/access-to-work Accessed 12

# Employment 6

publicly funded employment support programme that helps people with disabilities, including dyslexia/ SpLD, start or stay in work.

## 5 Navigating employment structures

NAVIGATING EMPLOYMENT STRUCTURES is very similar to NAVIGATING THE COURSE STRUCTURE which is written as a worked example for managing dyslexia/ SpLD during the processes of undertaking a course of study.

The diagram of the model for developing organisation only needs 'course structure' to be changed to 'employment structures', as in FIGURE 6.1.

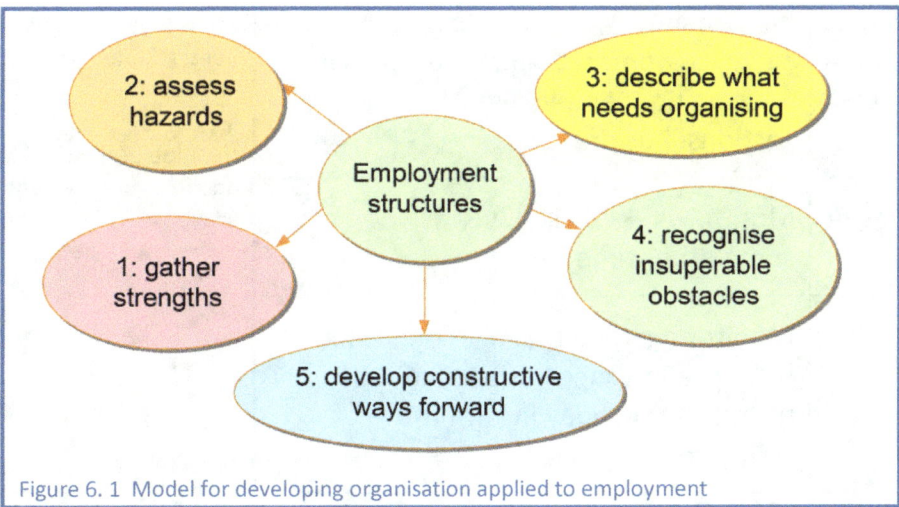

Figure 6. 1 Model for developing organisation applied to employment

June 2020

NAVIGATING THE COURSE STRUCTURE: p 175

 The quill, ink and parchment[1] icon has been used in NAVIGATING THE COURSE STRUCTURE, to show where the terms need changing to apply to employment.

The text can be adapted to navigating employment structures by changing the terminology so that it is suitable for employment. The table below shows how the terminology can be changed.

The EXERCISE: WHAT ARE STUDY PERIPHERALS and the list below the exercise can also be changed using the table below. The exercise is worth doing in relation to employment structures.

EXERCISE: WHAT ARE STUDY PERIPHERALS: p 180

---

[1] The ink, the quill and the parchment were made in materials containing electrons, so they belong to the electronic age.

# 6 Employment

| Table: Study | Employment<br>Possible employment structures: |
|---|---|
| Individual courses | Projects; areas of work: reception; office; catering; cleaning; finance department; production line; stock control; management |
| Qualification | Efficient work style; job satisfaction; outcomes |
| People; secretaries, librarians, tutors | Boss/manager; colleagues/ client/customer; team; employees in your section; employees of other sections; business reps |
| Terms/ semester | Month, week, season, year, some other time rhythm |
| Vacation/ holidays | Monitoring holiday allocation; using holiday allowance in specified time; fitting your holiday in with those of colleagues |
| Your peers: students on the course | Your peers: those working at the same level as you and with you. |
| Who knows you are dyslexic/ SpLD (characteristics of a helpful person set out) | The characteristics of the person I suggest you are looking for very much apply to people in the workplace, especially managers |
| Study peripherals | Conditions of employment |
| Study | The work you do |

The chapter mind map of STUDY PERIPHERALS (p 168) is colour coded:

the green branches are generic skills that will be useful in employments as well as study;

the red branches will need adapting to suit employment;

the blue branches apply to employment as well as study.

# Employment 6

| Table: Study | Employment<br>Possible employment structures: |
|---|---|
| Course materials | Job specifications; procedures involved; employees' handbook.<br>How do you know what to do?<br>Job appraisal systems |
| Tutors | Managers; team leaders; floor stewards |
| Overview of the course | Overview of your job: its aims and outcomes |
| Coursework | What you do; managing workload;<br>all the tasks in a manual job;<br>any paperwork that has to be completed |
| Group work | Teamwork |
| Materials left at home | Materials left in the office/factory/yard when you go somewhere else |
| Lectures, seminars, group discussions | General meetings; team meetings; seminars; presentations; briefings and de-briefings |
| Timetables and study time | Time at work:<br>you go there and just get on with a list of tasks<br>you have meetings that have specified time slots and preparation and time in between to deal with other work.<br>balancing time, having systems in place so that work flows is VERY important |
| Meeting deadlines for coursework | Projects can be treated in exactly the same way as coursework |

# 6 Employment

**Story: Study procedures transformed into employment ones**

On study courses, there are usually modules that change from one term to another. Gradually students learn how to approach each new module so that they stay on top of their work. They know:

- what topics will be covered
- how handouts will be given
- when lectures will be and where
- who will be giving them tutorials
- what work they have to produce and by when
- what assignments or exams are involved.

One medical student was moving into the clinical phase of her training. She would be changing hospital units every 6 weeks. She would have exams at the end of the next 3 years.

We used the MODEL FOR DEVELOPING ORGANISATION to see what was involved for her and what she could do to prepare for each unit.

MODEL FOR DEVELOPING ORGANISATION: p 57

In each unit, she would be learning about the patients, medical knowledge, procedures and drugs.

No clear goals are given by any supervisor; she had to set her own goals, realise what questions she had and where her interest lay for each new unit.

She had to organise her way of working, including having textbooks, notebooks and some idea of the technical language that would be used.

She needed to find a mentor in each unit so that she could ask useful questions, such as:

- What do I need to know about patients?
- What form does the continual assessment take?
- What books were good?
- What do you wish you had been told?

She also worked out how she was going to deal with learning about the drugs.

In summary, we took what she had learnt about herself as a student and developed ideas for her to go into the hospital units with confidence.

## 6  Handling people relationships[2] well

In most of life, relationships with other people need handling well. People with dyslexia/ SpLD have ways of thinking and processing information that are not readily understood by other people whose minds work in a different way.

See the *INDEX* for other sections of the book that discuss the differences between non-dyslexic/ SpLD and dyslexic/ SpLD people.

### Insight: Experiences shared

There was an occasion when the heating system had been turned off for the summer months but nobody had told the weather. At work we couldn't put on electric heaters because the number of them needed to warm the workforce blew the fuses. We were cold, though not cold enough to be sent home.

As we moved around the workplace, people could empathise with each other by giving a quick shiver as they passed in the corridor. There was a quick and easy camaraderie in this coldness because we all shared the same immediate experience.

I was struck by how difficult it is for a similar sharing of understanding to happen between dyslexic/ SpLD people and non-dyslexic SpLD people. The lack of understanding can lead to poor relationships.

---

[2] Many relationships work well without any special effort on either side to understand dyslexic/ SpLD issues. These relationships don't cause problems; enjoy them. They might be worth observing objectively to see if doing so helps with sorting out any difficult relationships. (G) p 283: objective

# 6 Employment

The points made here about achieving and maintaining good relationships apply also to everyday life and study. I have chosen to put them in this chapter on EMPLOYMENT because so much time is spent at work.

## 6.1 Culture at work

There is often an unspoken code that governs the behaviour that is expected at work.

It is thought that you will pick up this code just by being in the environment and observing how people treat you and each other.

Often dyslexic/ SpLD people don't become aware of the culture; there are parallels with the way most of us (the dyslexic/ SpLD group) don't learn subliminally.

ⓖ p 283: subliminal learning

### Examples: Different cultures

In building trade stores, you hear male banter at the counter;

at some stores, for example John Lewis, the shop assistants are very well mannered and willing to help a customer;

in some departments of a big organisation you are expected to follow your given routines and not raise questions;

in most scientific faculties you would be expected to want to understand the research and to ask questions.

All these different situations have their own ways for people to relate to each other.

# Employment 6

**Story: Not observing the culture**

One section I worked in for more than a decade had a culture of people bringing a cake to share when they had a birthday. Initially, I worked a few hours a week with no contract; later I was part-time and had a contract but there was no formal introduction to departmental ways.

After about 10 years, someone raised the question of cakes for birthdays at a department meeting. It was only then that I realised people always brought in cakes on their birthdays for everyone to share.

I had never done so. I said at the meeting "Oh my goodness! You must think I'm so mean! I never realised that we all brought in birthday cakes in all the years I've been working here."

It can be that easy for your behaviour not to fit the general culture.

There are many ways the effects of dyslexia/ SpLD mean you don't pick up the culture at all or you misread it and think something quite different is going on. Also others may find you quite unpredictable because they don't understand the patterns of thinking behind your actions and words.

You need to find someone who you feel comfortable with, who you can talk openly to and who you trust to be honest and kind. You need to be able to talk through difficulties that you are aware of so that you can own the PITFALLS of your dyslexia/ SpLD, and you can be appreciative of your strengths and the things you do well. With confidence coming from such a relationship, you are more likely to be able to deal with relationships at work in an open way.

*PITFALLS:* p 69

As long as the human reaction is to be reluctant to discuss the effects of differences openly, objectively and honestly, any outsider groups[3] are likely to have a hard time in relationships, at work, while studying, at home and in life in general.

---

[3] 'Outsider group' is used to refer to any groups of people outside the expected norm.

# 6 Employment

## 6.2 Dyslexic/ SpLD differences at work

The list below shows some of the ways differences at work can cause friction and what the root of the difference might be. The effects can be quite minor to begin with but they can develop into major issues. The differences may also occur between dyslexic/ SpLD people since not all of us work the same way. The solutions will come through:

- accurate observation as to why you work the way you do
- knowing what strengths you bring to the work and what benefits
- understanding the underlying dyslexia/ SpLD issues
- being able to explain them to your manager or team leader.

If you are in a job that suits you, you will probably find the differences are easier to deal with; see the discussion about choice of job in CHOICES.

MARGIN NOTE: it is my hope that people working with this book will increase the general understanding of the issues around dyslexia/ SpLD and so diminish some of these problems in relationships.

CHOICES: p 210

### Insight: Underlying dyslexia/ SpLD issues

| Point of friction | Possible cause |
|---|---|
| You may get protective of your workstation and develop body language that puts other people off invading your space. | You may find it very difficult to work in an environment that keeps changing; even the place where you expect to find your pencils may need to stay stable in order for you to work effectively, so you protect your space from other people. |
| You may get tense about keeping your work on time and organised. Your tension may feel brusque and unfriendly to other people in the way you speak to them. | You may be working to manage many different effects of your dyslexia/ SpLD; the efforts that you are making may not be obvious to your colleagues so they won't understand why you are under any particular stress. |

# Employment 6

| Point of friction | Possible cause |
|---|---|
| You may cause havoc in the filing system and not realise that is upsetting other people. | You may be very happy to do the filing, and not realise you're putting things away in the wrong place; your colleagues may be too polite to tell you that things are going wrong. |
| Others think you are lazy or indifferent to the consequences of being disorganised. | You may simply not realise that you are disorganised and that others are affected.<br><br>You may be trying to be organised, but you need some help with finding a good system that you can use. |
| Your level of organisation, either good or bad, may not match the level of organisation of others. | If you don't completely match the level of performance of the majority of those around you, you may find there are a lot of comments made about your organisation; it isn't particularly that anyone is unkind, it is just the number of comments eventually makes you feel an alien. |
| The way you handle information, for example a need to colour code everything, may be misunderstood by those you work with. | As with comments about level of organisation, the number of comments may highlight the fact that there is something different about you despite the comments being quite kind. |
| There may be accommodations agreed with your manager, or some other people, that are not understood by the majority of your peers and that may cause tension. For example, you may be in an office of your own or have a barrier that gives you some shelter from noise while others have to contend with an open office environment. | Part of your dyslexia/ SpLD may be that you cannot concentrate when distracted by noise from the environment; you may need to work in complete silence. |

# 6 Employment

## 6.3 Resolving interpersonal issues

The following suggested pattern for resolving misunderstandings uses ideas from *Nonviolent Communication* (Rosenberg, 2003) and *Happy Children: A Challenge for Parents* (Dreikurs and Soltz, 1984).

You need to be as objective as possible and not see anybody as being at fault; it is just a question of misunderstandings across the differences between dyslexic/ SpLD people and non-dyslexic/ SpLD people.

It is best if all the people involved in the situation contribute to finding the solution; otherwise you are second guessing the needs of absent people and you would possibly be putting energy into solving the wrong problem.

First you objectively describe the situation that needs changing. Then the people involved state what is happening for them and they state their needs.

There may need to be a preparatory step in which people keep records similar to the record-keeping about ideas in CHOICES IN EMPLOYMENT. If you keep your observations factual, it is often easier to make progress.

You should aim to reach a level of acceptance and understanding of each other's needs. From that you should be able to propose an objective way forward, or a solution. Both parties should have a willing attitude while the solution is tried out; there should be an agreed way of checking that progress is being made, that all is well or that some further modifications are required.

One major problem could be getting both parties to have 'a willing attitude'. Dyslexic/ SpLD people can seem very stubborn because experience has taught them there are some things they really cannot

Rosenberg (2003)
Dreikurs and Soltz (1984)

ⓖ p 283: objective

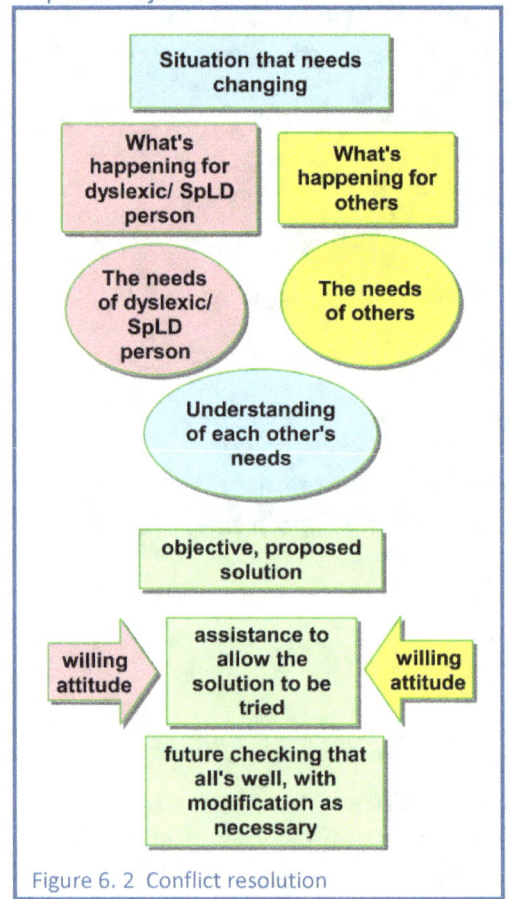

Figure 6.2 Conflict resolution

CHOICES IN EMPLOYMENT: p 213

change; other people sometimes simply cannot recognise the dyslexic/ SpLD issues. Understanding each other's needs can play a key part in enabling willing attitudes to be achieved.

The pattern looks rather formal, but it is possible to use it in an informal way just by having the elements in mind.

**Story: Communicating with the receptionist** (see *Margin Note*)

One dyslexic part-time worker used to give handwritten drafts to an office receptionist for word processing. There was uncertainty in the amount of time the receptionist would have available depending on the rest of her work.

The stress of dealing with paperwork and a poor short-term memory would make the dyslexic part-time worker quite anxious when he went to pick up the material and his manner was seen as putting pressure on the receptionist to complete work faster than she could.

Since the receptionist saw her position as inferior to that of the part-time worker, she didn't feel that she could say anything to him. Eventually, there was a meeting between the receptionist, her line manager and the part-time worker. The latter was very upset to find out the effect he was having on the receptionist; he was able to apologise but also explain the dyslexic problems he was facing.

With much better understanding of the work situation facing them all, the tensions in the office were reduced and friendly relationships restored. It was agreed that the line manager and the part-time dyslexic worker would check with each other from time to time that the receptionist felt her work was valued and appreciated by the part-time worker.

*Margin Note:* this example would include any person who supports your work.

# 6 Employment

## 6.4 Dyslexic/ SpLD impossibilities

We need to recognise when our dyslexia/ SpLD creates such a problem that it is better for somebody else to do all or part of the task.

**Story: Dictating instructions**

One dyslexic person was going to be away and had to leave instructions for several tasks to be carried out in his absence. The simplest solution was for him to do the tasks as normal while describing what he was doing to a colleague who wrote it down as instructions to be used in his absence.

Many competent dyslexic/ SpLD people get to a position in their work when they have a personal assistant (PA) or secretary. Some then naturally rely on the PA to sort out the dyslexic/ SpLD difficulties; this is the ultimate way of dealing with dyslexic/ SpLD impossibilities. Others can have a level of anxiety that means they still try to do some of the PA's work; if you find your work is overlapping with that of your PA you should probably step back and let him/her get on with it.

## References

Dreikurs, Rudolf and Soltz, Vicki, 1984, *Happy Children: A Challenge to Parents*, Fontant Paperbacks, Glasgow

Rosenberg, Marshall, 2003, *Nonviolent Communication: A Language for Life*, PuddleDancer Press, Encinitas, CA, 2nd ed.

Stacey, Ginny, 2021, *Gaining Knowledge and Skills with Dyslexia and other SpLDs*, Routledge, London

## Website information

Access to Work: https://www.gov.uk/access-to-work. Accessed 12 June 2020.
Series website: www.routledge.com/cw/stacey

# Employment 6

# Appendix 1: Resources

## Contents

Templates on the website ..... 232
1. General resources ..... 233
2. Collecting information together ..... 234
3. Prioritising ..... 236
4. Generating useful questions ..... 238
5. Surveying ..... 241
6. Recording as you scan ..... 242
7. Monitoring progress ..... 243
References and website information ..... 244

## Templates on the website

A1  JOTTING DOWN AS YOU SCAN

B1  COLLECTING IDEAS THAT RELATE TO YOU

B3  COMPARE EXPECTATIONS AND REALITY

B4  ACTION, RESULTS, NEXT STEP

B5  RECORDING TEMPLATE - 1 (4 COLS - NARROWER CODING COLUMN)

B6  RECORDING TEMPLATE - 2 (4 EQUAL COLUMNS)

B7  RECORDING TEMPLATE - 3 (5 COLS - NARROWER CODING COLUMN)

B8  RECORDING TEMPLATE - 4 (5 EQUAL COLUMNS)

B9  A CALENDAR MONTH FOR PRIORITISING – 5 WEEKS

B10  QUESTIONS TO ASK ONESELF TO HELP OBSERVATION

B11  MONITORING PROGRESS

TEMPLATES

## 1  General resources

This is a collection of resources and ideas that will help you to capture any ideas that seem important to you.  Ideas that are captured will then be available to you for use later on.

Notice anything that doesn't work for you, and use it to design your own way to capture and use information that seems relevant to you.

**Tip:  Margin**

You can use the right-hand margin to jot down your ideas as you scan or read the book.

I have used it for cross-referencing and for references to help you find these when you want them.

# Appendix 1   Resources

## 2   Collecting information together

- Create a mind map of the information; there are examples in the book. Experiment with different styles to find which work well for you. (Don't use mind maps if you don't like them.)
- Use a digital recording device; make sure you label the files so that you can remember what they are about.
- Create tables of information; this section has several suggestions for using tables.
- Use electronic note-collecting devices.

### B1 - COLLECTING IDEAS THAT RELATE TO YOU

This *TEMPLATE* will help with building your *INDIVIDUAL, PERSONAL PROFILE OF DYSLEXIA/ SPLD* and your *REGIME FOR MANAGING DYSLEXIA/ SPLD*.

Column 4 allows you to reflect whether you are learning more about
1   your profile
2   your regime for managing dyslexia/ SpLD.

Column 5 allows you to note which elements are involved:
>thinking preferences
>pausing
>pitfalls
>accommodations
>goals.

TEMPLATES

Ⓖ p 283: profile, regime

### B3 - COMPARE EXPECTATIONS AND REALITY

If you are going to observe objectively you need to keep a record of your expectations and what actually happens. The *TEMPLATE: COMPARE EXPECTATIONS AND REALITY* is one way of doing this. It can be easier to rule horizontal lines after writing in the template than forcing yourself to keep within lines already printed.

The template suggests you record the *situation* and *date*. It has 4 columns headed: *Events, Expected, Actual, Comments*.

TEMPLATES

## Resources   Appendix 1

For example:
*Situation*: to have everything ready for football on Saturday morning (include the date), in order to arrive on time.

| Events | Expected | Actual | Comments |
|---|---|---|---|
| wash kit | Tuesday | | |
| assemble kit | Friday | | |
| put boots with kit | Friday | | |
| get up | 8.30 am Saturday | | |
| breakfast | 9.00 | | |
| leave house | 9.45 | | |
| arrive at *venue* | 10.15 | | |

The Actual column would be filled in as close to the event as possible. The Comments could then reflect pleasure at success or any adjustments needed to achieve the desired result.

### B4 - ACTION, RESULTS, NEXT STEP

TEMPLATES

This TEMPLATE is very similar to COMPARE EXPECTATIONS AND REALITY. In COMPARE EXPECTATIONS AND REALITY you are planning ahead and monitoring how well the plan was executed. In ACTION, RESULTS, NEXT STEP, you are observing the results of actions, whether planned or not, and considering any implications for the *Next Step*, whenever that might be.

For example

| Event | Action | Results | Next Step |
|---|---|---|---|
| conversation with friend | I created pictures in my mind as we talked | I remembered the details next day | try putting pictures on my lists |
| shopping | I drew some of the items on the list and left the list at home! | I remembered the drawings and some connected items; forgot others | see what other line drawing I can use |

235

# Appendix 1   Resources

### B5, B6 - Recording Templates - 1 and - 2

These templates can be used for a number of different purposes. In *B5 - Recording Template - 1* the columns are uneven, which is suitable for those times when you want to use one column for a lot of detail while the others are only needed for brief information.
*B6 - Recording Template - 2* has 4 equal columns.

### B7, B8 - Recording Templates - 3 and - 4

These templates are similar to *B5, B6 - Recording Templates - 1* and *- 2*, but with a 5$^{th}$ column. Often the fifth column is very useful for a brief key word or symbol.  It allows you to code the information you are collecting so that you can find sections that belong together.  For instance, if you are exploring how you use different senses, you can put visual/ oral/ smell/ taste/ kinaesthetic or V/ O/ S/ T / K in the fifth column.  Then you only have to look for the V/ visual to find all the notes about the way you use your vision.

**Useful headings for linear lists or text notes**

Any of the column headings suggested for tabular forms of collecting information could be used as headings for lists or a sentence-based way of collecting information.

You might divide a page into spaces for different categories of information and label the spaces.

You might write down the information you are gathering and leave space to add in the headings later.

*TEMPLATES*

*MARGIN NOTE:* when these 4 templates are recommended, headings are usually suggested.

## 3  Prioritising

Given a collection of tasks, situations or topics (not an exhaustive list), what are the priorities for you?

1   You might have to prioritise bearing in mind limited time and resources.
2   You might be trying to decide the relative importance of each of a set of topics.
3   You might be deciding the order in which to do a series of tasks.

You can use any form of note-taking to collect the information together.  The suggestions here use a calendar, a mind map and a tabular form.

Resources   Appendix 1

**Step 1   With limited time or resources**

First you have to establish the constraints:

- Do you have enough time or resources to do everything?
- Does anything depend on another thing being done first?

Assessing the constraints first stops you trying to do more than you possibly can.

The TEMPLATE: B9 - A CALENDAR MONTH FOR PRIORITISING allows you to mark deadlines and block out sections of time.  You can often then decide the priority of the various tasks and the order in which to do them.

TEMPLATES

Put everything that is happening in your life onto the calendar.  In particular, include time for the ordinary, everyday tasks.

It can be helpful to highlight the beginning and end of the month, whether using paper or an electronic device.

You then continue with the second stage below.

**Step 2   What is involved?**

A second stage is simply to brainstorm about the tasks, situations or topics under consideration.  You can use any of the shapes of mind map used in the book.  You could make lists of ideas.

See the INDEX, p 295, for a list of mind maps

In terms of reading a book, a useful set of questions might be:
    What do I know already?
    Why have I picked up this book?
    What do I think it might give me?
    What am I interested in?  or  Who am I interested in knowing more about?
    What aspect would it be interesting to know more about?
    What do I really want to know?

MARGIN NOTE:
GENERATING USEFUL QUESTIONS, p 238, could help you find the right questions.

If you are prioritising actions, a set of useful questions might be:
    What do I want to achieve?
    What equipment do I need?
    Who else is involved?  How?  Why?
    What individual tasks are there?
    What do I need to find out?

# Appendix 1   Resources

### Step 3   Deciding relative priorities

When you have decided what is involved, you can put the information together in a table and then decide the relative priorities of the tasks.

B5, B6 - RECORDING TEMPLATES - 1 AND - 2 can be adapted to gather the information.

TEMPLATES

Title = the reason for sorting out a set of priorities.

      A = the priority assigned to each task once you've assessed them all

      B = name of a task

      C = details of the task

      D = resources or time requirements.

B7, B8 - RECORDING TEMPLATES - 3 AND - 4 could be used if a 5$^{th}$ column is useful.

TEMPLATES

      E = Vital/ important/ non-essential.

This information would help in assigning the priorities that are written in column A.

### Step 4   Plan of action

Use the priorities list in column A and the calendar to make a plan of action.  Keep monitoring your progress.  Adapt your plan as necessary.

---

## 4   Generating useful questions

Making a list of questions can be a very useful way to guide yourself through many different situations or tasks.  The purpose of the list is to clarify what you are attempting to do, to help you be realistic and to help you achieve the end goal.  Discussion around these ideas has come under: useful questions, ultimate goal, know your goal, research questions and probably a few other terms too.  It is hard to pick out any common themes that lead to a direct set of principles.  However, the idea of useful questions is sufficiently important that there is an INDEX entry: QUESTIONS, USEFUL, EXAMPLES.

INDEX: p 195

# Resources   Appendix 1

TEMPLATE: *B10 - QUESTIONS TO ASK ONESELF TO HELP OBSERVATION* is an example of a good set of questions.

The style and wording of the questions will be slightly different depending on the circumstances, for example:

> When you're organising something, you might think about how you're going to organise it and why you're organising it in a particular way.

> When you are reading something or listening, having some questions you want answered gives a structure to the material. You then understand it faster.

> When you're writing an essay, doing a presentation, or communicating by some means, the purposes for your work need to be defined clearly. This approach usually gives a coherence to the work.

> When you are making major decisions for your life, you can be helped by a set of questions about what you want to do, what you are most interested in, how your decisions will affect others. The list is not exhaustive.

> When you need to keep your attention focused on a specific task and stop yourself getting diverted, you can use a set of questions to:
>
> a) define the specific task
>
> b) relate what you are doing at any moment to the specific task.
>
> Pulling yourself back from distractions can make a task more enjoyable, or it can shorten a task you don't really want to do.

TEMPLATES

The Basic Set of
*USEFUL QUESTIONS*:
Why?
Who?
When?
Where?
How?
What for?

# Appendix 1   Resources

### Exercise: To practise generating useful questions 1

You are going to use USEFUL QUESTIONS to search the book in order to find any discussion on a specific topic:

- Think of a topic that interests you.
- What questions need answering to help you find out about the topic?
- List your questions.
- Use them as you scan the INDEX ENTRY: QUESTIONS, USEFUL, EXAMPLES. Then scan the rest of the INDEX, the CONTENTS and the book to find topics that are similar to the one you have in mind.
- How good were your questions? Did they help you to find the sections that deal with the topic you had in mind?
- What changes would you make to the questions for the next time?

*MARGIN NOTE*: this exercise could be applied to all 4 books in the series (Stacey, 2019, 2020a, 2020b, 2021)

*INDEX*: p 195
*CONTENTS*: p xv

### Exercise: To practise generating useful questions 2

You are going to use USEFUL QUESTIONS to search the book in order to find the nearest match to a specific task:

- Think of a task that needs doing.
- What questions need answering to help you find the best match, in the book, to your task?
- List your questions.
- Use them as you scan the INDEX ENTRY: QUESTIONS, USEFUL, EXAMPLES. Then scan the rest of the INDEX the CONTENTS and the book to find tasks that are similar to the one you have in mind.
- How good were your questions? Did they help you to find a good match to the task you had in mind?
- What changes would you make to the questions for the next time?

*MARGIN note*: this exercise will work best with *Organisation and Everyday Life with Dyslexia and other SpLDs* (Stacey, 2020a) and *Gaining Knowledge and Skills with Dyslexia and other SpLDs* (Stacey, 2021)

*INDEX*: p 195
*CONTENTS*: p xv

# Resources   Appendix 1

**Tip:  The skill of generating useful questions**

This skill is worth developing until it becomes natural.  You could add the EXERCISE: TO PRACTISE GENERATING USEFUL QUESTIONS 1 & 2, above, to the card index for SYSTEMATIC REVIEW.  It is a skill that could be usefully practised once a week until it is easy to use.

SYSTEMATIC REVIEW in *Finding Your Voice with Dyslexia and other SpLDs* (Stacey, 2019)

## 5  Surveying

In surveying you are looking over material to find out, in broad terms, what the material contains and where certain ideas are.  As part of the process you will probably decide your priorities for exploring the ideas.  'Material' could be instruction manuals for household goods, books, articles, web pages.

### Step 1  Key ideas

You need to establish a set of key ideas that you want to find out about.  These will be your focus of attention as you survey any material.

You can use one of the EXERCISES: TO PRACTISE GENERATING USEFUL QUESTIONS.
You can brainstorm around the associated topics to see if key ideas emerge.
You can look at other examples using QUESTIONS, USEFUL, EXAMPLES in the INDEX, and see if any of them help you to recognise the key ideas you want to read about.

You can discuss your interest with someone else and use ideas that come out of the conversation.

It doesn't matter how you do it, but find a set of key ideas.

The set of key ideas will still be helpful, even when they are not quite right.  They will help you to focus your mind as you survey.  You will be more attentive to the material than if trying to read with a wide open mind that is not looking for anything specific.

MARGIN NOTE: EXERCISE: INITIAL PURPOSE FOR READING, p 14 is a good example of surveying.

EXERCISES: TO PRACTISE GENERATING USEFUL QUESTIONS: p 240

ⓖ p 283: brainstorm

INDEX: p 195

# Appendix 1  Resources

**Step 2     Recording your survey**

Use *B5 - Recording Template - 1*.

Headings      A = key topic         B = where in the book

              C = main ideas        D = order to read.

                                    (Complete D at the end of Step 3)

TEMPLATES

**Step 3     Survey (as applicable to this book)**

- Use the *Index* and *Contents* of the book to find sections of the book that cover the topics you want to find out about.
- Scan the book for useful indications of important material, such as headings, words in bold or italic; scan graphs and other visual material.
- Cover all the topics you have identified in the key ideas list.
- Have a quick look at each section to gather its main ideas.
- Write in column D the order in which you would like to read the various sections.

*Index*: p 195
*Contents*: p xv

**Surveying other books**

Some books don't have an index or contents list.  You can use chapter headings.  You may have to use introductions and conclusions to chapters.  You may have to scan the beginnings of paragraphs every few pages.

Surveying can be used with any source of information.  It can be extended to work with several sources at the same time.  Column B would then be headed:  Source, and where in the source.  Or you could use the *B7 - Recording Template - 3*.

TEMPLATES

## 6  Recording as you scan

Scanning a section: you can randomly move through a section deciding roughly what it is about.  You don't try to understand the ideas.

Several times in this book you are recommended to scan several sections to find material and ideas that are relevant to you.
It is frustrating to see something interesting or useful and not be able to find it again.

## Resources   Appendix 1

TEMPLATE: *A1 - JOTTING DOWN AS YOU SCAN* allows you to make brief comments as you scan.

If you want to write more, and a landscape page would suit you better, use *B5 - RECORDING TEMPLATE - 1*.

The headings would be:

A = Source and page            B = Section/ Keywords

C = What is interesting        D = Priority.

Drawing a line after each entry can help to separate the ideas that you want to record.

TEMPLATES

---

## 7   Monitoring progress

It's really useful and encouraging to see how well you are doing.  It's useful to see anything that isn't working so well, because then you can do something about it.
You might want to see:

   your progress with a skill

   knowledge you are gaining

   how a situation is developing

   how you are managing a task

   other ... the list is not exhaustive.

You can collect the information by any means that suits you:
   notes                    on paper or electronic device
   voice recordings         art work.

Use the ideas below, in *USING TEMPLATES ON THE WEBSITE*, to help you decide what to record and how to label or annotate your information. You want to remember the key ideas and your reflections so that you can use them again later.

You can gather the information together by category, e.g. keep all the information about situations together.

# Appendix 1  Resources

**Using the templates on the website**

If you collect information using the TEMPLATES: B3 - COMPARE EXPECTATIONS AND REALITY and B4 - ACTION, RESULT AND NEXT STEP, you can use the last columns, Comment and Next Step respectively, to reflect on your progress and anything you want to change.

TEMPLATES

The TEMPLATE: B11 - MONITORING PROGRESS has 5 columns.

    1    = date
    2    = focus of interest
    3    = current state of play
    4    = last application
    5    = reflection.

TEMPLATES

Comments about the columns:

1    It is almost always useful to have the date recorded.
2    A few words that capture what you want to monitor.
3    Record your summary of how far you have progressed.
4    Describe what happened when you tried out your progress to date.
5    Reflect on your progress; maybe think about the next step; anyone you could usefully consult; anything that will bring further progress or satisfaction.

## References

Series: *Living Confidently with Specific Learning Difficulties (SpLDs)*
Stacey, Ginny, 2019, *Finding Your Voice with Dyslexia and other SpLDs*, Routledge, London
Stacey, Ginny, 2020a, *Organisation and Everyday Life with Dyslexia and other SpLDs*, Routledge, London
Stacey, Ginny, 2020b, *Development of Dyslexia and other SpLDs*, Routledge, London
Stacey, Ginny, 2021, *Gaining Knowledge and Skills with Dyslexia and other SpLDs*, Routledge, London

## Website information

Series website:  www.routledge.com/cw/stacey

Resources Appendix 1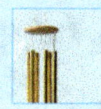

# Appendix 2: Individual, Personal Profile of Dyslexia/ SpLD and Regime for Managing Dyslexia/ SpLD

**Contents**

Templates on the website ... 247
1  Living confidently ... 248
    1.1  Individual, personal profile of dyslexia/ SpLD ... 248
    1.2  Regime for managing dyslexia/ SpLD ... 248
    1.3  Testing and developing your profile and regime ... 249
    1.4  Mental energy to manage dyslexia/ SpLD ... 249
2  Building up insights ... 250
3  The tool box for living confidently ... 253
4  Updating the tool box ... 256
5  Negotiating accommodation ... 258
References and website information ... 261

> **Series:** *Living Confidently with Specific Learning Difficulties (SpLDs)*
>
> Book 1: *Finding Your Voice with Dyslexia and other SpLDs*
> Book 2: *Organisation and Everyday Life with Dyslexia and other SpLDs*
> Book 3: *Gaining Knowledge and Skills with Dyslexia and other SpLDs*
> Book 4: *Development of Dyslexia and other SpLDs*

Stacey (2019, 2020a, 2021, 2020b)

## Templates on the website

TEMPLATES

| | |
|---|---|
| A3 | BOOK MARK – PROFILE AND TECHNIQUES |
| | |
| B1 | COLLECTING IDEAS THAT RELATE TO YOU |
| B2 | KNOW YOUR OWN MIND |
| B7 | RECORDING TEMPLATE - 3 (5 UNEQUAL COLUMNS) |
| B8 | RECORDING TEMPLATE - 4 (5 EQUAL COLUMNS) |
| | |
| C1 | INDIVIDUAL, PERSONAL PROFILE OF DYSLEXIA/ SPLD (SPATIAL) |
| C2 | EXAMPLE INDIVIDUAL, PERSONAL PROFILE OF DYSLEXIA/ SPLD (SPATIAL) |
| C3 | INDIVIDUAL, PERSONAL PROFILE OF DYSLEXIA/ SPLD (LINEAR) |
| C4 | 2 EXAMPLES OF AN INDIVIDUAL, PERSONAL PROFILE OF DYSLEXIA/ SPLD (LINEAR) |
| | |
| D1 | MANAGING DYSLEXIA/ SPLD (MIND MAP) |
| D2 | MANAGING DYSLEXIA/ SPLD (LINEAR) |
| D3 | REGIME FOR MANAGING DYSLEXIA/ SPLD (SPATIAL) |
| D4 | REGIME FOR MANAGING DYSLEXIA/ SPLD (LINEAR) |
| D5 | EXPERIENCES FOR MANAGING DYSLEXIA/ SPLD (LINEAR EXAMPLE) |
| | |
| E2 | TABLE OF THINKING PREFERENCES (SPATIAL) |
| E3 | EXAMPLE: TABLE OF THINKING PREFERENCES (SPATIAL) |
| E4 | THINKING PREFERENCES (SPATIAL) |
| E5 | THINKING PREFERENCES (LINEAR) |

# Appendix 2   Profile and Regime

## 1   Living confidently

The aim of the whole series LIVING CONFIDENTLY WITH SPECIFIC LEARNING DIFFICULTIES (SPLD) is that, as a dyslexic/ SpLD person, you have ownership of your dyslexia/ SpLD; therefore this appendix is addressed to you and is essentially the same throughout the series, with the addition of the sub-section in this section.  These sub-sections are summaries of key elements about the PROFILE and REGIME covered in *Finding Your Voice with Dyslexia and other SpLDs* (Stacey, 2019).

Stacey (2019)

### 1.1   Individual, personal profile of dyslexia/ SpLD

A profile is a summary of information.  This profile is about your dyslexia/ SpLD.  It contains:

| | |
|---|---|
| how you think best | THINKING PREFERENCES |
| how you pause well | THINKING CLEARLY |
| the pitfalls of your dyslexia/ SpLD | PITFALLS |
| any accommodations you need | ACCOMMODATION |

THINKING PREFERENCES: p 270

THINKING CLEARLY: p 264

PITFALLS: p 69

ACCOMMODATION: p 69

Thinking well and pausing at the right times allow you to deal with any pitfalls that come your way.  When you know what they are likely to be, you can recognise your pitfalls in advance.  You are in a better position to arrange necessary accommodations when you are clear about your pitfalls and the strategies you have tried to use in order to deal with them.

### 1.2   Regime for managing dyslexia/ SpLD

Your regime is about the day to day management of dyslexia/ SpLD in the light of life's unpredictable moments.  It has 3 elements in common with your profile; it has goals instead of accommodations.

In day-to-day life, you carry on assuming all's OK, then a pitfall looms. You may be able to notice it before it has become a problem.  You may be into a dyslexic/ SpLD way of functioning before you notice what is happening to you.  Either way, having a regime allows you options for managing the situation.

Noticing the pitfall as early as possible is the first step.  The second is pausing, being able to step back and take a moment to reflect on

## Profile and Regime   Appendix 2

what is happening.  Your thinking preferences are valuable tools for rescuing you.  If you are not clear as to what you are aiming to achieve (*Your Goal*), you are likely to fall back into the pitfall even after pausing well and deciding to use your best thinking.

*Know Your Goal:* p 275

### 1.3   Testing and developing your profile and regime

You test your profile and regime by using them and assessing how well each section works for you.  Your profile and regime are unlikely to be fixed for all time; they will develop as you use them and as you gain more insights into the way your mind best works.

### 1.4   Mental energy to manage dyslexia/ SpLD

(Copied from *Finding Your Voice with Dyslexia and other SpLDs*, Stacey 2019)

Stacey (2019)

---

### Insight:  Mental energy to manage dyslexia/ SpLD

By using thinking preferences and various strategies, it is possible to function at a level that is comparable to your best intelligence.

If you are a dyslexic person that means using language at a level that is much better than the dyslexic language, see *Figure Appendix 2.1*.

However, the dyslexia/ SpLD doesn't get removed.  It is still there in the mind and you can be triggered into using those thought processes.

Mental energy often has to be reserved to monitor progress in order to stay out of your dyslexic/ SpLD processing.

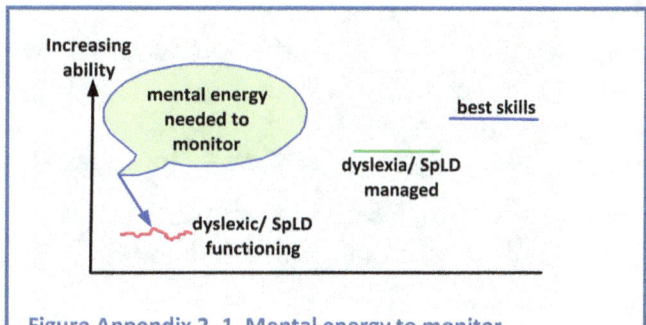

Figure Appendix 2. 1  Mental energy to monitor

# Appendix 2   Profile and Regime

## 2   Building up insights

The table shows the overlap between the elements of your individual profile and your regime for managing dyslexia/ SpLD.  It also shows the key way for developing and testing each element.

| Element | Individual, personal profile | Regime for managing dyslexia/ SpLD | For developing and testing processes | Covered in Book (or see Appendix 3 for summaries) | Page |
|---|---|---|---|---|---|
| Thinking preferences | 1 | 3 | recall & check | 1 | 268 |
| Pausing | 2 | 2 | practise & reflect | 1 | 264 |
| Pitfalls | 3 | 1 | observe & reflect | 2 & 4 partly in 1 | 69 277 |
| Accommodation | 4 |  | negotiate, use and reflect | 2, 3 & 4 partly in 1 | 69 277 |
| Goals |  | 4 | via applications | 3 partly in 1 | 275 |

The aim is to build up the insights into a TOOL BOX FOR LIVING CONFIDENTLY.  The tool box will develop and expand over time, see UPDATING THE TOOL BOX.

If you keep your records in a way that you can easily review, you will build on your insights in an effective way.  You will be able to use them and discuss them with others.

### B1 - COLLECTING IDEAS THAT RELATE TO YOU - TEMPLATE

Collect the stories, insights, examples, etc. from the book that relate to you.  Collect what happens when you try any of the exercises.

To fill in the 4th column, write 'profile' or 'regime/ managing'.
Use the elements in the table above to fill in the 5th column.
It is then easy to scan these two columns to bring your insights together.

TOOL BOX FOR LIVING CONFIDENTLY: p 253

UPDATING THE TOOL BOX: p 256

TEMPLATES

## Profile and Regime   Appendix 2

Look at the layout for the summary templates:

    D3 - REGIME FOR MANAGING DYSLEXIA/ SpLD (SPATIAL)
    C1 - INDIVIDUAL, PERSONAL PROFILE OF DYSLEXIA/ SpLD (SPATIAL)

    E2 - TABLE OF THINKING PREFERENCES

    D5 - REGIME FOR MANAGING DYSLEXIA/ SpLD (LINEAR EXAMPLE)
    C3 - INDIVIDUAL, PERSONAL PROFILE OF DYSLEXIA/ SpLD (LINEAR)

TEMPLATES

Which do you think will suit you best?

Which do you think would be worth trying out?

You can use them as soon as you start gathering insights. They may well change as further insights are gained.

**Observe and reflect**

Templates that can be used for gathering insights are:

    B2 - KNOW YOUR OWN MIND
    B7, B8 - RECORDING TEMPLATES - 3 OR - 4
    D1 - MANAGING DYSLEXIA/ SpLD (MIND MAP)
    D2 - MANAGING DYSLEXIA/ SpLD (LINEAR)

TEMPLATES

Suggestions for headings for the RECORDING TEMPLATES - 3 OR - 4 are:

A = date      B = situation      C = what I was trying to do

D = details, including strategies being used

E = notes on success or otherwise.

Column E could either be narrow for a single word that rated your success or it could be wider for more detailed notes. Choose the template depending on whether you want column E to be narrow or wide.

E4, E5 - THINKING PREFERENCES, one spatial, one linear, are two useful TEMPLATES for recording brief notes as you build your profile.

TEMPLATES

# Appendix 2   Profile and Regime

**Examples from a log book**

A log book is another way of recording incidents and reflections. You can pull the insights together by using key words in columns down the edges of the pages. You gradually have confidence in your insights because you have experience and evidence, which you are recording in a systematic way.

These notes were taken over several weeks while observing behaviour patterns:

MARGIN NOTE:
I usually shorten my headings to fit the columns
e.g. Th-Pref for Thinking Preferences

| Date | Details | Other | Pitfall | Th-Pref (Thinking Preference) |
|---|---|---|---|---|
| DD/ MM/ YY | Total absorption in what's current in my mind – nothing rings any bells to warn me that something else needs attention. (Example) Focusing on writing reports before a deadline meant I missed an evening class | | frequent problem | |
| DD/ MM/ YY | Can't remember from top of stairs to bottom that I need to add something to the shopping list. Crossing my fingers at top of stairs will remind me at the bottom that I have to remember something (that's enough to remember what to add). | | poor short-term memory | kinaesthetic |
| DD/ MM/ YY | A friend explained the mechanism of blood circulation and capillary healing; now I know how to look after my ankle injury. I had forgotten the list of instructions. When there is no logic behind information, I forget what I'm told; or I modify half-remembered instructions by trying to make sense of incomplete information. | | poor short-term memory | logic needed |

252

## Profile and Regime   Appendix 2

| Date | Details | Other | Pitfall | Th-Pref (Thinking Preference) |
|---|---|---|---|---|
| DD/ MM/ YY | Total confusion in my paperwork. If it isn't organised and doesn't stay organised, I've had it. I won't remember where any relevant other pieces of information are; I won't remember if it exists. Not having a printer in this room is causing major problems. I can't multi-task when paper is involved. | | reading problem & recall | |
| DD/ MM/ YY | After I've been reading black-on-white intently for a while, my vision has the black print lines across it. Bright images also leave a strong imprint. | eyes: after images | | |

### 3   The tool box for living confidently

If you consistently work through the ideas in this book and build a picture of how you think well, how you take-action well and how you manage your dyslexia/ SpLD well, you will accumulate a body of knowledge and skills. You can summarise what you learn in three templates:

    D3 - REGIME FOR MANAGING DYSLEXIA/ SPLD (SPATIAL)

    C1 - INDIVIDUAL, PERSONAL PROFILE OF DYSLEXIA/ SPLD (SPATIAL)

    E2 - TABLE OF THINKING PREFERENCES

or use the linear alternative templates:

    D4 - REGIME FOR MANAGING DYSLEXIA/ SPLD (LINEAR)

    C3 - INDIVIDUAL, PERSONAL PROFILE OF DYSLEXIA/ SPLD (LINEAR)

If some of the insights are more important than others, add this information to the summaries.

ⓖ p 283: taking-action

TEMPLATES

# Appendix 2   Profile and Regime

Make cross-references to any notes you have about the insights you put on the summaries.  For example, you could have a log book entry which gives a good example of you using your kinaesthetic strength.  You list 'kinaesthetic' in your thinking preferences table with cross-reference '(log book, date)'.

You could also have :

> a collection of stories that reflect your experiences
>
> a log book or other systematic collection of evidence that you can easily access.

What you know about yourself will change and develop over time, which is the same for everyone.  Any summary should be dated so that you know when it was the current one.

Even when nothing is causing you to update your tool box, it is worth reflecting on the whole tool box from time to time, to see whether any element needs to be developed further.

This accumulated knowledge and skills is your tool box for living confidently with your dyslexia/ SpLD.

You can use the *A3 - BOOKMARK – PROFILE AND TECHNIQUES* to record your profile and the techniques that help you.  Then use the bookmark when you are reading to make sure you are doing everything possible to ease your reading.

TEMPLATES

**Examples of insights of some other people are in *TEMPLATES*:**

> *D5 - EXPERIENCES FOR MANAGING DYSLEXIA/ SPLD (LINEAR EXAMPLE)*
>
> *C2 - EXAMPLE: INDIVIDUAL, PERSONAL PROFILE OF DYSLEXIA/ SPLD (SPATIAL)*
>
> *C4 - 2 EXAMPLES OF INDIVIDUAL, PERSONAL PROFILES OF DYSLEXIA/ SPLD (LINEAR)*
>
> *E3 - EXAMPLE: TABLE OF THINKING PREFERENCES (SPATIAL)*

TEMPLATES

It can be useful to see what insights other people have gained.

## Profile and Regime   Appendix 2

**General letter to employers**

It might be possible and useful to have a general letter in your tool box from someone who has given you dyslexia/ SpLD support. These are extracts taken from a single page for a student (PG) with dyslexia. He had decided that he wanted any future employer to know he was dyslexic.

### Example: Extracts from a letter to employers

To Whom it May Concern  (with qualifications of author somewhere)

Re:  PG and dyslexia in the workplace

*Dyslexia*
Short paragraph about dyslexia and giving a reference to a book that shows a positive approach to dyslexia.

*Dyslexia in the Workplace*
Short paragraph about management rather than cure of dyslexia and that suitable environment allows dyslexic people to be as effective as any others.

*PG's choice of career*
PG wants to work in pharmaceutical and medical marketing.  PG has done a biology and chemistry degree at Y University.  He has also discovered that he likes dealing with people and that he has appropriate, interpersonal skills.  He has chosen pharmaceutical and medical marketing as a career because he will be able to use both his degree and his interpersonal skills.

Most of the time in this job, PG does not expect his dyslexia to hinder him.  He may find certain electronic devices extremely useful, such as a voice recorder and an electronic organiser.  The one task he may need to take extra care with is report-writing.  He has found at university that he can deal with coursework assignments providing he leaves adequate time, does not work right up to the deadline and gets someone else to read his work before the final stage.  He will need to use the same strategies for any report-writing at work.

*Conclusion*
A couple of sentences about dyslexics in general having intellectual strengths.
PG should be able to contribute his knowledge and thinking strengths to any employer provided his different ways of working are accommodated so that he can effectively manage his dyslexia.

Appendix 2   Profile and Regime

## 4  Updating the tool box

Any time the tool box seems to be unhelpful:
- look after your confidence
- check you are pausing in ways that help you
- read (re-read) about fluctuations between the *4 Levels of Compensation*.

*4 Levels of Compensation:* p 275

**Observe and reflect**

Use any of the formats that have worked for you in building your tool box to find out what is undermining the management of your dyslexia/ SpLD and to develop any necessary new skills and knowledge.

In particular, the following could be table headings or arms of mind maps:

| | |
|---|---|
| Date, situation | *Insights as to why the strategy didn't work |
| What I want to do | *What was going well |
| Strategy I thought would work | *Insights as to why the strategy worked |
| *What was going wrong | What to try next. |

*In a table, I would combine these headings into one column, 'Details'. It would be wide enough to write quite a bit. I'd have a narrow column beside it which would categorise the details:

| | | |
|---|---|---|
| ✓ | or | OK |
| ✓ ? | | OK/ why? |
| x | | not OK |
| x ? | | not OK/ why? |

Working in this way, you can find new insights about the contents of your tool box. You may simply be adding to it. You may find some of the insights you had were not as robust as you thought they were. You may be replacing them or developing them. You may find the

## Profile and Regime   Appendix 2

source of your decreased management had nothing to do with the dyslexia/ SpLD.  The processes set out here should help you to identify the root of the problem.

**Tip:  Adding new significant insights to the tool box**

Whenever something significant comes to light:
- add it to the summaries
- date it.

Keep the stories that led to the new insight.
Make sure you can connect the summary to the stories.

**Progress report**

Progress reports can be useful.

- They can show you what you have achieved so far; they can demonstrate how those achievements have come about and what skills or capability you have.

- They can state the problems that remain.

- They can make the case for accommodations and continued support.  They can contribute to updating the tool box.

- They should have a declared benefit, especially for you.  The issues addressed need to be pertinent to you.

**Example:  Extracts from a progress report**

Name  XX - Progress report on dyslexia support tuition

This report outlines the progress that XX has made in study skills, and the support she is likely to need to complete her course successfully.

# Appendix 2   Profile and Regime

Five areas relevant to XX have been covered recently:

1) time management

2) organisation

3) reading and note-taking

4) essay-writing

5) exams stress control.

For example:  Reading and note-taking

XX has learnt to read more effectively.  She now scans contents lists and headings to get an overview and to find the sections of immediate relevance; she no longer works her way slowly through every word.  She continues to have difficulty understanding some texts, and benefits from translating them with the help of pictures.  For note-taking, she now uses mind maps.  She still needs support to group notes by topic.  She has developed various personal 'shorthand' symbols and also uses colour very effectively.

[Any significant comments about the other areas.]

General conclusion

XX has made considerable strides towards becoming a confident student, able to use appropriate strategies to overcome the range of difficulties caused by her dyslexia. She has become much more willing to try new approaches.  Her results in a number of modules show that she has the potential to achieve a good degree.

## 5  Negotiating accommodation

It is fairly hard to negotiate accommodation for yourself.  You may need to get someone, your advocate, who has been working with you or who knows you well, to put your case.

These are suggestions as to how to make the case for accommodation.  The request might be in a formal letter or in an email from your advocate.

Ⓖ p 283: accommodation

## Profile and Regime   Appendix 2

The role and expertise of the advocate need to be stated, and the contact they have with you in relation to the case being made. If these details are already known, they could be excluded.

The advocate should:
>Propose the requested accommodation directly and simply.

>Explain the situation that prompts the request. Include any information about dyslexia/ SpLD that may be relevant.

>Give any comparisons with the experiences of other people (if possible and useful).

>Explain any solutions that you have tried in order to deal with the situation and why nothing has worked.

>Give evidence of your capabilities (if not known to the person who would agree to the accommodation).

>Re-state the request, possibly in greater detail.

>End as fits the document being written.

---

### Example request for accommodation

Situation:  dyslexic mathematician receiving support at university, including:
  notes taken by a fellow student at lectures;
  a university department organising support;
  a support tutor;
  a system of feedback between support tutors and the university department.

It was necessary for the student to attend the lectures in order to be eligible to receive the notes from the note-taker.

# Appendix 2   Profile and Regime

**Email request: with copy going to subject tutor**
Dear [name of person, or person's job title],

Can XX opt out of lectures and still receive the notes from the note-taker?

I had email contact with XX before the beginning of term and then didn't hear from him. Last week I contacted him, asking whether the silence meant everything was OK or whether he was drowning. It was the latter.

He came to see me this morning. Last week he got so demoralised that he was considering giving up the course.

He has 9 lectures a week and is getting nothing from them. He has compared experiences with a couple of other students. One doesn't understand the lectures either, but she gets enough so that she is able to use the relevant sections to help her complete the problem sheets. The other finds that in the end everything falls into place, and that the maths doesn't all have to make sense immediately.

XX doesn't work like this; as I mentioned in the feedback sheet last term, he needs to understand everything as he goes, to build up the whole subject, and he cannot make progress when there are gaps in his knowledge. He has tried to use the on-line handouts before lectures so that he has some framework to listen with, but the lecturers don't follow the handouts and XX can't work out quickly enough how the lecture relates to the printed pages. Also, the handouts are very wordy so trying to understand them takes XX a long time. He records the lectures and finds that a bit useful. At the moment XX is spending 9 hours at lectures without understanding them, and is getting nowhere.

On Sunday he decided to go back to his preferred way of working and he solidly worked through all the maths relating to his problem sheets, making sure he understands everything. He managed to get the problem sheets done, albeit one was late.

# Profile and Regime   Appendix 2

> He used the notes made by the note-taker. They are bullet points, succinct and clear. Just occasionally he has had to find extra information from the on-line lecture handouts. They are a very good resource for him.
>
> We have worked on trying to find a solution to the problem of the lectures, but I am not very hopeful within the current situation; the lectures are really 9 hours that take time and destroy his motivation and morale.
>
> Can XX receive the lecture notes if he doesn't go to the lectures? Is an understanding of the way he needs to work and of the problems he is having with the lectures sufficient evidence? Can receiving the notes without going to the lectures be accepted as suitable accommodation for his dyslexia?
> Best wishes
> Support Tutor

**Result of this request**

XX was allowed to have the notes from the official note-taker even though he didn't go to the lectures. He had a conversation with the subject tutor, which resulted in a radical change to the way he worked on his course. He finished his degree.

## References

Stacey, Ginny, 2019, *Finding Your Voice with Dyslexia and other SpLDs*, Routledge, London

Stacey, Ginny, 2020a, *Organisation and Everyday Life with Dyslexia and other SpLDs*, Routledge, London

Stacey, Ginny, 2020b, *Development of Dyslexia and other SpLDs*, Routledge, London

Stacey, Ginny, 2021, *Gaining Knowledge and Skills with Dyslexia and other SpLDs*, Routledge, London

## Website information

Series website: www.routledge.com/cw/Stacey

# Appendix 3: Key Concepts

## Contents

Templates on the website ... 264
Context ... 264

1 Thinking clearly (pausing) ... 264
   1.1 Breathing    265
   1.2 Relaxation    266
2 Using the mind well ... 267
   2.1 Mind set    267
   2.2 Chunking    267
   2.3 Recall and check    268
   2.4 Memory consolidation    268
   2.5 Concentration    268
   2.6 Metacognition    268
   2.7 Objective observation    268
   2.8 Reflection    269
   2.9 Prioritising    269
   2.10 A model of learning    269
3 Thinking preferences ... 270
   3.1 The senses: visual, verbal and kinaesthetic    270
   3.2 Rationale or framework    271
   3.3 Holistic vs. linear    271
   3.4 Motivation    271
      3.4.1 Myers-Briggs Personality Type    272
      3.4.2 Multiple Intelligences    272
   3.5 'Other'    273

4 Useful approaches ... 273
   4.1 Materials and methods    273
   4.2 Model for developing organisation    274
   4.3 Comprehension    274
   4.4 Key words    274
   4.5 Know your goal    275
   4.6 Planning    275

5 Aspects of dyslexia/ SpLD ... 276
   5.1 Learned confusion    276
   5.2 Oldest memory trace    276
   5.3 Attention to learning    276
   5.4 Average level of language skills a disadvantage    276
   5.5 4 levels of compensation    276
   5.6 Pitfalls    277
   5.7 Accommodation    277
   5.8 Degrees of severity    278
   5.9 Stress    278
   5.10 Benefits of recognising the problems    278

References and website information ... 278

**Series:**
***Living Confidently with Specific Learning Difficulties (SpLDs)***

Book 1  *Finding Your Voice with Dyslexia and other SpLDs* (Stacey 2019)

Book 2 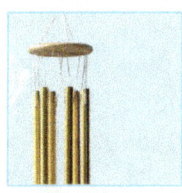 *Organisation and Everyday Life with Dyslexia and other SpLDs* (Stacey 2020a)

Book 3  *Gaining Knowledge and Skills with Dyslexia and other SpLDs* (Stacey 2021)

Book 4  *Development of Dyslexia and other SpLDs* (Stacey 2020b)

**Useful template on the website:**

B1  COLLECTING IDEAS THAT RELATE TO YOU

# Appendix 3   Key Concepts

## Templates on the website

B1   COLLECTING IDEAS THAT RELATE TO YOU
E1   LIST OF OPTIONS FOR THINKING PREFERENCES

## Context

The books in this series are written to be used individually, but people's lives can't be separated quite so neatly. In any situation, you may need information from more than one book.

*THINKING PREFERENCES are highlighted in orange in this appendix.*

This appendix has summaries of many of the skills and knowledge that I cover when going over all that is useful in managing dyslexia/ SpLD. It has been included to allow the books to be used individually.

The book that covers each key concept is indicated by the icons and the coloured lines in the CONTENTS, and the coloured lines on the left hand side of the text.

## 1   Thinking clearly (pausing)

Pausing is the second element in both your INDIVIDUAL, PERSONAL PROFILE OF DYSLEXIA/ SPLD and your REGIME FOR MANAGING DYSLEXIA/ SPLD. *Finding Your Voice with Dyslexia and other SpLDs* (Stacey, 2019) discusses the benefits of thinking clearly and gives you several different methods for doing so.

INDIVIDUAL, PERSONAL PROFILE OF DYSLEXIA/ SPLD: p 248

REGIME FOR MANAGING DYSLEXIA/ SPLD: p 248

Stacey (2019)

# Key Concepts   Appendix 3

*Thinking Clearly* in *Finding Your Voice with Dyslexia and other SpLDs* also discusses confidence and self-esteem.  Maintaining good levels in these two states of being is important.

You need to practise some of the methods for pausing in order to experience the benefits.  As you work with the ideas in this series of books, you will be able to reflect on what is happening for you.  You can add your insights to your PROFILE and REGIME.

This section repeats 2 of the exercises from *Finding Your Voice with Dyslexia and other SpLDs*.

## 1.1   Breathing

If you switch on good breathing, you switch off panic, anxiety and many other unhelpful emotional states.  Focusing on your breathing allows you mental space to stop and step back from the immediate situation.

### Tip: CAUTION

If you feel dizzy, get up and walk about, or hold your breath for a count of 10.  Dizziness, from poor breathing, is caused by too much oxygen and you need to use it up by walking about or to retain $CO_2$ by holding your breath awhile.

# Appendix 3   Key Concepts

If you carry a lot of tension in your body, you may find it more useful to work through the relaxation *Exercise: Physical Relaxation* before attempting the following exercise.

*Exercise: Physical Relaxation*: p 267

### Exercise: Breathing

First, see the *Tip: CAUTION* above.

During the exercise, as you breathe in you feel the sensations in different parts of your body; as you breathe out you let go of the sensations. You can imagine the out-breath flowing easily into each part of the body.

Sit comfortably and close your eyes.
    Breathe naturally while doing the exercise.
As you breathe in[1],
  feel the sensations in your:

| | |
|---|---|
| face | and let go |
| neck and shoulders | and let go |
| arms and chest | and let go |
| stomach | and let go |
| buttocks and legs | and let go |
| whole body | and let it relax further |

Repeat the cycle several times.

## 1.2   Relaxation

Being able to deliberately stop and relax is another way to give yourself the opportunity to pause well. Relaxation, however you do it, allows you to focus on the here and now and to step back from any situation that requires you to manage your dyslexia/ SpLD.

---

[1] When I lead this exercise, I usually say "As you breathe in" just once.
I say "feel the sensations in your (*name the part of the body*)" for at least the first cycle.
When it feels right, I just say the part of the body and "and let go".

## Key Concepts   Appendix 3

**Exercise:  Physical relaxation**

Sit comfortably and close your eyes.

| Tighten the muscles | of your face | and let go |
| --- | --- | --- |
| " | of your neck and shoulders | " |
| " | of your arms, clench your hands | " |
| " | of your chest | " |
| " | of your stomach | " |
| " | of your buttocks and legs | " |

Tighten your whole body and let go.

Repeat this cycle several times.

## 2   Using the mind well

*Using the Mind Well* is a chapter in *Finding Your Voice with Dyslexia and other SpLDs* (Stacey, 2019) which discusses many techniques and skills for thinking.  A selection of the techniques is summarised here.

Stacey (2019)

### 2.1   Mind set

If your mind is expecting a particular subject, it is able to handle relevant information more effectively.
Take about 5 minutes to switch your brain onto the subject you are about to deal with.  Recall to mind what you already know or what your most pressing questions are.

### 2.2   Chunking

Working-memory stores information more effectively when it is linked together in some way that makes sense to you.  The packages of linked information are known as 'chunks'.
Deliberately notice the links between pieces of information, or create your own links if necessary, or if you prefer.  The process of making links is known as 'chunking'.

ⓖ p 283: chunking, working memory

267

# Appendix 3   Key Concepts

## 2.3   Recall and check

You strengthen your memory of information, knowledge or skills by recalling what you know and then checking against a reliable source. Re-reading material is not nearly as effective.

## 2.4   Memory consolidation

Your memories of knowledge are made much more permanent by having a pattern of repeated recall and check.  You start by recalling your knowledge the next day, then after a week, then after a month, then after 6 months.

Done efficiently, memory consolidation is an extremely effective strategy.

The same memory consolidation is required for memories of skills. 'Little and often' is a better time scale for skills.

## 2.5   Concentration

Concentration is often a problem for dyslexic/ SpLD people.  As you observe the way you do things more precisely, you should look out for those places, times and conditions when you can concentrate easily. Gradually build up your knowledge of the things that help you and see how you can use them when you find concentration difficult.

## 2.6   Metacognition

Metacognition is the awareness of the fact that you are doing or thinking something; it is not awareness of how or why.  Just by noticing what is happening as you manage your dyslexia/ SpLD you will be developing the skill of metacognition.  Be positive about the things you notice: enjoy those things you do well; find ways that enable you to be positive about anything you don't do so well.

## 2.7   Objective observation

Ⓖ p 283: objective

Observation is most effective when it is objective.  If you keep factual records and reduce any emotional aspect to a minimum, the way forward with anything you want to change will be clearer.

## Key Concepts   Appendix 3

### 2.8   Reflection

Once you have collected some observations on a common theme, you can look at them all together and see what sense to make of the whole group together.  This is the skill of reflection, which is helpful in making decisions.

### 2.9   Prioritising

*PRIORITISING* is also a skill for using the mind well.  It is a section in *APPENDIX 1*.

*PRIORITISING:* p 256

### 2.10   A model of learning

There are various stages in learning when you need to pay attention to how you are processing information, these are:

Input: any time new information is given.

Immediate use: very shortly after input.

Feedback loop: when what is being learnt is checked against what is intended to be learnt.

Recall: information is brought back from memory some time after input.

Direct use: information and skills are used exactly as they were given.

Developed use: knowledge and skills are modified in some way.

Long-term memory: knowledge and skills are established in long-term memory, and can be recalled.

Understanding:  an appreciation of significant concepts has taken place.

You might use different ways of thinking:
- for each stage of a task
- for different tasks
- at different times for any particular task.

You need to experiment to find out what works for you.  You will often have to be quite determined about what's right for you, and not let others persuade you to adopt ways that you know don't suit you so well.

# Appendix 3  Key Concepts

## 3  Thinking preferences

THINKING PREFERENCES are part of both the PROFILE and REGIME (Stacey, 2019). They are often key to a dyslexic/ SpLD person being able to function well.  Often in this series there is a section on THINKING PREFERENCES.

It is unusual for people to pay attention to how they think, so the usual – orthodox – approach is to ignore how anyone is thinking. These thinking preferences can be seen as unorthodox simply because they are outside the orthodox approach.

The TEMPLATE: E1 - LIST OF OPTIONS FOR THINKING PREFERENCES has suggestions for using the different preferences.

One way to find out about your THINKING PREFERENCES is to use RECALL AND CHECK, together with MEMORY CONSOLIDATION; then to reflect on your ways of thinking.

Make sure you know what your preferences are and that you have the confidence to use them.

Attention is often given to visual and verbal aspects of communication and education.  The same attention should be given to the kinaesthetic sense and to the RATIONALE OR FRAMEWORK.  If the kinaesthetic sense and the need for a framework are part of your thinking preferences, do find ways to make sure these needs are met.

### 3.1  The senses: visual, verbal and kinaesthetic

(taken from the GLOSSARY, , p 283)
The five physical senses are vision, hearing, taste, smell and kinaesthetic which is made up of touch, position and movement.  The use of taste and smell to help use information is not covered in this series, although they are important for some people.

Words used in this series for acquiring and applying knowledge and skills through the different senses are:

| Sense | Acquiring | Applying |
|---|---|---|
| Visual | Reading | Writing |
| Oral/ aural/ verbal | Listening | Speaking |
| Kinaesthetic | Doing | Taking-action |

---

Stacey (2019)

INDIVIDUAL, PERSONAL PROFILE OF DYSLEXIA/ SpLD: p 248

REGIME FOR MANAGING DYSLEXIA/ SpLD: p 248

TEMPLATES

RECALL AND CHECK: p 268

MEMORY CONSOLIDATION: p 268

RATIONALE OR FRAMEWORK: p 271

G p 283:
kinaesthetic sense, rationale, framework

See INDEX for examples in this book.

G p 283:
taking-action

# Key Concepts   Appendix 3

'Kinaesthetic' is used as an umbrella term for the physical senses, by comparison with the visual sense or the verbal senses, aural or oral. The term also includes experiences that are primarily remembered through a connection with the physical part of the experience.

## 3.2   Rationale or framework

Some dyslexic/ SpLD people do not keep hold of information or understanding if they don't know what the overall rationale or framework is.  Their minds don't retain the seemingly random information long enough for the framework to emerge; it has to be given in advance.

ⓖ p 283: rationale, framework

## 3.3   Holistic vs. linear

'Holistic thinking is happening when a large area of a topic is held in the mind and processed simultaneously.  An example is when you look at a scene in front of you, you see that scene as a whole.  This type of thinking doesn't involve words, but you are definitely thinking.' (Stacey, 2019)

(Stacey, 2019)

'Linear thinking involves analysing and breaking topics into their component parts.  Linear thinking is thought to be localised to definite areas for specific tasks, whereas holistic thinking is diffused over larger areas.' (Stacey, 2019)

## 3.4   Motivation

Two schemes for looking at individual differences between people are used in *Finding Your Voice with Dyslexia and other SpLDs* (Stacey, 2019):

    Myers-Briggs Personality Type

    Multiple Intelligences.

In the context of this appendix, the most interesting characteristics from both schemes are the motivations that people have, and which some dyslexic/ SpLD people can use to help themselves think well.

Stacey (2019)

271

# Appendix 3   Key Concepts

## 3.4.1   Myers-Briggs Personality Type (MBPT)

The Myers-Briggs scheme is based on 4 mental functions and 4 attitudes.  The scheme characterises people as:

| 4 mental functions: | 4 attitudes: |
|---|---|
| sensing | extroverted |
| intuiting | introverted |
| thinking | perceiving |
| feeling | judging (deciding). |

The motivations of the different types come from their approach to the world around them.

*Margin Note:*
Judging is used in the sense of being able to make decisions, not in judging right or wrong.

*Mental functions*

- **Sensing** people are practical, pay attention to the here-and-now, like practical skills and learning with their hands.
- **Intuiting** people focus on concepts, ideas and plans.
- **Thinking** people tend to be logical, to like structures and organisation.
- **Feeling** people engage with people dynamics and feelings.

*Attitudes*

- **Extroverted** people sort out their ideas with the people and environment around them.
- **Introverted** people sort out most of their ideas on their own, before engaging with anyone else.
- **Perceiving** people like to carry on gathering information.
- **Judging** people like to come to a decision.

## 3.4.2   Multiple Intelligences (MI)

The Multiple Intelligences scheme includes 8 different, independent intelligences.  Most of the intelligences have overlap with the Myers-Briggs system, as far as motivation is concerned, so I don't use them.  However there is one intelligence that is distinct and worth noting.

The **Naturalist Intelligence** involves accurate observation of the world around.  People skilled with this intelligence are able to see parallels between topics or within a group of objects.  They are able to classify

# Key Concepts   Appendix 3

ideas or objects and they instinctively sort information into categories.

## 3.5  'Other'

The list of thinking preferences has grown as I have worked with dyslexic/ SpLD people and tried to make sense of what happens to or for them.  There was no point in trying to make them fit already known patterns, so I have always worked with a category titled 'Other'.

'Other' is a holding category that allows you to keep hold of experiences that don't fit any category you already know.

## 4   Useful approaches

You will be managing your dyslexia/ SpLD during everyday events and while you tackle tasks.  *Organisation and Everyday Life with Dyslexia and other SpLDs* and *Gaining Knowledge and Skills with Dyslexia and other SpLDs* deal with the practical application of using your PROFILE and REGIME.  The approaches summarised here are those that help you make a good start with most tasks.

Stacey (2020a, 2021)

### 4.1  Materials and methods

For many situations or tasks, you will want to collect information together.  You should find out your best way of doing it.  The options depend on how you think best.

Materials include: paper, recording device, computer; using colour; using pen or pencil with a suitable grip.  You need to think how you manage your materials, e.g. being able to spread out can make a significant difference.
Methods include: making lists (**linear** thinkers); mind maps (**holistic** thinkers); doing for yourself (**kinaesthetic** learners); bouncing ideas off other people (Myers-Briggs **feeling**, **extroverted** people).

When something is working well for you, notice what you are using and how you are doing it.

MATERIALS AND METHODS: p 56

# Appendix 3   Key Concepts

## 4.2   Model for developing organisation

The model puts forward 5 steps that need attention in organisation:

| Step 1 | gather strengths |
| Step 2 | assess hazards |
| Step 3 | describe what needs organising |
| Step 4 | recognise insuperable obstacles |
| Step 5 | develop constructive ways forward. |

By changing the text at step 3, this model can be adapted to work with different situations or tasks when no organisation is required.

As you work with the tasks and situations, record what happens for you.  Have a system so that you can see what is working for you and you can deliberately make the progress you want.

MODEL FOR DEVELOPING ORGANISATION: p 57

Ⓖ p 283: hazard, obstacle

## 4.3   Comprehension

To comprehend something is to have a mental grasp of it.

You need your mind to hold information together and for long enough so that you can understand, comprehend, what it is all about.

All the skills in this appendix will help with comprehension.  Observe how you comprehend anything.  Keep records so that you can reflect on your experience over time.  Explore different approaches until you find the ones that work best for you.

## 4.4   Key words

Key words are the words that hold the essence of
 an idea, a paragraph, a subject ...

Take something that you are very familiar with.  Jot down some words that are most important for describing it.  Cut the number of words down and find the fewest words that you feel comfortable with.  These words should be the keywords of your chosen topic.  Repeat the exercise over time, until you are good at producing a minimum collection of words to hold the essence of a subject.

274

# Key Concepts   Appendix 3

When you can work well with key words, you can use them to give an overview of something or to help you sort out a main theme from minor details.

## 4.5  Know your goal

Knowing your goal is the 4$^{th}$ element of your REGIME FOR MANAGING DYSLEXIA/ SPLD.  Quite often, when you are using MENTAL ENERGY TO MANAGE DYSLEXIA/ SPLD, you can do all the right things:

- observing what is happening
- pausing well
- deciding how to use your thinking preferences

but you still can't get matters under control and you still find yourself struggling in a circle.
Knowing what you want to achieve can help you to see the way out, or the way to resolve the situation.

Key words can help with knowing your goal.  Learning how to hold your goal in a few keywords means it is much easier to stay focused and not get lost in a maze of ideas.

REGIME FOR MANAGING DYSLEXIA/ SPLD: p 248

MENTAL ENERGY TO MANAGE DYSLEXIA/ SPLD: p 249

## 4.6  Planning

Planning is when you consider all the steps necessary to achieve a given outcome.

Almost all dyslexic/ SpLD people need to plan their work in order to minimise problems; for example, dyslexic people often write well when they have a good plan, but without a plan their writing will rarely reflect their ideas.

You need to find the level of detail that yields the result you want.

A big project can be broken down into smaller sections and separate plans constructed to achieve each section.  This process makes the big plan less daunting and allows you to tackle it more readily.

# Appendix 3  Key Concepts

## 5  Aspects of dyslexia/ SpLD

You need to stay confident and positive in order to manage dyslexia/ SpLD. The aspects summarised here help you to know more about the characteristics of dyslexia/ SpLD so you are prepared for the inevitable fluctuations; the full discussions are in *Development of Dyslexia/ SpLD* (Stacey, 2020b).

Stacey (2020b)

### 5.1  Learned confusion

As a dyslexic/ SpLD person develops, certain patterns of confusion tend to become established in your brain, see USEFUL PREFACE CONTEXT. When you are older, you probably learn in better ways but you don't erase the original confused ways; they remain in your brain. They are there for your brain to activate.

USEFUL PREFACE CONTEXT: p 3

### 5.2  Oldest memory trace

When you unexpectedly need to think of something it is often the oldest memory trace that is used, not a later one. For example, you have learnt correct spellings, but when you use the words the older incorrect versions spring to mind.

### 5.3  Attention to learning

Most dyslexic/ SpLD people have to pay attention to all levels of a task; they do not learn subliminally. Reading a large number of books does not teach spelling.

ⓖ p 283: subliminal learning

### 5.4  Average level of language skills a disadvantage

Intelligent students are often first recognised as being dyslexic/ SpLD at college or university, when they can no longer find ways round underlying problems. They have language skills that lift them above the group who are recognised as being in need of extra help at school, but those skills are not at the level of overall intelligence and the difference makes its mark in Higher Education.

### 5.5  4 levels of compensation

As you work on managing dyslexia/ SpLD, you gain skills and you become a 'compensated' dyslexic/ SpLD (McLoughlin *et al.*, 2001).

McLoughlin *et al.* (2001)

## Key Concepts   Appendix 3

There are different levels of compensation:

1. 'People at level 1 are not aware of their weaknesses and have developed no strategies to overcome them.
2. 'Those at level 2 are aware of their weaknesses but have not developed strategies to overcome them.
3. 'People at level 3 are aware of their weaknesses and have developed compensatory strategies, but have developed them unconsciously.
4. 'Finally, people at level 4 are aware of their weaknesses and they have consciously developed strategies to overcome them.'

The most important aspect is to realise that you do not remain consistently on any particular level.  Even when you mostly operate as a 'compensated' dyslexic/ SpLD, i.e. on level 4, you may find you have dropped back into one of the less compensated ways of managing.

### 5.6   Pitfalls

Gradually as you learn to manage your dyslexia/ SpLD, you will recognise certain things that often tip you into dyslexic/ SpLD functioning: these things are called pitfalls in the context of these books.

('pitfall, n.4b', OED Online, 2020)

A pitfall is defined as 'a hidden or unsuspected danger, drawback, difficulty or opportunity for error' (OED Online, 2020).

I've divided pitfalls into 'hazards' and 'obstacles'.  I've used the term 'glitch' for those moments when you notice a potential pitfall and deal with it immediately.

Ⓖ p 283: hazard, obstacle, glitch

### 5.7   Accommodation

Accommodations are adaptations put in place to address or reduce the problems caused by dyslexia/ SpLD; sometimes called 'reasonable adjustments' or 'provisions'.

There are certain situations in which a PITFALL of your dyslexia/ SpLD is very likely to be a significant issue, and it is known in advance.  For some of these situations, e.g. exams and tests, accommodations are well established.  Other situations may be specific to your circumstances.

# Appendix 3  Key Concepts

## 5.8  Degrees of severity

Dyslexia/ SpLD is not like short- or long-sightedness: there is no equivalent pair of glasses that you can put on and find that the problems are reliably sorted.  Learning 'coping strategies' gives you ways of dealing with issues, but you will constantly have to be putting effort into doing so.

I argue that 'degrees of severity' is not a useful concept.  The statements usually used are that someone is 'mildly dyslexic/ SpLD' or 'severely dyslexic/ SpLD' as if this describes a static level of being dyslexic/ SpLD.  The lived experience of dyslexia/ SpLD is that how you will be is variable and unpredictable.

It would be more useful to talk in terms of McLoughlin's 4 compensation levels (McLoughlin *et al.*, 2001).  For each person:

> What does level 4 consist of?
>
> How well can the person maintain level 4?
>
> How often does the person get triggered out of level 4?
>
> How much time and effort are required to get back to level 4?

*4 Levels of Compensation*: p 276

McLoughlin *et al.* (2001)

## 5.9  Stress

Stress usually makes the problems of dyslexia/ SpLD worse.  You and those around you need to recognise this.

## 5.10  Benefits of recognising the problems

It is very difficult to do anything about problems that are not being recognised.  When you know what your strengths are, and you realise you can make useful contributions, it is easier to acknowledge the problems and discuss them fruitfully with those around you.

## References

McLoughlin, David, *et al.*, 2001, *Adult Dyslexia: Assessment, Counselling and Training*, Whurr, London, 6th re-print

Series: *Living Confidently with Specific Learning Difficulties (SpLDs)*

Stacey, Ginny, 2019, *Finding Your Voice with Dyslexia and other SpLDs*, Routledge, London

# Key Concepts   Appendix 3

Stacey, Ginny, 2020a, *Organisation and Everyday Life with Dyslexia and other SpLDs*, Routledge, London
Stacey, Ginny, 2020b, *Development of Dyslexia and other SpLDs*, Routledge, London
Stacey, Ginny, 2021, *Gaining Knowledge and Skills with Dyslexia and other SpLDs*, Routledge, London

## Website information

*OED Online*, June 2020, Oxford University Press  Accessed 21 August 2020.
Series website:  www.routledge.com/cw/Stacey

# Glossary

## Contents

1. Table: Symbols ... 280
2. Table: Specific Learning Difficulties (SpLDs) descriptions ... 280
3. Table: Acronyms ... 282
4. Table: Words and phrases, alphabetical list ... 283

References and website information ... 288

## 1 Table: Symbols

| Symbol | Explanation |
|---|---|
| § | Symbol used to denote a section. |
| Ⓖ | Symbol used to indicate an entry in the GLOSSARY. The page number is to the beginning of the appropriate section of the glossary. |
| (companion website @ icon) | The symbol signifies material on the companion website, www.routledge.com/cw/stacey. The section of the website is indicated. |
| text | Thinking preferences are highlighted in orange. |
| Book icon and blue line | Used in Useful Preface to show text that is significantly different from one book to another. |

## 2 Table: Specific Learning Difficulties (SpLDs) descriptions

Dyslexia/ SpLD is used in most of this book because dyslexia is the most researched and recognised form of SpLD and because the dual term keeps the variations in mind.

| SpLD | Definition from DfES Report (2005) |
|---|---|
| Dyslexia | 'Dyslexia is a combination of abilities and difficulties; the difficulties affect the learning process in aspects of literacy and sometimes numeracy. Coping with required reading is generally seen as the biggest challenge at Higher Education level due in part to difficulty |

| SpLD | Definition from DfES Report (2005) |
|---|---|
| | in skimming and scanning written material. A student may also have an inability to express his/her ideas clearly in written form and in a style appropriate to the level of study. Marked and persistent weaknesses may be identified in working memory, speed of processing, sequencing skills, auditory and/or visual perception, spoken language and motor skills. Visuo-spatial skills, creative thinking and intuitive understanding are less likely to be impaired and indeed may be outstanding. Enabling or assistive technology is often found to be very beneficial.' |
| Dyspraxia / Developmental Co-ordination Disorder (DCD) | 'A student with dyspraxia/DCD may have an impairment or immaturity in the organisation of movement, often appearing clumsy. Gross motor skills (related to balance and co-ordination) and fine motor skills (relating to manipulation of objects) are hard to learn and difficult to retain and generalise. Writing is particularly laborious and keyboard skills difficult to acquire. Individuals may have difficulty organising ideas and concepts. Pronunciation may also be affected and people with dyspraxia/DCD may be over/under sensitive to noise, light and touch. They may have poor awareness of body position and misread social cues in addition to those shared characteristics common to many SpLDs.' |
| Dyscalculia | 'Dyscalculia is a learning difficulty involving the most basic aspect of arithmetical skills. The difficulty lies in the reception, comprehension, or production of quantitative and spatial information. Students with dyscalculia may have difficulty in understanding simple number concepts, lack an intuitive grasp of numbers and have problems learning number facts and procedures. These can relate to basic concepts such as telling the time, calculating prices, handling change.' |

# Glossary

| SpLD | Definitions from DfES Report (2005) |
|---|---|
| Attention Deficit Disorder ADD<br><br>AD(H)D indicates ADD with or without hyperactivity | 'Attention Deficit Disorder (ADD) exists with or without hyperactivity. In most cases people with this disorder are often 'off task', have particular difficulty commencing and switching tasks, together with a very short attention span and high levels of distractibility. They may fail to make effective use of the feedback they receive and have weak listening skills. Those with hyperactivity may act impulsively and erratically, have difficulty foreseeing outcomes, fail to plan ahead and be noticeably restless and fidgety. Those without the hyperactive trait tend to daydream excessively, lose track of what they are doing and fail to engage in their studies unless they are highly motivated. The behaviour of people with ADD can be inappropriate and unpredictable; this, together with the characteristics common to many SpLDs, can present a further barrier to learning.' |

## 3 Table: Acronyms

| Acronym | Explanation |
|---|---|
| ADD, ADHD, AD(H)D | Attention Deficit Disorder with or without Hyperactivity |
| DCD | Developmental Co-ordination Disorder |
| DfES | Department for Education and Skills |
| MBPT | Myers-Briggs Personality Type |
| MI | Multiple Intelligences |
| NLP | Neuro-Linguistic Programming |
| OED | Oxford English Dictionary |
| SpLD | Specific Learning Difficulty |
| STM | Short-term memory |

# Glossary

## 4  Table:  Words and phrases, alphabetical list

| Entry | Explanation |
|---|---|
| Accommodation | Accommodation refers to adaptations put in place to address or reduce the problems caused by dyslexia/ SpLD; sometimes called 'reasonable adjustments' or 'provisions'. |
| Autonomy autonomous | Control over your life by self-determination: acting and thinking for yourself; independent; free; self-governing.<br>An autonomous person has autonomy. |
| Brainstorm | Collect all your ideas or thoughts about something; collect them in a concrete way, either on paper or on a white board, etc., straight into a computer or using a recording device; the collection of ideas is then available for further processing.  The initial stages of brainstorming are often not selective; all ideas are captured even if they don't seem very relevant. |
| Chaotic chaos theory | Chaos theory is a field of mathematics. 'Behaviour of a system which is governed by deterministic laws but is so unpredictable as to appear random owing to its extreme sensitivity to initial conditions' ('chaos, n.6' OED Online, 2020). |
| Chunk | A chunk is 'a package of information bound by strong associative links within a chunk, and relatively weak links between chunks' (Baddeley, 2007).  The capacity of working-memory is discussed in terms of chunks that can be stored. |
| Chunking | The process of making strong links between pieces of information so that more can be stored in chunks in working-memory (Baddeley, 2007). |
| Confidence | Assurance arising from reliance on oneself (OED, 1993). |
| Doing<br>See also KINAESTHETIC and SENSES | In this series of books, 'doing' is used to refer to acquiring knowledge and skills using the kinaesthetic sense. |

# Glossary

| Entry | Explanation |
|---|---|
| Framework | 'A structure made of parts joined to form a frame; especially one designed to enclose or support; a frame; a skeleton' ('framework, n.1a' OED Online, 2020). |
| Glitch | 'A sudden short-lived irregularity in behaviour' (glitch, n.1' OED Online, 2020). A glitch is a time when dyslexia/ SpLD has an effect on your behaviour, but you see it immediately and correct it. Any error is short-lived and there is no impact to prolong dyslexic/ SpLD functioning. |
| Goal | The end result of a task or activity. Knowing the goal of anything is often an important element in managing dyslexia/ SpLD. |
| Hazard | A hazard is a danger or a risk which you can take steps to deal with. 'Hazard' is used to describe one category of the pitfalls of dyslexia/ SpLD. |
| Kinaesthetic See also PROPRIOCEPTION and TAKING-ACTION. | Used as an umbrella term for the physical senses, by comparison with the visual sense or the verbal senses, aural or oral. The term also includes experiences that are primarily remembered through a connection with the physical part of the experience. |
| Mind map | To map ideas in an organised, spatial way, with relationships shown by linking lines or branch structures. Sometimes called a spider diagram. |
| Mind set | A process of switching your mind on to the topic you are about to work on: for study, for a meeting, for planning a project, etc. It is the equivalent of warm-up exercises before vigorous exercise.<br><br>(Mindset as one word is something quite different.) |
| Mnemonics | Memorable phrases, words or sounds that help you to remember something. For example: Naughty Elephants Squirt Water gives the directions north, east, south and west round a compass or map; HONC gives the four most common elements in organic chemistry, hydrogen, oxygen, nitrogen and carbon. |
| Neural networks | Neural networks are established when neurons repeatedly fire in set patterns. These set patterns are related to learning. |

# Glossary

| Entry | Explanation |
| --- | --- |
| Neuro-Linguistic Programming (NLP) | NLP is about the mind and how we organise our mental life; about language, how we use it and how it affects us; about repetitive sequences of behaviour and how to act with intention.  Some of the ideas from NLP are used in THINKING CLEARLY (Stacey, 2019).  For further information, see O'Connor and McDermott (1996). |
| Neuron | A basic cell of the nervous system. |
| Neuron firing | A neuron fires a signal along its axon when the conditions in the neuron rise above a certain threshold; the conditions depend on all the many other neurons that input to that neuron. |
| Objective vs. subjective | Objective: existing as an object of consciousness, as opposed to being part of the conscious [person]. (OED, 1993)<br><br>Subjective: of or belonging to the thinking [person]; proceeding from or taking place within the individual's consciousness. |
| Obstacle | An obstacle is something that blocks your way or prevents progress; you have to go round it, or avoid it.  'Obstacle' is used to describe one category of the pitfalls of dyslexia/ SpLD. |
| 'Other' | 'Other' is a useful category.  Whenever I'm sorting something out, for myself or a student, I keep the category 'other' in mind or give it space on the sheet of paper I'm working on.<br><br>I use it for anything that I don't want to forget and that doesn't fit into the categories I already have. |
| Paradigm | 'A conceptual or methodological model underlying the theories and practices of a science or discipline at a particular time; (hence) a generally accepted world view' ('paradigm, n.4' OED Online, 2020). |
| Pitfall | 'A hidden or unsuspected danger, drawback, difficulty or opportunity for error' ('pitfall, n.4b' OED Online, 2020). Used as part of an individual's profile with respect to dyslexia/ SpLD. |

# Glossary

| Entry | Explanation |
|---|---|
| Profile: Individual or personal | '(A representation of) a structured set of characteristics of someone or something. A description of a person, organisation, product, etc.' ('profile, n.II.10' OED Online, 2020).<br><br>The dyslexia/ SpLD profile used in this book is an outline of:<br>1   the thinking preferences<br>2   the dyslexia/ SpLD pitfalls<br>3   strategies for pausing<br>4   accommodations that need to be made.<br>The profile is highly personalised and is the foundation for managing the dyslexia/ SpLD. |
| Proprioception | Part of the kinaesthetic senses. 'The perception of the position and movements of the body, esp. as derived from proprioceptors'. A proprioceptor is 'a sensory receptor which responds to stimulate … from muscle or nerve tissue' ('proprioception , n.' 'propiroceptor, n.' OED Online, 2020). |
| Pruning | Has been proposed as an idea to account for the reduction in synaptic connections that occurs during normal development (Kolb, 1995, p154). |
| Rationale | 1   'A reasoned exposition of principles; an explanation or statement of reasons'<br>2   'The fundamental or underlying reason for or basis of a thing; a justification'<br>('rationale, n.2.1 and 2.2' OED Online, 2020). |
| Regime | 'A way of doing things, esp. one having widespread influence or prevalence' ('regime, n.2a' OED Online, 2020).<br><br>The regime for managing dyslexia/ SpLD profile used in this book includes:<br>1   recognising the pitfalls<br>2   pausing<br>3   using best thinking preferences<br>4   knowing the relevant goal.<br>The regime is highly personalised. |

# Glossary

| Entry | Explanation |
|---|---|
| Schema | An (unconscious) organised mental model of something in terms of which new information can be interpreted or an appropriate response made (OED, 1993). |
| Self-esteem | Esteem: value, worth, favourable opinion (OED, 1993); hence self-esteem is valuing oneself. |
| Senses | The five physical senses are vision, hearing, taste, smell and kinaesthetic, which is made up of touch, position and movement. The use of taste and smell to help use information is not covered in this book, although they are important for some people.<br><br>Words used in this book for acquiring and applying knowledge and skills through the different senses are:<br><br>| Sense | Acquiring | Applying |<br>|---|---|---|<br>| Visual | Reading | Writing |<br>| Oral/ aural | Listening | Speaking |<br>| Kinaesthetic | Doing | Taking-action | |
| Study peripherals | Are the network of systems supporting and enabling anyone to study. |
| Subliminal<br>Subliminal learning | Subliminal: below the level of consciousness.<br>Subliminal learning is learning which happens without conscious effort or attention; it simply happens alongside other learning or through everyday life. |
| Taking-action | Used in this book to mean: 'applying knowledge and skills in a practical way through the kinaesthetic sense'. The hyphen is deliberate.<br><br>See SENSES for the words used for acquiring and applying knowledge and skills via the different senses. |
| Thinking preferences | A major component of dealing with your dyslexia/ SpLD is to know how you think best (Stacey, 2019). |

# Glossary

| Entry | Explanation |
|---|---|
| Working memory | Part of the mind/ brain which has the capacity for complex thought; it has temporary storage and its workings can be monitored and directed by conscious attention. |

## References

Baddeley, Alan, 2007, *Working Memory, Thought, and Action,* Oxford University Press, Oxford

Kolb, Bryan, 1995, *Brain Plasticity and Behaviour,* Lawrence Erlbaum Associates, Mahwah, NJ

OED[1], Brown, Lesley, Ed in Chief, 1993, *The New Shorter Oxford English Dictionary on Historical Principles*, Clarendon Press, Oxford

O'Connor, Joseph and McDermott, Ian, 1996, *Principles of NLP,* Thorsons, London

Stacey, Ginny, 2019, *Finding Your Voice with Dyslexic and other SpLDs,* Routledge, London

## Website information

DfES Report, 2005, https://www.patoss-dyslexia.org/Resources/DSA-Working-Guidelines Accessed 10 June 2020

*OED Online*, June 2020, Oxford University Press. Accessed 21 August 2020.

---

[1] The online OED has been consulted every time, and the meanings are consistent. Sometimes the words used in the hard copy of OED (1993) are clearer, or more to the point in the context of this book; in which case the reference is to the hard copy edition that I have consulted.

# Glossary

# List of Templates on the Website

This table lists the TEMPLATES on the companion WEBSITE  that are recommended in each chapter.

The sections on the WEBSITE are:

A: Aids for Reading

B: Gathering Insights

C: Individual, Personal Profile of Dyslexia/ SpLD

D: Regime for Managing Dyslexia/ SpLD

E: Thinking Preferences

F: Organisation and Problem Solving

There is no significant difference between ✓ and ◊; having 2 symbols just makes tracking easier.

## Website information

Series website: www.routledge.com/cw/stacey

| Name of Template<br>U-P is Useful Preface<br>A1 – A3 are Appendices 1 – 3 | | | ✓<br>U-P | ◊<br>1 | ✓<br>2 | ◊<br>3 | ✓<br>4 | ◊<br>5 | ✓<br>6 | ◊<br>A1 | ✓<br>A2 | ◊<br>A3 |
|---|---|---|---|---|---|---|---|---|---|---|---|---|
| Jotting down as you scan | A | 1 | ✓ | ◊ | ✓ | ◊ | ✓ | ◊ | ✓ | ◊ | | |
| Bookmark – purpose | A | 2 | ✓ | ◊ | | | ✓ | ◊ | ✓ | | | |
| Bookmark – profile & techniques | A | 3 | | ◊ | | | | | | | ✓ | |
| Jotting down as you read, with a few guiding questions | A | 4 | ✓ | | ✓ | ◊ | ✓ | ◊ | ✓ | | | |
| Collecting ideas that interest you | A | 5 | ✓ | | | | | | | | | |
| Collecting ideas that relate to you | B | 1 | | ◊ | ✓ | ◊ | ✓ | ◊ | ✓ | ◊ | ✓ | ◊ |
| Know your own mind | B | 2 | | | | | | | | | ✓ | |
| Compare expectations and reality | B | 3 | | ◊ | ✓ | ◊ | | ◊ | ✓ | ◊ | | |
| Action, results, next step | B | 4 | ◊ | | | | | | ✓ | ◊ | | |
| Recording template - 1<br>(4$^{th}$ column narrower for coding) | B | 5 | | | | | | | | ◊ | | |
| Recording template - 2<br>(4 equal columns) | B | 6 | | | | | | | | ◊ | | |
| Recording template - 3<br>(5$^{th}$ column narrower for coding) | B | 7 | | | | | ✓ | | | ◊ | ✓ | |
| Recording template - 4<br>(5 equal columns) | B | 8 | | ◊ | | ◊ | ✓ | | | ◊ | ✓ | |
| A calendar month for prioritising – 5 weeks | B | 9 | | | | | | | | ◊ | | |
| Questions to ask oneself to help observation | B | 10 | | | | | | | | ◊ | | |
| Monitoring progress | B | 11 | | ◊ | | | | | | ◊ | | |

# List of Templates

| Name of Template<br>A2 – A3 are Appendices 2 and 3 | | | ✓<br>A2 | ◊<br>A3 |
|---|---|---|---|---|
| Individual, personal profile of dyslexia/ SpLD (spatial) | C | 1 | ✓ | |
| Example individual, personal profile of dyslexia/ SpLD (spatial) | C | 2 | ✓ | |
| Individual, personal profile of dyslexia/ SpLD (linear) | C | 3 | ✓ | |
| 2 Examples of an Individual, personal profile of dyslexia/ SpLD (linear) | C | 4 | ✓ | |
| Managing dyslexia/ SpLD (mind map) | D | 1 | ✓ | |
| Managing dyslexia/ SpLD (linear) | D | 2 | ✓ | |
| Regime for managing dyslexia /SpLD (spatial) | D | 3 | ✓ | |
| Regime for managing dyslexia /SpLD (linear) | D | 4 | ✓ | |
| Experiences for managing dyslexia/SpLD (linear example) | D | 5 | ✓ | |
| List of options for thinking preference | E | 1 | | ◊ |
| Table of thinking preferences (spatial) | E | 2 | ✓ | |
| Example: Table of thinking preferences (spatial) | E | 3 | ✓ | |
| Thinking preferences (spatial) | E | 4 | ✓ | |
| Thinking preferences (linear) | E | 5 | ✓ | |

# List of Templates

| Name of Template<br>U-P is Useful Preface | | | ✓<br>U-P | ◊<br>1 | ✓<br>2 | ◊<br>3 | ✓<br>4 | ◊<br>5 | ✓<br>6 |
|---|---|---|---|---|---|---|---|---|---|
| Developing organisation - mind map | F | 1 | | ◊ | | | | ◊ | |
| Developing organisation - spatial | F | 2 | | ◊ | | | | ◊ | |
| Developing organisation - linear | F | 3 | | ◊ | | | | ◊ | |
| Problem solving - mind map | F | 4 | | | ✓ | | | | |
| Problem solving - spatial | F | 5 | | | ✓ | | | | |
| Problem solving - linear | F | 6 | | | ✓ | | | | |
| Root cause of a problem - mind map | F | 7 | | ◊ | | | | | |
| Root cause of a problem - spatial | F | 8 | | ◊ | | | | | |
| Root cause of a problem - linear | F | 9 | | ◊ | | | | | |
| Understanding time or place problems | F | 10 | | | ✓ | ◊ | | | |
| Exploring time | F | 11 | | | ✓ | | | | |
| Week with hours | F | 12 | | | ✓ | | | | |
| Calendar week – 5 weeks | F | 13 | | | ✓ | | | | |
| Half a year – 27 weeks - 2021<br>pdf 2 pages for 2021 | F | 14 | | | ✓ | | | ◊ | |
| Half a year – 27 weeks - 2022<br>pdf 2 pages for 2022 | F | 15 | | | ✓ | | | ◊ | |
| Half a year – 27 weeks -<br>pdf no dates | F | 16 | | | ✓ | | | ◊ | |
| Half a year – 27 weeks -<br>Excel spread sheet | F | 17 | | | ✓ | | | ◊ | |
| Half a year – 27 weeks -<br>Open Source spreadsheet | F | 18 | | | ✓ | | | ◊ | |

293

# Index

*in front of an entry marks a word or phrase that is in the GLOSSARY, ⓖ, p 283

The following may be useful INDEX entries:
(sub-entries are shown in brackets)

| *Reason* | *Entries* | |
|---|---|---|
| to engage with the book | reading<br>scanning | exercises (reading style,<br>         initial purpose for reading) |
| to organise | organisation, model for materials and methods<br>new | paperwork<br>questions, useful: examples |
| to think well | mind (prime your)<br>mental techniques | techniques |
| to understand the impact of SpLD | everyday life organisation<br>employment | study peripherals |
| to understand SpLD issues | SpLD experience<br>new<br>pitfalls | time<br>space, place and direction |
| to manage SpLD | SpLD, managing | SpLD, managing (working with the chapter) |

**Tip: To find a word in the text**

If the word you are looking for doesn't show quickly, try running a ruler or envelope or other straight edge down the page. Doing this makes your eyes look at each line and you are more likely to find the word.

Occasionally, the entry refers to the context and not a specific word; so sometimes you need to read the text.

*accommodation 45, 69, 277
    employment 212-213, 214-217, 256
    evidence and negotiation 250,
        257-261
    identifying 234
    profile of SpLD, component of 248
    request for 259-261
    space 113
    time 85

*AD(H)D:
    description 282
    organisation and 77
    *See also* SpLD

appointments:
    preparation 97
    problems with 46, 48, 94
    reminders 135

autonomy 16, 33

book:
    about this 18-19
    aims and outcomes 20
    chapters, summary of x
    what to expect 1

*brainstorm 63, 73, 180, 237, 241

breathing 265-266

choices 210
    changing jobs 214
    declaring SpLD 212
    for study 178
    in employment 213
    records 214

colour coding 78, 94, 114

*confidence 129
    feeling confident 45, 211
    living confidently 248-249, 252, 256
    thinking preferences 270-273

cultures, different:
    education 202
    employment 224-225

# Index

deadlines 87, 187-188
    managing 142, 188, 218
    response to 100
    timetables 172-173

decisions, remembering 140
    solutions 141-143

diaries 89, 95-96, 133, 139, 142-143, 165
    reminders 69, 158

direction, meaning of 108
    good sense of 108-109
    no sense of 115
    taking directions 116
    updating strategies for 115
    words not having a meaning 117
    *See also* space, place and direction

dyscalculia:
    description 281
    organisation and 77
    *See also* SpLD

dyslexia:
    description 280
    organisation and 74
    *See also* SpLD

dyspraxia:
    description 281
    experience 110
    organisation and 75-76
    *See also* space, place and direction
        SpLD

emails, dealing with 217
    *See also* paperwork

employer 213

employment:
    accommodation 215-217, 230
    career 210-211, 213, 214, 218
    cultures, different 224-225
    declaring SpLD 212, 255-256
    management 212-214, 217-223
    other people 223-229
    SpLD issues 217-219, 226-227, 255-256
    *See also* navigating course structures
        other people
        space, place and direction

environment 118-120
    *See also* space, place and directions

everyday life, organisation of 18-20, 126, 130-133
    different styles for 131
    holidays 133
    SpLD experience 127-130
    useful questions for 132
    while studying 205
    *See also* decisions
        objects
        organisation, model for
        other people
        paperwork
        tasks
        vital for dyslexic/ SpLDs, good practice for all

exam provisions 194-199

# Index

exercises:
- avoid more problems 8
- breathing 265-266
- criteria for good organisation 73
- how will you benefit? 148
- initial purpose for reading 14
- physical relaxation 267
- questions, practise generating useful 240
- reading style 11
- realise your present organisational skills 60
- to be clear about a pitfall 68
- to resolve problems in your paperwork system 149
- to work out what is needed for an activity 136

finances 204

*goal, know your 234, 238, 248, 250, 275

*hazards 66-69
- example 139
- *See also* organisation, model for, step 2
  - organisation, model for, step 4
  - pitfalls

information, collecting together 234-236
- materials and methods, for collecting information 56-57

instructions:
- learning 252
- misunderstanding 52

IT: assistive technology 190
- clearing memory 165-167
- dealing with emails 217
- exam provision 195
- in the work place 216
- recording decisions 143
- try devices before buying 117
- using electronic devices 56, 69, 96, 114, 136, 138, 142

key ideas, identifying 241-242

key words 274
- use of 243

lists, making 69, 133
- good use 136-139
- example 144

log book, use of 252

managing dyslexia/ SpLD, *regime for 234-236, 248-261
- insights into potential and problems 69, 250, 257

materials and methods, for collecting information 56-57

297

# Index

maths and organisation 77-78
    colour coding 78
    individual style of working 259-261
    observe working 78

meetings 134-138
    *See also* everyday life, organisation of

memory, SpLD experience 7, 52, 75, 112, 252, 253

memory, techniques:
    *chunking 267
    consolidation 268
    mind set 267
    recall from memory, remember 268

mental energy to monitor SpLD 249

mental techniques:
    comprehension 274
    concentration 268
    key words 274
    planning 275
    *See also* prioritising

metacognition 268

mind:
    comprehension 274
    know how your mind works 3-4, 88, 235
    out of sight out of mind 48, 157
    prime your 12-17, 241
    using well 267-269
    *See also* profile of SpLD

*mind map examples ii, iii, 0, 23, 25, 27, 29, 36, 41, 56, 58, 63, 84, 104, 122, 145, 168, 176, 206, 219

*mind set 267

monitoring progress 72, 81, 236, 243-244
    example progress report 257-258

monitor SpLD functioning 249

navigating course structure 175-189
    course materials 181-183
    course work 184
    exam provisions 194-199
    *See also* deadlines
        organisation, model for SpLD support
        time
        timetables

navigating employment structure 219-223
    *See also* navigating course structure

*neural networks 3-6
    biological, constitutional level 5
    *chaotic 5
    pruning 4

new, importance of 7-8, 50, 52
    directions 115
    disturbs organisation 44
    exercise to avoid more problems 8
    learning new systems 218
    study and changes 172

# Index

non-dyslexic/ SpLD people 4, 16-17, 45, 67-68, 79, 127
    use SpLD systems 51
    *See also* other people
        vital for dyslexic/ SpLDs, good practice for all

objects to be organised 136-139
    exercise: to work out what is needed for an activity 136
    not remembered in time 92
    nothing missed 70
    study materials 186
    taking everything 43

observe objectively 234, 250-253, 256, 268
    observe maths working 78

*obstacles 66-69
    dyspraxia 75
    *See also* organisation, model for, step 2
        organisation, model for, step 4
        pitfalls

organisation 42-45, 55
    issues affecting 50-54
    SpLD and 73-79
    SpLD disorganised 50
    SpLD experience 45-49
    SpLD ultra organised 49
    SpLD unorganised 54
    *See also* new, importance of

organisation, model for 57-66
    check-list 70-72
    criteria for good organisation 72
    decisions 143
    materials and methods 56-57
    recording 65
    skills for organising 173
    step 1 gather strengths 60, 70, 130, 148, 176
    step 2 assess hazards 60, 70, 130, 149, 177-179
    step 3 describe what's to be organised 61, 71, 130, 150, 180
    step 4 recognise insuperable obstacles 64, 71, 130, 149-150, 181
    step 5 constructive organisation 59, 65, 71, 130, 151-159, 181
    useful questions for 61-63
    *See also* objects
        paperwork
        pitfalls
        problem-solving, general
        tasks
        time

*'other' 6, 139, 273

# Index

other people 133-135, 204
    bouncing ideas off others 57
    conflict resolution 228-230,
    culture differences 20, 223-227
    disorganised 175
    education 183
    group work 185
    support 179
    too helpful 45
    using SpLD systems 51

out of sight out of mind 48, 157

paperwork 144-159
    filing 152-156
    responding 156-159
    *See also* decisions
        organisation, model for
        other people
        throw away

pausing 250, 256, 264-267
    know your goal 275
    *profile of SpLD and managing SpLD 248
    recording 234

philosophy of the series 4-6

*pitfalls 67-69, 234-236, 248-253
    contrast 66
    exercise to be clear about a pitfall 68
    *glitch 277
    *hazards 66
    *obstacles 66, 75
    root cause 82-83
    story including pitfall 64
    variations 68
    *See also* organisation, model for >
        step 2
        organisation, model for >
        step 4

place, meaning of 108
    good sense of 109-110
    no sense of 114
    words not having a meaning 109
    *See also* space, place and direction

precautions, major 7-8

preparation 98-99
    SpLD issues 47

prioritising (priority and related words) 236-238, 241, 243

problem-solving, general 79-83
    root cause of 82-83
    solutions overview 130-131

*profile of dyslexia/ SpLD 248-261
    building profile 68, 250-257, 234-236
    progress report 257

# Index

questions, generating useful 238-241
    adapting questions 132

questions, useful: examples:
    about a pile of stuff, with answers 63
    assessing hazards 177
    basic set 239
    be aware of the details of your exam 196
    criteria for good organisation 73
    dealing with pitfalls 177
    gathering strength 60
    going away for the weekend 132
    guiding question for paperwork 164
    learning new skills, avoiding problems 8
    preparation for a conversation 150
    prioritising 237
    reading style 11
    reading, to help 237
    relating to the space around you 119
    time management 89
    to assess skills needed for course work 183
    to be clear about a pitfall 69
    to brainstorm about a department 203
    to choose template style 251
    to help with paperwork 155
    to survey course material 182
    to throw objects away 160
    what needs organising 62
    when observing maths 77
    your present organisational skills 60

reader groups 15-17

reading:
    bookmark 254
    different ways for 9-11
    explore different ways for 11
    prioritising topics 237
    problems 11-12, 253
    surveying and scanning 241-243
    using themes 12-15, 17

reflection 269
    questions, useful 8
    noting progress 243-244
    recording 252

*regime *see* managing dyslexia/ SpLD, regime for

regulations, study 199-203

relaxation, physical 266

reminders 156-159

resources:
    collecting information 234-236
    generating useful questions 238-241
    monitoring progress 243-244
    prioritising 236-238
    surveying and scanning 241-243

root cause of a problem 82-83

scanning 241-243

*senses 270
    choosing between 236
    reading style 10
    words for using the 270

# Index

series: *Living Confidently with SpLDs* 21-34
    aims and outcomes 31
    philosophy of 4-6

shopping 137
    See also everyday life, organisation of

skills for organising 173

space, meaning of 108

space, place and direction 108-110
    accommodation 113
    concentration affected by 268
    dyspraxia 110
    environment 118-120
    exercise: relating to the space around you 119
    meaning of 108
    no sense of your body 111-113
    no sense of direction 115-117
    no sense of place 114
    no sense of your environment 113
    words have no reliable meaning 117

spelling 82

SpLD:
    descriptions of 280-282
    analogy 4
    and organisation 73-79
    aspects of dyslexia 270-276
    biological, constitutional level 5
    declaring 179, 189
    degrees of 278
    distinctions, where made 32
    persistence of SpLD 249
    SpLD behaviours 191-192
    view of 4-6
    *See also* new
        pitfalls
        SpLD experience
        SpLD progress
        SpLD support

SpLD experience 45-49, 65, 157
    adult experience 6
    concentration affected by time and space 268
    differences at work 226-227
    everyday life 127-131
    learning 7
    new 44
    organising objects 42-43
    reading 11-12
    thinking preferences 3
    variation of experience 50, 61, 118
    *See also* employment, SpLD issues

# Index

SpLD support 189-199, 218
    communication 52-53
    negotiating provisions 194-199, 258-261
    See also vital for dyslexic/ SpLDs, good practice for all

SpLD, managing 248-261
    mental energy to manage 249
    progress report 257-258
    working with the chapter 38, 85, 106, 124, 170, 208

stress 100
    managing 264-267

*study peripherals 172-173, 180

study, organising 172-175, 182
    institution 199-203
    See also everyday life, organisation of
        navigating course structure
organisation, model for other people

success, routes to 6


tasks, organising 93, 132-133, 243
    accommodation 69
    employment issues 216-219, 221
    methods and materials 56-57
    people involved 65, 230
    prioritising 236-238
    SpLD systems used by others 51
    time issues 88-90, 95, 101
    useful questions 61-63, 238-241

techniques:
    collecting information together 234-236
    generating useful questions 238-241
    monitoring progress 243-244
    prioritising 236-238
    recording 242-243
    surveying 241-242
    techniques for using the mind well 267-275

templates, list of 290-293
    how to use 234-236, 242-244
    table headings 256

thinking clearly 264-267

*thinking preferences summaries 270-273
    enabling 9-11
    exploring 235
    materials and methods for collecting information 56-57
    *profile and management *regime of dyslexia/ SpLD 234, 250-253
    See also *thinking preferences assisting reading

# Index

*thinking preferences assisting reading:
    *framework 9
    *kinaesthetic 10
    linear 9
    motivation, interest-oriented 10
    senses 10
    spatial 9

thinking preferences, examples:
    holistic 57
    *kinaesthetic 54, 56, 57, 92, 94, 116, 131, 136, 252
    linear 57, 131
    MBPT 57, 92, 131, 136
    motivation 211
    *rationale, *framework and logic 252, 260
    verbal/ oral/ aural 10, 56, 116, 131, 136
    visual 10, 54, 56, 78, 92, 94, 96, 116, 131, 136
    visualising/ visualisation 131, 136, 137

throw away 159-167
    electronic delete 165
    objects 160
    paperwork 161

time 87
    build your knowledge of 93
    letting go 100-103
    problems 46, 88, 91-92, 94
    solutions 89-91, 92-94, 95-100
    study, organising 187
    *See also* deadlines
        paperwork

timetables 94-98
    revision 97
    study 88, 187
    travel 96
    *See also* diaries

tools for living 34
    tool box 253-256
    updating 256-258

trial and error:
    fail safe 72
    learning from what's wrong 62, 174
    benefit from mistakes 54

vital for dyslexic/ SpLDs, good practice for all 4, 38, 85, 105, 123, 169, 207
    system used by others 51

worked example 174-175
    exam provisions 194-199
    navigating course structure 175-189

# Taylor & Francis eBooks

www.taylorfrancis.com

A single destination for eBooks from Taylor & Francis with increased functionality and an improved user experience to meet the needs of our customers.

90,000+ eBooks of award-winning academic content in Humanities, Social Science, Science, Technology, Engineering, and Medical written by a global network of editors and authors.

## TAYLOR & FRANCIS EBOOKS OFFERS:

- A streamlined experience for our library customers
- A single point of discovery for all of our eBook content
- Improved search and discovery of content at both book and chapter level

## REQUEST A FREE TRIAL
support@taylorfrancis.com

# BBC SOUNDS

BRITISH LIBRARY

The BBC Listening Project records conversations between different people about many different kinds of experiences between people with a wide range of relationships.

## Ginny and Sally — A Dyslexic Brain

Sally and I have enjoyed our journey working together on these four books and we recorded our thoughts about the experience for The Listening Project in April 2018. Though we are both dyslexic, our experience of dyslexia is quite different; we have different processing strengths and different ranges of problems. We are both positive about dealing with any problems and we both enjoy our various strengths. It has been huge fun working together, as we hope you can hear from our conversation.

An extract from our conversation is available on the BBC website at
https://www.bbc.co.uk/sounds/play/b0b1tmbl

The whole conversation is archived at the British Library and will be made available later this year (2020) at https://sounds.bl.uk

Full details of the recording can be found on the British Library's Sound and Moving Image catalogue at http://sami.bl.uk (search for C1442/1554).

Ginny Stacey and Sally Fowler
Photo by Louise Pepper for the BBC Listening Project

For Product Safety Concerns and Information please contact our EU representative  GPSR@taylorandfrancis.com
Taylor & Francis Verlag GmbH, Kaufingerstraße 24, 80331 München, Germany

www.ingramcontent.com/pod-product-compliance
Lightning Source LLC
Chambersburg PA
CBHW080523020526
44112CB00046B/2774